Inclusion, Diversity and Innovation in Translation Education

LITERATURE AND TRANSLATION

Series Editors: Timothy Mathews, Geraldine Brodie and Ana Cláudia Suriani da Silva

Literature and Translation is a series for books of literary translation as well as about literary translation. Its emphasis is on diversity of genre, culture, period and approach. The series uses the UCL Press open-access publishing model widely to disseminate developments in both the theory and practice of translation. Translations into English are welcomed of literature from around the world.

Timothy Mathews is Emeritus Professor of French and Comparative Criticism, UCL.

Geraldine Brodie is Professor of Translation Theory and Theatre Translation, UCL.

Ana Cláudia Suriani da Silva is Associate Professor of Brazilian Studies, UCL.

OTHER TITLES IN THE SERIES

Selected Essays and Dialogues by Gianni Celati
Edited and translated by Patrick Barron
https://doi.org/10.14324/111.9781800086395

The Bankruptcy
Júlia Lopes de Almeida, edited by Ana Cláudia Suriani da Silva, and translated by Cintia Kozonoi Vezzani and Jason Rhys Parry
https://doi.org/10.14324/111.9781800085664

In the Face of Adversity
Edited by Thomas Nolden
https://doi.org/10.14324/111.9781800083691

Contemporary Afro-Brazilian Short Fiction
Edited by Ana Cláudia Suriani da Silva, Julio Ludemir and Maria Aparecida Andrade Salgueiro
https://doi.org/10.14324/111.9781800086692

Paradise from behind the Iron Curtain
Miklós Péti
https://doi.org/10.14324/111.9781787358539

Reflexive Translation Studies
Silvia Kadiu
https://doi.org/10.14324/111.9781787352513

Eva
Carry van Bruggen, translated and with a commentary by Jane Fenoulhet
https://doi.org/10.14324/111.9781787353299

Ethics and Aesthetics of Translation
Harriet Hulme
https://doi.org/10.14324/111.9781787352070

Inclusion, Diversity and Innovation in Translation Education

Edited by
Alejandro Bolaños García-Escribano
Mazal Oaknín

Foreword by
Olga Castro

UCLPRESS

First published in 2024 by
UCL Press
University College London
Gower Street
London WC1E 6BT

Available to download free: www.uclpress.co.uk

A CIP catalogue record for this book is available from The British Library.

ISBN: 978-1-80008-714-9 (Hbk.)
ISBN: 978-1-80008-713-2 (Pbk.)
ISBN: 978-1-80008-712-5 (PDF)
ISBN: 978-1-80008-715-6 (epub)
DOI: https://doi.org/10.14324/111.9781800087125

To the brave trailblazers who navigated unchartered territories in education.
To the courageous colleagues and students who persevere despite a lack of sense of belonging.
To the bold people who go beyond ticking boxes.
We learn from you; we see you; we celebrate you.

To our families and friends who have inspired us and supported us.
We thank you and love you.

Contents

List of figures

List of tables

List of contributors (in order of appearance)

Editors

Alejandro Bolaños García-Escribano (SFHEA) is Associate Professor in Audiovisual Translation and Programme Director at UCL, UK, where he teaches (audiovisual) translation and Spanish language and culture at both the Centre for Translation Studies and the Department of Spanish, Portuguese and Latin American Studies (SPLAS). He is an associate editor of *The Interpreter and Translator Trainer* (Taylor & Francis, ISSN: 1757-0417) and the book reviews editor of *HIKMA: Translation Studies Journal* (UCOPress, ISSN: 1579-9794).

Mazal Oaknín (FHEA) is Associate Professor (Teaching) and Language Coordinator, as well as project lead of the Tackling the BAME-BIPOC Awarding Gap in SELCS project, at UCL, UK. She mainly teaches Spanish language, translation and literature and has also taught in other higher education institutions in Malaga, New York, Paris and Birmingham. She is the co-editor of *Literatura política y política literaria en España: Del desastre del 98 a Felipe VI* (Peter Lang, 2015) and her work has appeared in journals such as *Espéculo, Fahrenheit 452, Hikma, Alfinge and Journal of Spanish Cultural Studies*. Her current research interests revolve around the teaching of Spanish as a foreign language, contemporary Spanish literature, gender and identity, and representations of minorities. Her book *Feminism, Writing and the Media in Spain* appeared in 2019 (Peter Lang).

Chapter authors

Sergio Portelli is Professor of Translation Studies at the University of Malta, where he is Head of the Department of Translation, Terminology and Interpreting Studies at the Faculty of Arts. He teaches Terminology and Translation in the MA course in Translation and Terminology Studies. He also teaches computer-aided translation, translation and intercultural communication, and Italian-Maltese/English translation. Most of his publications are in the fields of literary translation, comparative literature and cultural history. He is also a literary translator and a former translator of the European Parliament.

Beatriz Cerezo Merchán is Lecturer of Translation and English Language at the Department of English and German Philology, Universitat de València, Spain. In 2013 she won the Young Scholar Prize of the European Society for Translation Studies (EST) for the best doctoral thesis in the area of translation and interpreting. Her main areas of research are audiovisual translation and the didactics of translation.

María del Mar Ogea Pozo is Lecturer in Translation at the University of Córdoba, Spain. She holds a BA in Modern Languages and Translation and Interpreting (Italian-Spanish-English) from the University of Salford, UK, and a PhD in Translation and Interpreting from the University of Córdoba. After completing an MA in Audiovisual Translation applied to Subtitling and Dubbing (ISTRAD, Spain), she worked as a translator specialised in biomedical and audiovisual texts. Currently her research focuses on audiovisual translation and specialised language in audiovisual texts. She is a member of the research group Oriens HUM-940, chief editor of the journal *Transletters* and coordinator of the TradAV project.

Noa Talaván is Professor of English Studies and Translation in the Foreign Languages Department of the Universidad Nacional de Education a Distancia (UNED), Spain. She obtained her PhD in 2009 with a thesis on the didactic applications of audiovisual translation in foreign language education. Since then, this has been her main research interest, and she has contributed to translation studies scholarship with more than 30 peer-reviewed publications. She has coordinated 14 teaching innovation projects since 2008 in the area of the didactic applications of audiovisual translation to foreign language education. Since 2016, she has been the coordinator of the teaching innovation research group ARENA (Accessibility, Audiovisual Translation and Language Learning) and the international research group TRADIT (Didactic Audiovisual Translation).

Soledad Díaz Alarcón is Senior Lecturer at the University of Córdoba, Spain, where she teaches Translation and Interpreting. Her research areas include literary translation, particularly French narrative and nineteenth-century detective novels, and translation didactics. Her works include over 30 publications, including articles, book chapters and books on detective novels. She has also participated in numerous conferences and international research stays. She is currently editor-in-chief of the Spanish translation journal *Hikma* and UCOPress's *Nuevos Horizontes Electrónicos*.

Carmen Herrero is Reader of Spanish Studies at Manchester Metropolitan University, UK. She leads the research group Film, Languages and Media Education (FLAME) and is a co-founder, with Isabelle Vanderschelden, of the Film in Language Teaching Association (FILTA). Her research focuses on film and screen studies, in particular their pedagogical applications for language learning and teaching. She has published, in English and Spanish, numerous articles on Spanish and Latin American cinema and the use of movies, media and transmedia in the language class. She co-edited, with Isabelle Vanderschelden, *Using Film and Media in the Language Classroom: Reflections on research-led teaching* (Multilingual Matters, 2019). She has participated in international projects including Communication in Virtual and Mobile Work [CoMoViWo] (2014–2016) and Open World Research Initiative Cross-Language Dynamics: Reshaping Community (2016–2021).

Isabelle Vanderschelden taught French Studies, Translation and Film at Manchester Metropolitan University, UK, until 2021. She is now an independent researcher affiliated with the Remelice Lab at the University of Orleans and an Associate Lecturer at Lancaster University. She has published *Screenwriters in French Cinema*, co-authored with Sarah Leahy (Manchester University Press, 2021) and *Studying French Cinema* (Columbia University Press, 2013). She co-founded the Film in Language Teaching Association (FILTA) with Carmen Herrero and is an active member of Film, Languages and Media Education (FLAME). She co-edited, with Carmen Herrero, *Using Film and Media in the Language Classroom: Reflections on research-led teaching* (Multilingual Matters, 2019).

Xiaofan Amy Li is Lecturer in Comparative Cultural Studies at UCL. She earned her PhD at Queens' College (University of Cambridge, UK). Her research spans French and East Asian literatures and cultures. She has published on key topics in comparative and world literature, including comparative poetics, translation and cultural representations.

John Gray is Professor of Applied Linguistics and Education at UCL, UK. His research interests include literature in the language classroom and issues of language, gender and sexuality. Recent publications include a special issue of *Gender and Language* (2018) on intersectionality, language and queer lives, co-edited with Melanie Cooke; 'Narratives of queer migration' in *The Oxford Handbook of Language and Sexuality* (2020), co-written with Mike Baynham; and 'Addressing LGBTQ erasure through literature in the ELT classroom' in the *ELT Journal* (2021).

Haydn Kirnon is Lecturer (Teaching) in Spanish into English translation at UCL, UK, where he teaches in the Department of Spanish, Portuguese and Latin American Studies (SPLAS). He has been a professional translator and subtitler for over 30 years and also worked as a lexicographer on several dictionaries at Oxford University Press, including the *Oxford Beginner's Spanish Dictionary*, thereby developing a strong liking for the teaching of translation to linguists in training.

Foreword

An ever-growing interest in new pedagogical approaches seeking to promote equality, diversity and inclusion in higher education has been noticeable in recent times. In Western academic settings, this is arguably linked to an increased awareness of the important role that inclusive pedagogies have in maximising students' learning potential, while also possibly influenced by patterns of mobility, migration and displacement defining our globalised world today. Understanding the classroom as a radical transformational space (hooks 1994), over the past few years we have witnessed numerous institutional and student-led campaigns aimed at incorporating an inclusive approach in higher education programmes. Their stated aims have often included challenging racial inequality, decolonising the curriculum, implementing neurodivergent-friendly practices, raising awareness of non-normative sexualities and promoting a conscious consideration of educators' assumptions and biases, to name but a few. These would all be examples of what Carolyn Shrewsbury (1987, 8) once envisioned as 'engaged teaching/learning processes'. The multi-level engagement described by the author still seems very valid today: processes of teaching and learning which are

> engaged with self in a continuing reflective process; engaged actively with the material being studied; engaged with others in a struggle to get beyond our sexism and racism and classism and homophobia and other destructive hatreds and to work together to enhance our knowledge; engaged with the community, with traditional organizations, and with movements for social change. (Shrewsbury 1987, 8)

Yet, the particularities of each academic subject will require specific tools, strategies and critical reflections about the challenges and opportunities that an inclusive pedagogy necessarily entails. And with very few notable exceptions thus far, this remains uncharted territory in translation studies. In this pioneering collection, the editors – Alejandro Bolaños García-Escribano and Mazal Oaknín – fill this gap by addressing the crucial question of equality, diversity and inclusion (EDI) in translation by combining research-led teaching practices with teaching-focused research projects. Their joint editorial work has produced a highly compelling volume that offers ground-breaking perspectives and inspiring examples of how audiovisual and literary translation is, and can be, taught and learnt today and in the years to come, carefully considering the ways in which technology-driven transformations are affecting our understanding of translation. These practices and proposals are mostly contextualised in the Anglo-Saxon and Spanish academic traditions and university settings, as they have been inspired by the highly successful e-Expert Seminar Series: Translation and Language Teaching, an international collaboration between UCL and the Universidad de Córdoba, Spain, since 2018.

All the chapters in *Inclusion, Diversity and Innovation in Translation Education* share a common goal of developing teaching approaches that promote social justice in the classroom and beyond. They all seek to bring EDI to the forefront of students' learning experiences as a catalyst for social change. In their thought-provoking chapters, twelve experts showcase the latest research advancements in translation curricula and cover a diverse range of practices and proposals, including literary translation, film adaptation, didactic audiovisual translation, media accessibility (and more specifically, subtitling for the deaf and the hard of hearing), machine translation in the wake of artificial intelligence, intersectional feminism, queer studies and critical race theory, among others. This collection unequivocally addresses exclusion in higher education and concludes with a compelling piece in which a translation trainer, who has over 30 years of experience in the profession, argues for the need to increase the sense of belonging experienced by BAME-BIPOC (Black, Asian and Minority Ethnic and Black, Indigenous and People of Colour) students. Ultimately, the latter could maximise their learning potential while bridging the damaging degree awarding gap in higher education. It is to be expected, then, that this will have positive implications for students' employability in the translation profession, helping overcome what Corine Tachtiris (2024, 1) describes as the 'unbearable whiteness in translation' in the West, which has traditionally excluded racialised translators and scholars. In this regard, it is quite revealing that the author of the closing chapter acknowledges his African-Caribbean background and argues that his ethnic and cultural identities inform his practice as a racialised educator in a city as racially diverse as London.

This commitment to creating a critical space for underrepresented scholars also highlights the crucial role that both experiential knowledge (that is, knowledge learnt through lived experience) and representativeness have in critical debates about EDI in higher education. Both concepts are relevant for any subject matter, and in translation studies they have sparked some of the most heated debates in recent times, as exemplified by the passionate responses posted on the forum of the journal *Translation Studies*, triggered by the article entitled 'Representing experiential knowledge: Who may translate whom?' by Şebnem Susam-Saraeva (2021).

In light of the above, a highly valuable aspect that enriches the discussions in this volume is the fact that the contributors identify with a variety of minority backgrounds, including BAME-BIPOC and LGBTQI+ communities as well as different ethnicities, genders, nationalities and religions. In this regard, this collection serves as a platform where diverse voices engage in meaningful discussions on how to engage students and train future language and translation professionals, doing so from an intersectional perspective that considers how different layers of identity interact. As such, situated at the crossroads of translator training research, translation technology and intersectional feminist translation studies, among others, *Inclusion, Diversity and Innovation in Translation Education* promises to be a landmark in both educational and EDI approaches to translation.

Olga Castro
Universitat Autònoma de Barcelona, University of Warwick

References

hooks, bell. 1994. *Teaching to Transgress: Education as the Practice of Freedom*. London: Routledge.
Shrewsbury, Carolyn. 1987. 'What is feminist pedagogy?' *Women's Studies Quarterly* 15, no. 3/4: 6–14.
Susam-Saraeva, Şebnem. 2021. 'Representing experiential knowledge: Who may translate whom?' *Translation Studies* 14, no. 1: 84–95.
Tachtiris, Corine. 2024. *Translation and Race*. London: Routledge.

Preface

As editors of this book, we are very proud of this exploratory work that addresses the urgent need to focus on equality, diversity and inclusion in language and translation education. There is little doubt that this book has taken precious time from everyone, especially chapter authors, in the past few years, but we believe that it has also helped us to reflect on *what*, *how* and *why* we teach languages and translation in the twenty-first century. If anything, this editorial project, which stems from the e-Expert Seminar Series: Translation and Language Teaching (2018–), has been the perfect platform for fostering closer collaboration between us and with external contributors who are leading experts in their field. More importantly, this book has forced us to further reflect on *who* we are as educators and what our position is in the face of an ever-changing educational landscape. By challenging traditional approaches and engaging in two-way conversations with contributors, we have strived to foster and encourage much-needed reflection on how to make our classrooms more diverse, egalitarian and inclusive. We believe that maintaining a student-centred approach is essential in today's higher education landscape, and it is with great pleasure that we now offer the results of these reflections in the form of this book.

Acknowledgements

We would like to hereby thank all authors for their hard work, enthusiasm and trust. We are also grateful to the Literature and Translation series editors at UCL Press – Timothy Mathews, Geraldine Brodie and Ana Cláudia Suriani da Silva – as well as Chris Penfold and Elliot Beck for their support throughout the publication process. Many thanks to Lydia Hayes and Irene Collazo Lugo, who have contributed as translators and editors of some of the chapters. We are also indebted to Azahara Veroz González, Marga Navarrete and Soledad Díaz Alarcón (also one of this book's contributors), co-creators of our e-Expert Seminar Series: Translation and Language Teaching. Much of the inspiration in this book stems from the innovative connections and incursions that our seminar series has explored since its inception in 2018.

1

Introduction: why inclusion, diversity and innovation matters in translation education

Alejandro Bolaños García-Escribano
Mazal Oaknín

Translation studies (TS) is a multidisciplinary academic field with solid theoretical foundations. It is therefore no surprise that publications abound on topics related to the teaching of different practices and specialisms (for instance medical, technical and scientific translation) as well as the use of (pedagogical) translation as a tool in foreign language education. The growing and changing nature of translation scholarship has prompted translation researchers to explore societal issues by looking at different translation disciplines or practices, thereby enhancing the multidisciplinary nature of our field. In this book, we endeavour to establish a closer dialogue between two disciplines that are not often approached together – audiovisual translation (AVT) and literary translation. Moreover, we set out to showcase teaching-focused research happening at the intersection of these two disciplines, while observing factors such as gender, feminism, accessibility and LGBTQI+ identities, which are scarcely found in the literature and are virtually absent from some settings. We as editors set out to explore the latest innovations in research-led education and student–teacher collaborative projects by building on the lessons learnt from a seminar series (see below), with a special emphasis on innovative research on equality, diversity and inclusion (EDI) and its presence in the translation classroom.

This book stems from the e-Expert Seminar Series: Translation and Language Teaching, an international initiative devised by UCL in the UK and the University of Córdoba (UCO) in Spain. Since its inception in

2018, this seminar series has sought to open a forum for discussion on the contributions offered by practitioners, stakeholders and scholars to the study of translation and modern foreign language teaching. First conceived as international hybrid and online seminars, the series has served as a platform for leading experts in TS to discuss how the latest research can be better weaved into the teaching of translation and modern languages at a global scale. The demand for this type of forum is evidenced by the growing number of participants in each edition – totalling over 1,500 participants at the time of writing – as well as the new perspectives on online conferences following the COVID-19 pandemic. Technical innovation and greater social empowerment have inevitably been fuelled by the democratisation of new information and communication technologies, but also because of the ever-increasing consumption of audiovisual programmes, websites, video games and multimedia content. Indeed, we could argue that, just like future generations of translators, our experiences as translator educators are heavily influenced not only by constant exposure to information on screens, but also by an increasing awareness of the importance of accessibility to the media. This accessibility has developed greatly in recent decades, particularly thanks to seminal legislative work carried out by international bodies such as the European Union (European Accessibility Act, 2019) and the United Nations (Convention on the Rights of Persons with Disabilities, 2006). This book builds on the understanding that, in light of these new scenarios, the learning and teaching of modern foreign languages and translation have to keep up with societal changes and strive to be more diverse and inclusive.

If we look at the TS scholarship, we can establish that the teaching of translation has attracted much interest among researchers and educators alike. Seminal works on the practice of teaching translators-to-be how to translate include those by Delisle (1980), Nord (1988), Robinson (1991), Kussmaul (1995), Kiraly (1995), Gile (1995/2009), Hurtado-Albir (1999), Kiraly (2000), González-Davies (2004), Kelly (2005) and Robinson (2020). Academics have approached the teaching of translation from different perspectives; whereas some prioritise the practical nature of our discipline – 'translator training' (Massey et al. 2019) – others have stuck to more academic-sounding nomenclatures, such as 'translator education' (Way 2020). In spite of these terminological disparities, TS scholars have long devoted research efforts to understanding *how* translation can be taught. Publications on matters arising from the teaching of translation abound in TS journals, not least because it is often easy for trainers (or educators) to obtain data from trainees, with whom they have contact on a regular basis.

As a result, today's body of scholarship on translator education is vast and thriving. It suffices to take the peer-reviewed journal *The Interpreter and Translator Trainer* as a primary example. First conceived in 2007 (Kelly and Way 2007), it had more than 20 volumes at the time of writing (with often as many as four issues each year); it constantly features in the first quartile of subject category rankings and holds one of the highest impact factors among TS journals worldwide. A quick search on the University of Alicante's BITRA (Bibliography of Translation and Interpreting), which comprises over 92,000 entries at the time of writing, reveals some impressive results: 5,167 for *training*, 4,711 for *teaching*, 2,930 for *education*, 2,886 for *translator training*, 1,993 for *translation education*, 527 for *pedagogy* and 501 for *didactics*.[1] Without undertaking a detailed analysis of each result, this indicates that 18,715 entries (20 per cent of all TS publications on this database) arguably have a direct connection with the teaching of translation or interpreting.

Indeed, there have been many efforts to discuss *how* translation is taught. González-Davies's (2004) and Kelly's (2005) seminal books inspired much of the subsequent research, with edited volumes following, such as those by Venuti (2017) and Laviosa and González-Davies (2020), among others. These works tend to offer holistic views of the teaching of translation by focusing on translation specialisms (for instance literature, science and film), whereas others provide insights into curriculum design. It could be argued, on the one hand, that the teaching of literary translation has featured significantly in most of the early translator education publications, but Landers's (2001) practical guide remains one of the few dedicated pedagogical resources in this field. More efforts have perhaps been devoted to the teaching of foreign literature in translation (Maier and Massardier-Kenney 2013; Baer and Woods 2022), although we would argue that most pedagogical translation textbooks make lesser or greater use of literary texts (see, for instance, Carreres et al. 2017) for the teaching of languages and translation. When it comes to the learning and teaching of AVT, on the other hand, the volume edited by Díaz-Cintas (2008) remains a one-of-a-kind resource. Likewise, Seel et al. (2023) put an innovative emphasis on foreign language teaching in translator and interpreter education; they argue that for this approach to fully enhance students' competences it should differ from conventional language teaching practices.

Although the aforementioned volume recommends a multicultural approach, it appears that the topic of EDI is still scarcely explored in TS research. Among the very few attempts to embed EDI issues in translation education are the works by Castro and Ergun (2017), who focus on feminist translation understood as political activism, and by Gould and Tahmasebian (2017), who highlight the role of translation as a tool to fight injustice. More recently, analyses of linguistic representations of identities in translated texts have also included transgender and genderqueer identities (Larkosh 2011; Bassi 2017; Santaemilia 2017, 2018) and 2023 has seen the launch of the first feminist translation journal (*Feminist Translation Studies*). Given that each language shows a different degree of adaptability to non-binary expression, as editors we consider it important to champion the use of non-sexist language and to celebrate non-heteronormativity in translation (Baxter 2005; Expósito-Castro and Rodríguez-Muñoz 2023). Hence, the present volume honours the commitment to the belief that by being exposed to inclusive language in the honing of their translation skills, students can learn how to recognise and use the tools necessary to make the classroom (and thereby their future role in society) more diverse and inclusive. We believe these tools should both come from and spread to the teaching of foreign languages.

Of particular interest is the Translation Practices Explained series, first launched by St Jerome and now published by Routledge under the direction of Kelly Washbourne. At the time of writing it included as many as 27 coursebooks on the teaching of specific translation practices, ranging from scientific and technical to localisation, subtitling, consecutive interpreting and marketing, among others. Despite the fact that AVT education has generally received little attention (Cerezo Merchán 2018), five publications in Routledge's series are related to AVT. Conversely, only one is related to literary translation and none of them, unfortunately, seems to (directly) touch on EDI issues, such as gender, feminism, race and ethnicity, or LGBTQI+ identities. And yet, Castro and Ergun (2017, 139) avow that pedagogical intervention is of paramount importance to 'help us engage in more ethical translational encounters with one another – encounters that do not otherwise assimilate or fetishise our differences, but rather bring us eye-to-eye and connect us across those differences without pursuing oneness or sameness'.

This book notes the gains made by the above-mentioned scholarly publications and constitutes a step forward insofar as it combines AVT and literary translation through an EDI lens. We showcase case studies that delve into teaching-related experiences and research by a wide and diverse body of authors. Apart from comprehensive literature reviews, the chapters propose a refreshing attempt to align translation teaching with twenty-first-century skills and industry demands in light of the greater commitment to EDI values in higher education. As new and innovative language and translation practices mushroom and universities increasingly commit to EDI agendas and more inclusive curricula, the need to update our research on translation pedagogy is inevitable. This book therefore revisits how translation is traditionally taught and proposes new connections with industry and a stronger commitment to EDI values, which are currently driving the agendas of many universities, including translator training institutions. This book explores synergies between different research areas, such as accessibility, feminism, plurilingualism and transmedia, in both AVT and literary translation, while maintaining a pedagogical approach overall.

In terms of demographics, this book aims to set an example by giving a platform to scholars who are accomplished experts in translation and modern languages and who also come from a variety of backgrounds and minorities. They include representatives of the BAME-BIPOC – which stands for Black, Asian and Minority Ethnic (often used in the UK) and Black, Indigenous and People of Colour (often used in the US and increasingly frequent nowadays across the Anglosphere) – and LGBTQI+ communities as well as different religions, nationalities and ethnicities. The great potential of this diversity of researchers to have a positive impact on how the pilot and case studies have been presented in this volume is supported by Dhanda (2010) and Ambrose et al. (2010). These studies concluded that modelling inclusiveness has the capacity to improve the chances of BAME-BIPOC students engaging in pastoral and academic support and also offers a powerful learning experience for all students.

This book showcases carefully selected research studies that can potentially make a broader impact on *how* translation is taught and learnt – and, perhaps more importantly, *who* teaches it. The chapters give accounts of current research-led pedagogical experiences that have been piloted and have proven useful in incorporating the latest research and student–teacher collaborations into the classroom. A particular emphasis is put on how these case studies can inform learning and teaching practices in TS and the alignment of modern languages and translation curricula with twenty-first-century demands.

We have divided the book into three main sections, which provide contemporary debates on three main challenges concerning translation students and teachers nowadays. The following paragraphs briefly describe the contents of each chapter and highlight the main impact they strive to make on TS scholarship, with a particular focus on learning and teaching practices.

The uses of new technologies in language and translation education

Translation professionals have long been using digital solutions, especially computer-assisted translation tools such as translation memories (TM) and machine translation (MT) engines. For a number of years now, neural MT has been a major technological advancement that yields better results than its predecessors (that is, statistical approaches) in terms of fluidity and quality of the target text. The world of translation has undergone significant changes in recent years, and neural MT is now part and parcel of the discipline's landscape. Currently, the field is looking at generative technologies with large language models such as Google's Bard, OpenAI's ChatGPT and Microsoft's Copilot, all of which have text translation capabilities. The past years have seen researchers, teachers and translators pondering the value of such innovative tools as well as their ethical and professional implications (Kenny 2022). Neural MT has not only revolutionised our understanding of the profession, but also had a major impact on the ways in which educators are teaching and assessing would-be translators in higher education. Artificial intelligence poses a variety of challenges to academic practice as well as curriculum and assessment design, and the pressing need for educators to explore the transformative role of artificial intelligence in the field of language learning and teaching is reflected by the global emergence of fora and conferences that aim to tackle this debate.

Based on a case study concerning the German-to-English translation of a nineteenth-century tragedy, Sergio Portelli's chapter aims to analyse the extent to which computer-aided literary translation (CALT) may be reliable in the translation of literary works where the researcher or student does not know the source language. Researchers in comparative literature who focus on texts in different languages may find themselves in situations where a literary work has not been translated into any of the languages they know. In such cases, the work would be effectively inaccessible and commissioning a translation would be expensive and time consuming. The chapter duly fleshes out the methodology applied in the study, the choice of MT tool and the analysis of the raw output according to error types and the post-editing process required to render the target text adequate for the needs of the researcher. The further steps required to produce a publishable target text are discussed in the final part of the chapter and the conclusion sums up the challenges and limitations of CALT, specifically in the genre of tragedy, with comments on how the findings may be pertinent, or not, in other literary genres.

Technology also plays a fundamental part in Alejandro Bolaños García-Escribano and Beatriz Cerezo Merchán's chapter. Against the backdrop of soaring university fees and skyrocketing living costs, the UK left the Erasmus+ exchange programme (1987–) following Brexit. Fortunately for UK-based language and translation students, the democratisation of new information and communication technologies, such as telecollaboration programmes, can pave the way for a more accessible international exchange. Bolaños and Cerezo's chapter centres on telecollaboration and expounds on a virtual mobility case study between a British university and its Spanish counterpart. The use of telecollaboration practices has been growing steadily as an accessible alternative to develop students' linguistic, intercultural, digital and collaborative skills, but the authors' focus on pedagogical translation with didactic AVT solutions makes this case study particularly original and refreshing. This chapter presents a detailed methodological proposal for a telecollaboration project that other institutions can emulate. The authors' methodology builds on an experience from pre-pandemic times in which students were exposed to innovative tasks involving international collaboration. Thanks to the use of a variety of synchronous and asynchronous exercises and online tools and platforms, English- and Spanish-speaking students could work collaboratively in international teams to study, analyse, compare, translate and revise active AVT tasks that embed EDI topics such as disability, sexual orientation and gender. Due to the effects of globalisation, interaction between people from different linguistic and cultural backgrounds is highly significant nowadays, and work environments are changing, with an increasing number of professionals working in cross-cultural teams and communicating via digital platforms. Therefore, the authors posit that university education must train professionals who can work in multilingual and multicultural teams. In recent years, interest in telecollaboration, which can be understood as a form of virtual mobility, has grown significantly. It is increasingly being adopted by university educators in Europe and elsewhere through projects involving students from a wide variety of schools and universities. It allows for the fostering of twenty-first-century competences, including linguistic, intercultural, digital and teamwork skills.

The third contribution in this section is María del Mar Ogea Pozo and Noa Talaván's chapter, which focuses on expanding consciousness of gender issues, particularly gender-based violence, in the translation classroom. They make an interdisciplinary teaching proposal in which media accessibility meets gender studies for the purpose of fostering language learning. Indeed, the authors highlight the importance of didactic media accessibility in the classroom as a vehicle for raising students' awareness of gender violence. Their chapter describes a didactic proposal, based on the use of subtitles for the deaf and hard of hearing (SDH), which seeks to teach students how to analyse audiovisual products through a gender lens, reporting inequalities and examining the different types of violence against women. Audiovisual content is ever more present in everyone's lives, and it is therefore paramount that media content be accessible to all. The authors argue that audiovisual content has the potential to raise awareness about socially relevant issues, such as gender and violence, and that didactic media accessibility (including SDH) constitutes a field of study that has received increasing attention during the past decade. The objective of their study is to assess the impact of transferable contents, together with the enhancement of communicative L2 skills. As a point in case, their focus is on how sensibility towards gender violence can be explored through didactic SDH practice in the classroom. To that end, a lesson plan based on the short film *The Mirror* (Reithmayr 2017) prompts students to use didactic SDH to complete pre-viewing, viewing and post-viewing tasks. Students thereby learn to analyse audiovisual products that have included gender on their agendas. This allows for exploring inequalities and the different types of violence against women that exist today. The student feedback obtained is surprisingly positive – not only on the awareness raised about existing gender-based violence but also on the need for further embedding media accessibility in everyone's lives. Overall this is an interdisciplinary proposal, where gender studies, media accessibility and language learning are intertwined to raise students' awareness about the role played by accessibility to media while they enhance their communicative skills in the foreign language.

Unlocking the untapped possibilities of transmedia studies

The second section of the book is devoted to transmedia, understood as the interaction and convergence of different forms of media, as well as the synergies that exist between literature and film. Drawing on a seminal essay by Jakobson (1959/2021), scholars have previously looked into the cinematographic adaptation of literature as a form of intersemiotic translation (García-Luque 2021). The process of converting literature (including canonical works) into audiovisual products (for instance films) can yield much fruit in the language classroom, where learners are exposed to the many different understandings of translation beyond traditional linguistic approaches.

Soledad Díaz Alarcón's chapter discusses the use of technology to tackle another barrier often met by literary translation students. Indeed, when it comes to the learning of literary translation practice, the lack of sufficient knowledge in literary studies is a frequent obstacle which can impact negatively on the development of students' literacy in their native language. This chapter proposes the incorporation of audiovisual materials into the literary translation classroom. The fruits yielded by combining cinema and literature have traditionally been acknowledged in the literature. Being artistic expressions full of creative language, films require viewers to actively decode the different layers of meaning that create a given literary or audiovisual product. By projecting and analysing French film adaptations of literary classics in the classroom, audiovisual resources are used to exploit students' motivation and encourage them to work proactively with and on literature by fostering their translation skills. In particular, students are asked to hone their critical thinking skills by analysing linguistic features (phonetic, morphosyntactic, lexical, semantic, pragmatic and so forth) and literary devices (discursive structures, style figures, symbols, symmetries and so forth) present in the scripts and the corresponding literary texts before they rewrite them in the target language. A particular emphasis is placed on identifying intertextuality and references to other literary and cinematic texts to further consolidate the literary knowledge built in the learning process.

Capitalising on the importance of the visual medium in an era of global convergence cultures, Carmen Herrero and Isabelle Vanderschelden's chapter examines the pedagogical potential that results from combining transmedia studies and TS to enhance the relevance of literature among language students who may be unfamiliar with media artefacts and literary texts. In the current digital media environment, transmediality allows for intermedial phenomena not connected to a specific medium to be realised in many different media, such as literature, art, film or music. Following a theoretical discussion of the key concepts and theories, the last section of the chapter proposes several examples of transmedia applications in language education. It describes how pedagogical approaches can prompt students to engage in critical readings of classical and modern literary texts across diverse cultures. Transmedia research, understood as a diversification across different cultural industries, is now used in the field of education, particularly for looking at the affordances, challenges and opportunities brought about by the current digital media environment. However, there remains a paucity of work that has critically explored the pedagogical potential of transmedialisation as an effective approach to translation practice and training. After analysing different concepts such as transmedia, transmedia storytelling, transmedia worlds and transmedia adaptation, the authors introduce the models of multimodality and multimodal composition, which have become particularly relevant in contemporary communicative landscapes with the decline of the writing medium. The authors propose several examples of transmedia applications in language teaching settings and critically analyse the process of transmedia adaptation. The latter provides students with a deeper understanding of the steps involved in the design of a transmedia adaptation and the strategies involved in the process of transmedialisation (cross-media and trans-genre storytelling and narrative expansions). The two case studies – *Josep* (Aurel 2020) and *Intemperie* (Zambrano 2019) – illustrate how pedagogical approaches allow students to engage in critical reading of classical and modern literary texts across different cultures.

The relevance of cross-disciplinary intersections in the classroom

This section aims to showcase the latest trends in TS research and its growing cross-pollination with a number of disciplines, such as gender and sexuality studies, cultural and media studies, sociology, politics, linguistics and literary criticism. For the past few decades, EDI policies have enjoyed a prominent place on most universities' agendas, furthering the inclusion of underrepresented groups and embracing more inclusive research, reading lists and modules, and these are some of the most immediate goals of this book. When it comes to TS, there are productive interactions between the fields of modern languages and translation and disciplines such as gender and queer studies, and there is an ever-growing number of researchers and teachers who champion the use of feminist translation and teaching materials that recognise LGBTQI+ identities as vehicles to pursue social and gender equality and to empower minority groups. Against this backdrop, the chapters in this section emphasise the importance of liberating the curriculum to further integrate and embrace inclusivity in the classroom and, therefore, enable diversity and foster equality. From a gender perspective, engagement in pedagogy-focused research helps to promote interdisciplinarity and collaborative thinking in our quest for teaching excellence and leadership driven by women. Likewise, we strive to build bridges between students and teachers with the purpose of establishing a long-lasting allyship that would ensure LGBTQI+ inclusion, recognition and awareness in the modern language classroom.

Despite recent works such as De Marco and Toto's (2019) edited volume on gender approaches in translator education, few attempts have been made to tackle how language and translation teaching materials have traditionally erased sexual, ethnic, class, religious and gender diversity in language and translation curricula. Indeed, current teaching resources – including handbooks, textbooks and manuals – still tend to focus on the portrayal of the world through a Eurocentric, heteronormative, white lens. Our volume champions gender training for translators as a means of promoting social justice inside and outside the classroom. Since the turn of the century, there has been a steady growth in the production of research and scholarship on gender and language, mainly in Western languages, but our volume also seeks to challenge traditional understandings of feminism, which are often preoccupied solely with disparities and gender oppression. Indeed, these mainstream feminisms may come with the cost of overlooking other intersections, contexts and geographies.

In this sense, Xiaofan Amy Li's chapter focuses on contemporary Sinophone poetry written by the women writers Xi Xi and Zhai Yongming. The alliance between feminism and translation has fostered the development of studies centred on the agency and performativity of the translator or the interpreter, as well as their role in society. Nowadays, translation has become a privileged space of agency, activism and resistance. By exploring these writers' poetry and their recent English and French translations, and the cross-pollination of translation with comparative literature, Li reflects on the power of translation as a tool that can change the dynamics between gender, poetic language and power. Her chapter examines translation as a textual force that both genders and de-genders poetic language. Li understands translation in two ways: translation as inherent to the creation of the original text and translation as afterlife – that is, something done to the original text that transforms and multiplies it. Both translational processes are prominent in contemporary Sinophone poetry, in which the female body and feminine perspectives feature, albeit in fragmented, ambiguously gendered ways.

Blending in questions of gender and intersectionality, Mazal Oaknín's chapter proposes a didactic approach to feminist translation, used as a pedagogical act in support of social and gender equality. The chapter describes some translation exercises based on Bernardine Evaristo's *Girl, Woman, Other* (2019) and highlights the potential that pedagogical translation has to bring about social, political and cultural transformation. In order for students to fully understand the excerpts selected – which include instances of discrimination and oppression – and to achieve a successful translation in spite of the many cultural references and unique literary style, it is necessary for them not only to foster their linguistic and translation competence but also to develop their interlinguistic and intercultural abilities and their documentation skills. This chapter champions the use of mediation as a tool to guide students' approach to translating EDI issues. Rather than simply focusing on gender, the excerpts selected raise issues of race, sex, culture, social class, physical ability, sexuality and education. The proposed exercises prompt students to work collaboratively, with both their tutor and peers, to achieve a translation that capitalises on this intersectionality. *Girl, Woman, Other* follows the lives and struggles of twelve characters – eleven women and one non-binary person – all of whom share a common denominator: they are Black and British. This polyphonic novel spans different decades and contexts and presents the protagonists' struggles and acts of resistance as instances of intersectional feminism in modern Britain. Their stories are often interconnected and are defined by the concepts of identity and Otherness. However, said Otherness is not subject to one single interpretation in the novel; the women are matter-of-factly Othered in different ways and even by each other at times. This chapter proposes that, at a time when most universities are increasingly committed to ever-more present EDI agendas, the use of novels that have appealed to the public constitutes an excellent opportunity to expose our students to more inclusionary feminist politics, thus raising awareness of difference (as can be the case of Otherness and Blackness as opposed to normalness and Whiteness), whilst allowing them to fine-tune their translation skills.

The chapter also presents hands-on translation exercises focusing on selected excerpts from the novel. The value of this is twofold. First, the exercises promote classroom discussion on the micro-politics and everyday sexism and misogyny described in the novel as part of a pre-translation analysis. This provides students and tutors with the means to foster gender equality, acknowledge gender diversity and empower minorities through peer discussions. Secondly, the novel's unconventional, experimental style is a form of protest against our contemporary patriarchal, racialised society. The instances of different language used to challenge conventional writing include erratic line breaks and direct and indirect speech mix-ups, with little punctuation and run-on sentences, among other features. The author's peculiar representation of her stream of consciousness is ever-present throughout the novel, and so is her mastery of a myriad of cultural and ideological terms, which she uses to again tackle societal concerns in her fiction. This chapter ultimately aims to demonstrate how translating intersectionality can bring about considerable benefits in literary translation education. On the one hand, in exploring intersectional feminism, tutors can play a pivotal role as agents of resistance and societal change. On the other, these translation exercises give students the means to improve their linguistic and translation skills, foster their interlinguistic and intercultural abilities and develop their documentation skills, all by leading change using a most powerful tool – *Other* words.

Next, John Gray's chapter denounces the rampant lack of recognition of non-normative sexualities and gender diversity in language and translation materials. In this chapter, both explicitly queer and implicitly queer texts are proposed to tackle this erasure and examine how translation practices can contribute to encouraging or foreclosing queer readings. One of the features of much foreign language teaching, certainly in terms of commercially produced textbooks, is the erasure of non-normative sexualities and gender diversity. Teachers, concerned with the impact of this denial of recognition on their LGBTQI+ students and the message this transmits to those who do not identify as LGBTQI+, have frequently been advised to consider the use of well-chosen literary texts by way of redress. This chapter considers the use of what has been described as explicitly queer and implicitly queer literary texts in the classroom from the perspective of the challenges and affordances posed by translation. Gray examines the translation issues raised by the language of insult, as well as that of contemporary sexual and gender politics, in Jarlath Gregory's explicitly queer young adult novel, *What Love Looks Like* (2021). He also peruses existing translations in French and Spanish of the implicitly queer poem *The Owl and the Pussycat* by Edward Lear (1867) and explores how queer readings can be encouraged or foreclosed through translation practices.

In line with the importance of diversity and inclusion in the translation classroom, the last chapter of this volume contains the reflections of an experienced translator trainer who zooms out from the teaching materials and shifts the focus towards in-class discussions and personal experience. Haydn Kirnon concludes our volume by arguing that universities should be welcoming havens for all students and educators, irrespective of background, class, race or sexual orientation. It is thus crucial that all members of the community feel comfortable about their identities to maximise their learning potential and overall educational experience. Teachers can and should play a key role as advocates for LGBTQI+ and other minority students and as creators of safe spaces. This is especially important for the teaching of pedagogical translation in language learning environments, where students are exposed to other ways to experience and communicate with the rest of the world. In this chapter, Kirnon delves into his vast experience as a translator, translation teacher, subtitler and lexicographer in the UK, spanning over three decades. As a proud member of the BAME-BIPOC community, Kirnon reflects on how his translation classes address questions of diversity and inclusivity, and how both trainers and trainees can be allies in the translation classroom.

To conclude this introductory chapter, we understand that this book sets a much-needed precedent in TS scholarship. It not only endeavours to tie closer together two disciplines that are often approached separately – literary translation and AVT – but also sustains a strong focus on research-led education while observing the EDI-related needs in today's higher education sector. In light of the technology-driven transformations affecting our very understanding of translation, and amid ever-more diverse cultures and societies, it is perhaps more necessary than ever to reflect on how we teach languages and translation and to fully embrace change by incorporating a new EDI lens into our research.

Note

1 See https://aplicacionesua.cpd.ua.es/tra_int.

References

Ambrose, Susan A., Michael W. Bridges, Michele DiPietro, Marsha C. Lovett, and Marie K. Norman, eds. 2010. *How Learning Works: Seven research-based principles for smart teaching*. San Francisco, CA: John Wiley and Sons.

Baer, Brian James, and Michelle Woods, eds. 2022. *Teaching Literature in Translation: Pedagogical contexts and reading practices*. London: Routledge.

Bassi, Serena. 2017. 'Displacing LGBT: Global Englishes, activism and translated sexualities'. In *Feminist Translation Studies: Local and transnational perspectives*, edited by Olga Castro and Emek Ergun, 235–48. London: Routledge.

Baxter, Robert Neal. 2005. 'On the need for non-sexist language in translation'. *Language, Society and Culture* 15. Accessed 29 June 2023. https://aaref.com.au/wp-content/uploads/2020/05/15-1.pdf.

Carreres, Ángeles, María Noriega-Sánchez, and Carme Calduch. 2017. *Mundos en palabras. Learning advanced Spanish through translation*. London: Routledge.

Castro, Olga, and Emek Ergun, eds. 2017. *Feminist Translation Studies: Local and transnational perspectives*. London: Routledge.

Cerezo Merchán, Beatriz. 2018. 'Audiovisual translator training'. In *The Routledge Handbook of Audiovisual Translation*, edited by Luis Pérez-González, 468–82. London: Routledge.

Delisle, Jean. 1980. *L'analyse du discours comme méthode de traduction: initiation à la traduction française de textes pragmatiques anglais*. Ottawa: Presses de l'Université d'Ottawa.
De Marco, Marcella, and Piero Toto, eds. 2019. *Gender Approaches in the Translation Classroom: Training the doers*. Cham: Palgrave Macmillan.
Dhanda, Meena. 2010. *Understanding Disparities in Student Attainment: Black and minority ethnic students' experience*. [Report]. Wolverhampton: University of Wolverhampton.
Díaz-Cintas, Jorge, ed. 2008. *The Didactics of Audiovisual Translation*. Amsterdam: John Benjamins.
Evaristo, Bernardine. 2019. *Girl, Woman, Other*. London: Penguin.
Expósito-Castro, Carmen, and María Luisa Rodríguez-Muñoz, eds. 2023. *Guía de buenas prácticas de lenguaje inclusivo para la redacción y la traducción*. Córdoba: UCOPress.
García-Luque, Francisca. 2021. *La adaptación cinematográfica desde una perspectiva traductológica: nuevas vías de investigación*. Granada: Comares.
Gile, Daniel. 1995/2009. *Basic Concepts and Models for Interpreter and Translator Training*. Amsterdam: John Benjamins.
González-Davies, Maria. 2004. *Multiple Voices in the Translation Classroom: Activities, tasks and projects*. Amsterdam: John Benjamins.
Gould, Rebecca Ruth, and Kayvan Tahmasebian, eds. 2017. *The Routledge Handbook of Translation and Activism*. London: Routledge.
Gregory, Jarlath. 2021. *What Love Looks Like*. Dublin: O'Brien Press.
Hurtado-Albir, Amparo, ed. 1999. *Enseñar a traducir: Metodología en la formación de traductores e intérpretes*. Madrid: Edelsa.
Jakobson, Roman. 1959/2021. 'On linguistic aspects of translation'. In *The Translation Studies Reader*, 4th ed., edited by Lawrence Venuti, 113–18. London Routledge.
Kelly, Dorothy. 2005. *A Handbook for Translator Trainers*. Manchester: St Jerome.
Kelly, Dorothy, and Catherine Way. 2007. 'Editorial: On the launch of ITT'. *The Interpreter and Translator Trainer* 1, no. 1: 1–13. https://doi.org/10.1080/1750399X.2007.10798747.
Kenny, Dorothy. 2022. *Machine Translation for Everyone: Empowering users in the age of artificial intelligence*. (Translation and Multilingual Natural Language Processing 18). Berlin: Language Science Press.
Kiraly, Don. 1995. *Pathways to Translation: Pedagogy and process*. Kent, OH: Kent State University Press.
Kiraly, Don. 2000. *A Social Constructivist Approach to Translator Education: Empowering the translator*. Manchester: St Jerome.
Kussmaul, Paul. 1995. *Training the Translator*. Amsterdam: John Benjamins.
Landers, Clifford E. 2001. *Literary Translation: A practical guide*. Clevedon: Multilingual Matters.
Larkosh, Christopher, ed. 2011. *Re-engendering Translation: Transcultural practice, gender/sexuality and the politics of alterity*. London: Routledge.
Laviosa, Sara, and Maria González-Davies, eds. 2020. *The Routledge Handbook of Translation and Education*. London: Routledge.
Lear, Edward. 1867. 'The Owl and the Pussy-Cat'. Poetry Foundation. Accessed 11 September 2023. https://www.poetryfoundation.org/poems/43188/the-owl-and-the-pussy-cat.
Maier, Carol, and François Massardier-Kenney, eds. 2013. *Literature in Translation: Teaching issues and reading practices*. Kent, OH: Kent State University Press.
Massey, Gary, Don Kiraly, and Maureen Ehrensberger-Dow. 2019. 'Training translator trainers: An introduction'. *The Interpreter and Translator Trainer* 13, no. 3: 211–15. https://doi.org/10.1080/1750399X.2019.1647821.
Nord, Christiane. 1988. *Textanalyse und Übersetzen: Theoretische Grundlagen, Methode und didaktische Anwendung einer übersetzungsrelevanten Textanalyse*. Heidelberg: Groos.
Robinson, Douglas. 1991. *Becoming a Translator: An accelerated course*. London: Routledge.
Robinson, Douglas. 2020. *An Introduction to the Theory and Practice of Translation*. London: Routledge.
Santaemilia, José, ed. 2017. *Traducir para la igualdad sexual/Translating for Sexual Equality*. Granada: Comares.
Santaemilia, José. 2018. 'Sexuality and translation as intimate partners? Toward a queer turn in rewriting identities and desires'. In *Queering Translation, Translating the Queer: Theory, practice, activism*, edited by Brian James Baer and Klaus Kaindl, 11–25. London: Routledge.
Seel, Olaf Immanuel, Silvia Roiss, and Petra Zimmermann-González, eds. 2023. *Instrumentalising Foreign Language Pedagogy in Translator and Interpreter Training*. Amsterdam: John Benjamins.
Venuti, Lawrence, ed. 2017. *Teaching Translation: Programs, courses, pedagogies*. London: Routledge.

Way, Catherine. 2020. 'Training and pedagogical implications'. In *The Bloomsbury Companion to Language Industry Studies*, edited by Eric Angelone, Maureen Ehrensberger-Dow, and Garey Massey, 179–208. London: Bloomsbury Academic.

Filmography

Aurel, dir. 2020. *Josep*. Les Films d'Ici Méditerranée. 74 minutes.
Reithmayr, Matthew, dir. 2017. *The Mirror.* Go West Creative [Producer]. 1 minute, 47 seconds.
Zambrano, Benito, dir. 2019. *Intemperie*. Morena Films, Movistar Plus+, RTVE, Aralan Films, Ukbar Filmes. 103 minutes.

Part I
New technologies

2
Translating the unknown: a case study on the usefulness of machine translation in comparative literature research

Sergio Portelli

Introduction

Despite the uneasiness with which the discipline of comparative literature (CL) long regarded translation, at least until the 'cultural turn' in translation studies (TS) in the last decades of the twentieth century (Bassnett 1993; Lefevere 1995; Apter 2006; D'hulst 2007; Tee 2012; Ning and Domínguez 2016), new areas of research in the latter field of study have provided CL with interesting tools that are being increasingly tested, evaluated and used in contemporary scholarship. Apart from translation theory, which, since Walter Benjamin, has increased its relevance within CL (see Apter 2006), the sub-discipline of computer-aided literary translation (CALT), together with the emergence of the digital humanities, has introduced technology as a potentially useful tool in comparative literary research.

CL researchers who deal with non-canonical works may find themselves in a position where their studies are limited by language barriers. Some minor texts, which may be of interest within a wider research topic, may never have been translated, thus rendering it impossible for the researcher to access them without human or technological assistance. Since a fully fledged, publishable translation by a competent literary translator may be expensive and possibly unnecessary for the scope of a research project, machine translation (MT) can prove to be a useful tool. This chapter investigates the extent to which MT may come to a CL researcher's aid in accessing untranslated literary works for specific types of analysis. It limits itself to the genre of historical drama and derives the data for its conclusions from a case study conducted on the German nineteenth-century tragedy *Marino Faliero* by Heinrich Kruse (1876). The text was machine translated, post-edited by the researcher and reviewed by a professional German linguist to obtain an adequate translation in English for CL research purposes.

Comparative literature and translation

D'hulst (2007, 96) states that 'for comparatists, translations are an important source of information to understand the *rapports de faits* between literatures'. However, earlier generations of CL scholars were reluctant to use translations and regarded them as unreliable sources due to the intervention of the translator in the source text (Ning and Domínguez 2016). The only alternative was that comparatists had to be polyglots with a profound knowledge not just of various languages, but also of their respective cultures. In Bassnett's (1993, 139) words, 'a comparatist [...] would read original texts in the original languages, an infinitely superior form of reading than any which involved translation'. Such competence is not very common, especially when it involves languages that are not widely known in the West; this constituted a serious obstacle for prospective researchers interested in the field (Bernheimer 1995). An ever-increasing attention to the literatures of non-Western countries rendered direct access to texts more problematic (Apter 2006). Consequently, the issue of translation could not be ignored much longer (Tee 2012).

The emergence of TS as an academic discipline in the 1970s was a significant step towards the legitimisation of translation in comparative literary studies. The contribution of scholars such as Itamar Even-Zohar on the need to study translations as an important aspect of national literature cannot be underestimated. He expressed his conviction in no uncertain terms when he wrote, 'I conceive of translated literature not only as an integral system within any literary polysystem, but as a most active system within it' (Even-Zohar 1990, 46). The importance of translated literature as literature proper, as well as the need to overcome the focus on the issue of equivalence between source and target texts, was taken further by the scholars of the Manipulation School, who advocated 'a descriptive method [that] takes the translated text as it is and tries to determine the various factors that may account for its particular nature' (Hermans 1985, 13). They focused on the reasons why texts are translated into a specific language, the conditions under which a translation is produced and the intention(s) behind the process and the product itself. In the early 1980s, Lefevere introduced the concepts of 'refraction' and 'rewriting' in the manipulation of literature. He defined refraction as 'the adaptation of a work of literature to a different audience, with the intention of influencing the way in which that audience reads the work' (Lefevere 1982, 4), whereas in his later elaboration of the concept of rewriting he emphasised the role of power dynamics, where patronage, ideology and poetics all play a part in the manipulation of literature, also by means of translation (Lefevere 1992). Together with Bassnett, he overturned the generally accepted hierarchy between CL and TS by stating that:

> translation has been a major shaping force in the development of world culture, and no study of comparative literature can take place without regard to translation. We have both suggested on occasions, with a deliberate intention of subverting the status quo and drawing attention to the importance of Translation Studies, that perhaps we should rethink our notions of Comparative Literature and redefine it as a sub-category of Translation Studies instead of vice versa. (Bassnett and Lefevere 1990, 12)

Bassnett (1993, 161) reaffirmed this position by declaring that CL was on its way out and that it should be considered as a 'subsidiary subject area' with respect to TS. The affirmation of the cultural turn in TS in the 1990s brought the two disciplines closer together. At the beginning of the new century, translation became an important feature in CL at a time when world literature was gaining prominence (Ning and Domínguez 2016). The potential for collaboration between the two disciplines with reference to world literature was highlighted by Bermann (2009, 432, 443), who, in her 2009 American Comparative Literature Association (ACLA) presidential address, envisaged the creation of an '*and* zone', a space of interaction between TS and CL that 'becomes the site for articulating an interpretation, or a theoretical meditation on the qualities or limitations of the text, or a critical reflection on literature more generally'.

The success of academic programmes in TS worldwide in recent decades has put the discipline on a firm standing and affirmed its interdisciplinarity. In light of this development, CL can only gain from the potential insights provided by TS. D'hulst (2007, 103) recognised this when he rhetorically asked, 'why should comparative literature be reluctant when it comes to recognizing the conceptual apparatus and methodology that has been developed for the study of translation?'

Computer-aided literary translation

Apart from literary translation and translation theory, which are the two sub-fields of TS that are most readily considered to be close to CL, another area that has recently been gaining more attention is CALT. It may be classified within the emerging research area of the digital humanities, where digital technology is applied to the various fields in the humanities. The application of computers to the study of literary translation began in the 1960s, when machines became capable of processing elements of texts in electronic format (Zanettin 2017). As digital technology improved, the possibility of obtaining data from text processing opened new avenues for research in various areas of literary studies. Zanettin (2017) has identified two main areas to which computer-assisted research has more readily been applied, namely the creation of searchable electronic archives of texts in digital format and textual analysis within the wider context of stylistics. Searches at a lexical and syntactic level may shed light on the linguistic and stylistic characteristics of one or more translations of a particular author and pave the way for broader comparative analyses. The creation of corpora of literary translations allows for a vast range of studies based on the analysis of statistical data, such as the visibility of translators, the latter's lexical and stylistic choices and differences between translations of a particular text across time.

Another important aspect of CALT concerns the types of translation technology applied to literary texts, especially MT. In recent years, the quality of MT has improved greatly (Toral and Way 2015). The transition from rule-based and statistical methods to neural networks has resulted in the production of higher-quality raw output that requires less human post-editing (see Castilho et al. 2017). Whereas MT is generally used for non-literary texts, in recent years studies have been carried out to evaluate the extent to which such tools may be used in the actual production of literary translations. Genzel et al. (2010, 163) used a custom statistical phrase-based MT tool to produce translations of poetry with meter and rhyme, reaching the conclusion that 'it seems that at the present state of MT, one does indeed have to choose between getting either the form or the meaning right'.

Greene et al. (2010) used statistical machine tools to analyse and generate love poetry in English and then to translate rhythmic poetry from Italian to English. What is of interest here is their attempt to translate Dante's rhymed hendecasyllables of the *Divine Comedy* into English rhymed iambic pentameters. The quality of the translations, bound as they were by prosodic and rhyme constraints, apart from the need to render the meaning and effect of the source text, was unsatisfactory. This led the researchers to suggest that rather than seeking such an objective, a text generation and translation program may be used 'for inspiration' rather than for the production of poetic texts (Greene et al. 2010, 532).

Jones and Irvine (2013) analysed samples of machine-translated French literature into English in order to gauge the extent to which a machine can convey the 'experience' of reading a text, since literature elicits a special type of involvement by the reader that other text types do not. More specifically, they analysed the raw output in terms of textual fidelity and the ethical aspect of the translator's (in)visibility, as discussed by Venuti (2008). They used both a custom phrase-based tool and Google Translate for comparison in order to see how MT deals with domestication and foreignisation. The results of their study showed that statistical MT cannot adopt translation strategies considering the issue of ethnocentricity. The issue of the translator's 'voice' in CALT has more recently been discussed by Taivalkoski-Shilov (2019) and Kenny and Winters (2020), from an ethical perspective.

In a pilot study, Besacier (2014) used MT to translate a previously untranslated text by American writer Richard Powers into French. The raw output was then post-edited by non-professional translators and subsequently evaluated by a professional translator, who noted that the final version had certain linguistic and stylistic shortcomings, namely syntactic calques, the presence of anglicisms and the incorrect rendering of culture-specific elements (Besacier 2014, 393). Besacier concluded that such a low-cost process may have some benefits, such as the possibility for authors to have their books quickly translated into many languages. However, he wondered if sacrificing quality for a wider diffusion would be worthwhile for a writer. From the readers' perspective, potential benefits would be faster access to translations of their favourite author's works, and having the translation as an aide for non-native readers, who may struggle to understand certain passages in the original text (Besacier 2014, 394).

Like Besacier's study, that of Toral and Way (2015) also focused on the quality of machine-translated literary texts. They built custom statistical MT systems to translate novels from Spanish into Catalan and from Spanish into English. In order to investigate whether statistical MT may be used successfully to translate literary texts, they compared the degree of freedom of the translation and the narrowness of parallel corpora in the domain of literature to other non-literary domains. They also focused on two specific parameters: the closeness of the languages and the literary genre. Their most interesting claims, based on their results, are that the closeness of related languages is a primary factor in translation freedom and that MT 'can be useful to assist with the translation of novels between closely related languages' (Toral and Way 2015, 130).

Recently, a stronger focus has been placed on the post-editing of literary texts, in which professional literary translators have been asked to post-edit statistical and/or neural machine-translated texts, thus providing analysable data (Moorkens et al. 2018; Toral and Way 2018; Toral et al. 2018; Kenny and Winters 2020; Castilho and Resende 2022). Toral and Way (2018) trained both a phrase-based statistical and a neural MT engine on large amounts of literary texts (over 100 million words) and then used the engines to translate 12 widely known modern and contemporary novels. The Bilingual Evaluation Understudy (BLEU) automatic evaluation metric showed that neural MT performed better than phrase-based MT, whereas an additional human evaluation of three of the novels showed that in some cases the automatic translations were deemed of similar quality to those done by human translators.

In another study, Toral et al. (2018, 1) claimed that theirs was 'the first experiment in the literature in which a novel is translated automatically and then post-edited by professional literary translators'. As a case study, they translated a chapter of an English-language fantasy novel into Catalan, using both phrase-based statistical and neural MT. The raw output from both tools was then post-edited by six experienced professional translators, who also translated the text from scratch for comparative purposes. In all three cases, the researchers recorded all the keystrokes, the time taken to translate each sentence, the number of pauses and their duration. The results showed that the use of both types of MT led to an increase in productivity, a reduction in the number of keystrokes and a reduction in pauses, though the pauses tended to be longer. In all cases, neural MT performed better than its statistical counterpart. The data collected for this study was used by Moorkens et al. (2018), who collected feedback from the participants before and after the post-editing and translation. The researchers found that the participants unanimously preferred to translate from scratch because the option allowed them greater freedom, but those with less experience appreciated the usefulness of the raw output from MT.

Another study on literary translators' perspectives regarding post-editing was conducted by Kenny and Winters (2020). They sought to investigate to what extent the raw output produced by neural MT influences the *textual voice* of the literary translator who post-edits it. A professional translator from English into German was asked to post-edit an excerpt from a novel he had previously translated and to comment on his task. The researchers concluded that post-editing affected the translator's textual voice, which was deemed less perceivable than in the version he had previously translated from scratch.

Another very recent study on literary post-editing was carried out by Castilho and Resende (2022), who investigated the phenomenon of post-editese in literary texts. The term post-editese refers to the difference between the characteristics of texts translated by a human translator and those of the respective post-edited versions, in relation to the raw output produced by an MT tool (Castilho and Resende 2022, 4). The researchers carried out a study on two novels, Lewis Carroll's *Alice's Adventures in Wonderland* and Paula Hawkins' *The Girl on the Train*. The texts were translated from English into Brazilian Portuguese using Google Translate and analysed to identify the nature and extent of post-editing features present in them. The post-edited translations were then compared to human translations to highlight the differences. The results showed, among other things, that the Hawkins text required less post-editing than the one by Carroll, leading the researchers to conclude that 'while literary texts whose author's style is full of figurative language pose a harder challenge to the MT system, texts that emphasise action over language style are less challenging' (Castilho and Resende 2022, 19).

Scope of the study

The present study brings together both CL and CALT in that it investigates how CL researchers may resort to MT in order to overcome the not-uncommon problem of not knowing the language of a text they need to access for a specific research project. When studying groups of lesser-known and often untranslated works across languages, researchers may be faced with a potentially unsurmountable language barrier. As a possible solution to the problem, the present researcher sought to devise a methodology that could allow access to untranslated literary works for comparative studies specifically focused on plot and narrative structure. The methodology was tested on a German text, which the researcher could not read because he does not know the language. A freely available neural MT tool was used to obtain a raw output before the text was post-edited by the researcher himself to obtain a version that was comprehensible enough for him to follow. The third and final stage consisted of a revision of the post-edited version by an experienced literary translator who works out of German into English. If successful, the model could be replicated for other works and other languages, thus allowing CL scholars to access literature in a wider range of languages.

The object of the study was a German five-act tragedy written in the nineteenth century, entitled *Marino Faliero*. It was published in 1876 by Heinrich Kruse, a liberal journalist and writer who believed in a united German state led by Prussia (Kruse-Jarres 2008). His 16 historical dramas focus on issues such as justice, morality and uprightness. They were never successful, neither during his lifetime nor after, and no English translations have been traced.[1] *Marino Faliero* was never reprinted, and therefore only one version of the text exists. It consists of 2,893 verses (mostly unrhymed iambic pentameters), stage directions and a small number of footnotes.

Methodology

In the pre-translation phase, the first step was to prepare the source text for MT. The text is copyright-free and freely available on the internet (such as on Google Books). The book is printed in the Gothic Fraktur typeface, which initially made the text difficult to read. Moreover, since the PDF document is a scanned version, the text could not be digitally copied. The commonly used optical character recognition (OCR) tool for Fraktur, ABBYY FineReader, could not be used, for technical and financial reasons – the software does not run on a Mac operating system and its license is too expensive for a one-off text conversion. Moreover, any character recognition errors would have been difficult for the researcher to identify because of the language barrier. Consequently, the text was manually transcribed into an editable document.

As previously mentioned, reading the text was initially complicated because it required getting used to the typeface. In the beginning, the transcription process was considerably slow, because every letter had to be distinguished from the others, especially those that are graphically very similar; however, eventually the researcher got accustomed to the script and proceeded at a faster pace. Transcribing an unknown language requires great attention and a relatively slow pace, but once the most common words become familiar, the process becomes quicker. Typing errors and mistakes were corrected with the help of a spellchecker. There were a few cases where spelling mistakes were identified in the post-editing stage because the raw output of a specific verse was wrong or out of context. In fact, correct spelling was always checked first whenever the corresponding raw output was difficult to understand. The transcription strictly followed the page layout of the book, so that the verses could be easily located in the book for verification purposes. This was very important, since the researcher could not understand the source text and orient himself accordingly.

Once the transcription was completed, the source text was ready for translation. It was decided to use an open-access neural MT tool, DeepL, which has been found to be the best performing engine for the German–English language pair (Savenkov 2019). The translation was carried out in batches of not more than 10 verses at a time; this allowed the researcher to make sure that no verses were skipped or only partially translated due to errors in copying and pasting from the text document to the browser and vice versa. At this stage it was important to make sure that the verses had been fully translated. This was done by checking that the raw output reflected the source text in terms of punctuation and sentence completeness, but no other validation of the translation output was carried out. The process was time consuming, but the lack of source language competence required a particularly cautious approach. It also ensured that no errors were made in the input stage and provided a first, basic check of the completeness of the output.

Subsequently, the raw output from DeepL was post-edited by the researcher to obtain a version that could be useful for an analysis of the plot and narrative structure of Kruse's drama. This was done by resorting to online dictionaries and other resources, as well as by consulting colleagues from the University of Malta's Department of German. Such a step was crucial for this specific study, because the researcher could log all the instances where problems of comprehension arose and had to be solved. The post-edited version was then submitted to an experienced literary translator for revision. This was necessary to obtain a high-quality version to use as a reference for back translation, in the absence of a previously published English translation of the play.

In order to assess the usefulness of the raw output from the MT as a CL research tool, it was necessary to focus on its adequacy for the scope of the study. In this specific case, adequacy meant allowing the researcher to follow the plot and the text with ease. The priority being comprehension, not the linguistic correctness of the target text, the evaluation criteria were necessarily different from the ones normally applied in other areas of research on MT (see, for instance, Daems et al. 2017; Popović 2018). This sort of evaluation, for research purposes, requires a specific focus on certain error types rather than on others that may be equally if not more important for studies on MT quality.

In this study, the term 'comprehensibility issues' is used to refer to the translation errors that hindered the researcher's comprehension of the raw output. This is because a distinction was made between MT errors that did not create comprehensibility problems for the researcher and those which made it necessary for the researcher to consult dictionaries and other resources in order to follow the text. In many cases, errors that would normally require correction in the post-editing process were not an obstacle to comprehension, since the meaning could be taken from the context. Two examples where translation errors were not counted as comprehensibility issues are '*Erster Aufzug*' and '*Erster Auftritt*' (Kruse 1876, 5), which were translated by DeepL as 'first elevator' and 'first appearance' respectively. From the context, it was clear that their meanings were 'Act One' and 'Scene One', so they did not pose any obstacles to comprehension. All the other instances where *Aufzug* and *Auftritt* were translated in a similar way were thus ignored.

The peculiar nature of this study required an ad hoc taxonomy of comprehensibility issues. These were categorised as follows:

- Lexical: Where a term hindered comprehension by altering the meaning of a phrase or verse. Examples of such instances are '*Dienertroß*' (Kruse 1876, 18), translated as 'servant's horse' (post-edited as 'group of servants'), and '*Ruf*' (Kruse 1876, 34), translated as 'call' (post-edited as 'reputation').[2]
- Semantic: Where a phrase or verse was unclear and could not be inferred from the context. An example of such issues is '*Doch will ich mir die Wahrheit eingesteh'n, / Ist aller meiner Sorgen schlimmste noch, / Es könnte dennoch nicht Verleumdung sein!*' (Kruse 1876, 40), translated by DeepL as 'But I will admit the truth to myself, / Is the worst of all my worries, / Yet it could not be slander!' The verses were post-edited as 'But I must admit to myself that in truth, / The worst of all my worries / Is not the defamation'.
- Grammatical: Where there was ambiguity, mainly caused by incorrect pronoun agreement. An example of such instances is 'The Doge does it like a chestnut woman, / That makes a great noise before the judges, / Showing the naked parts of *his* head, / Where the neighbour tore out *his* hair, / But quite forgets to tell the judges, / That it was *she* who started it / And went into the neighbour's hair'. The italicised pronouns should all be feminine because they refer to the 'chestnut woman' (a female peasant). The source passage reads: '*Der Doge macht's wie ein Kastanienweib, / Das vor den Richtern großen Lärm verführt, / Die nackten Stellen auf dem Kopfe zeigend, / Wo ihm die Nachbarin die / Haare ausriß, / Doch ganz vergißt den Richtern zu erzählen, / Daß sie es war, die angefangen hat / Und in die Haare fuhr der Nachbarin*' (Kruse 1876, 18). Another example is the translation of '*Ich kann sie fragen*

– *(unwillig mit dem Fuße stampfend)*' (Kruse 1876, 42) as 'I can ask her – (reluctantly stamping *my* foot)', where the italicised pronoun should read 'his'.

- Word order: Where awkward word order caused ambiguity or lack of clarity. Since German syntax differs considerably from that of English, certain phrases and verses that were translated literally were not easily understood. An example of word-order comprehensibility issues is '*Dann laß ich läuten mit der großen Glocke, / Die nur auf meinen schriftlichen Befehl / Gezogen werden darf*' (Kruse 1876, 81), which was machine-translated as 'Then let me ring with the great bell, / Which may only be rung by my written command / To be pulled'. The post-edited version read: 'Then I will give orders to ring the great bell, / Which may only be rung by my written command'. Another example is '*Jawohl, an seinem Thron, / Auf welchem fremde Fürsten und Gejandte / Im Staat der doge zu empfangen pflegt*' (Kruse 1876, 5), which was translated as 'Yes, at his throne, / On which foreign princes and envoys / In the state of the doge to receive' and post-edited as 'Yes, on his throne, / Where the Duke receives foreign princes and envoys / As head of state'.
- Cultural: Where culture-specific terms, expressions or allusions remained unadapted or obscure. For example, the noun *Fuder* in '*Und Trunk'nen muß sogar ein Fuder Heu / Ausweichen*' (Kruse 1876, 9) refers to an old liquid measure, which was mainly used for wine. However, DeepL translated the verse as 'And drunkenness must even win a cartload of hay / Evade it'. Originally, *Fuder* meant the carriage load of a two-horse carriage. However, the measure was also used for many other products, such as hay, ore or coal, or as a meadow measure (the area that provided one load of hay). As a measure for wine, there were large regional differences, which varied between about 800 to 1,800 litres. Today the term refers to a type of wine barrel still in use in Germany. Since this is a pun to mean that the person addressed must avoid drinking, it was post-edited as 'And drunkards must avoid even a barrel'. The pun is lost in translation, but the meaning is thus conveyed to the target reader. Another example is the word *Flatterhans* in '*Der Flatterhans hat mich verlassen*' (Kruse 1876, 37). The word is an appellation referring to levity or inconstancy and was left untranslated in the raw output. It was then post-edited as 'shallow man' in the phrase 'That shallow man left me'.

- Additions: Terms, strings of words or phrases, mostly repetitions, which are not found in the source text. Verification was needed to make sure that these repetitions were not used for emphasis in the German version. An example is DeepL's translation of '*Als Sodom und Gomorrha / Der Sünden voll war, wollte die Gerechten / Der Herr doch scheiden von den Ungerechten*' (Kruse 1876, 82) as 'When Sodom and Gomorrah / Were full of sins, the Lord would separate / The Lord wanted to separate the righteous from the unrighteous'. Another example is '*Ihr sollet alles Volk in Kanaan / Vertilgen mit dem Schwert, verschonet Niemand!*' (Kruse 1876, 82), which contains the following italicised addition: 'You shall *destroy* all the people of Canaan / Destroy with the sword, spare none!'. Another instance of an addition is '*Heut Morgen fanden sich am Dogenstuhl / Schmähverse angeschrieben*' (Kruse 1876, 5), which was rendered by DeepL as 'This morning at the Doge's Chair / Verses of invective written on the Doge's chair' and post-edited as 'This morning / Offensive words were written on the Doge's throne'.
- Non-translations: Where untranslated words, left in German, hampered comprehension. An example is 'Up the stairs I found myself / *Grad'* on the place of execution between the two columns' (German: '[...] *da fand ich mich / Grad' auf dem Richtplatz zwischen beiden Säulen*', Kruse 1876, 28). The post-edited version read: 'Up the steps I found myself / On the place of execution between the two columns'. Another example is '*Ab*. Behind him *Steno*' (German: '*Ab. Hinter ihm Steno*', Kruse 1876, 21), which was post-edited as 'He leaves. Steno follows him out'. Untranslated words in Italian found in the source text were not considered as comprehensibility issues, since the researcher understands the language.
- Mistranslations: Where the translation in the raw output was pragmatically incorrect. An example is 'We didn't need to punish Steno at all; / The slight cancels itself out' for '*Wir brauchten Steno gar nicht zu bestrafen; / Die Kränkung hebt sich auf*' (Kruse 1876, 23). These verses were post-edited as 'We did not need to punish Steno at all; / The offence will be forgotten'. Another one is the German verse '*Kein finst'rer Ernst hält seiner Laune Stand*' (Kruse 1876, 44), translated as 'And he's not a man to be taken lightly'. The post-edited version was 'No seriousness can withstand his humour'.

Every comprehensibility issue encountered during the post-editing process was colour coded. The identification and categorisation of each instance was inevitably subjective, since what may be an issue for one reader may not be so for another, and some of the issues were not clear-cut cases in terms of which category they fitted into. A case in point is the above-mentioned example of *Flatterhans*, where the issue could well have been classified in the 'Non-translations' category. Consequently, the number of issues per category should not be considered in absolute terms. What is indicative is the proportion between them, which sheds light on the overall nature of the challenge posed by using MT to understand a nineteenth-century German historical drama.

Findings and analysis

The table below lists the total number of comprehensibility issues encountered in the raw output provided by DeepL, together with the number of occurrences for each category described above.

As can be seen from Table 2.1, a total of 380 comprehensibility issues were encountered. Of these, the most frequent were semantic issues and mistranslations. Lexical issues were less frequent, but their percentage is still significant. The prevalence of these categories is to be expected, since they are the ones that most depend on context and require the pragmatic competence of a human translator. An unexpected indication from these results is the relatively high percentage of additions, which, despite not impeding overall comprehension, had to be checked every time to make sure that they were not found in the source text and that they were not a stylistic expedient used by the author.

The most significant result of this study from a CL perspective is that the translation of Heinrich Kruse's historical tragedy *Marino Faliero*

Category	Frequency	Percentage
Semantic	100	26.32%
Mistranslations	86	22.63%
Lexical	64	16.84%
Additions	52	13.68%
Grammatical	28	7.38%
Non-translations	20	5.26%
Word order	16	4.21%
Cultural	14	3.68%
Grand Total	**380**	**100%**

Table 2.1 Occurrences of comprehensibility issues in raw output, in descending order

using DeepL achieved the goal of allowing the researcher to obtain direct access to the text despite not knowing the source language. The raw output required post-editing to clarify comprehensibility issues, as described above. However, considering that the text is in verse form and was written in nineteenth-century German, and considering its length, the number of issues was deemed reasonable. The post-editing process required time and external assistance from German specialists and a reviser. The latter's intervention was especially important for the identification of some expressions that had not been adequately rendered by DeepL and could not be identified as such by the researcher. A case in point was the rendering of '*Dem Dogen mag die Galle überlaufen*' (Kruse 1876, 7), which in the raw output was rendered as 'The Doge's gall may run' and was post-edited as 'The Doge's gall may be too much'. However, the reviser noted that the source text refers to the expression '*jemand läuft die Galle über*', which resulted in the final translation reading 'The Doge may well be very angry'. Such instances were counted as semantic incomprehensibility issues, since they altered the meaning of the specific phrase. Apart from possible better translation alternatives, the reviser identified only 9 mistranslations, such as the example above, and 16 partially correct renderings, mostly due to missing modifiers such as adjectives and adverbs. At the end of the process, the translation was deemed adequate for research purposes, allowing for a reliable analysis of the narrative elements of the text, which was the ultimate scope of the exercise.

The applicability of the model above is subject to many conditions. Firstly, its feasibility depends on the time at the researcher's disposal. The time element is crucial when deciding whether translating a work this way would be advisable or not, and if the process would benefit the CL research project at hand. In most cases, the time-consuming transcription phase would be much shorter, since most texts are printed in fonts for which OCR is widely available and only revision would thus be required. A more important factor is the availability of human assistance in the source language. In this study, the researcher could rely on the help of German scholars and a literary translator to solve issues that could not be settled by an online search. If the source text had been written in a lesser-used language for which no human assistance was available, the final target text would not have been validated and thus would have been unreliable. Other limitations may be the length of the source text and its stylistic characteristics, especially if it relies heavily on metaphors, allegories, allusions, neologisms, unconventional use of language, and the sound and rhythm of the words.

Conclusion

Using MT to access literary works in a language which a researcher cannot understand comes with many caveats. Before making such an attempt, the feasibility of obtaining a useful target text must be carefully evaluated. Not all literary genres and texts can be machine-translated usefully for comparative purposes. Despite the significant improvements brought about by neural MT, especially for the most widely used languages, the raw output must be relied upon with great caution, because not all mistranslations are easily identifiable. This renders the interpretation of the target text much more difficult; mistakes can easily be made. If a source text is strongly characterised by figurative language, wordplay, puns, allusions and other stylistic elements, it would not be a suitable candidate for MT. The time, effort and expertise required to post-edit the target text would make the exercise unviable, and anything short of professional human literary translation would not be enough to attain reliable access to the source text. However, the MT post-editing of Kruse's historical drama *Marino Faliero* was successful enough to provide a reliable target text. The length and format of the text –around three thousand unrhymed verses mainly consisting of dialogue – made it suitable for the case study. The fact that the source text was written in the nineteenth century did not have a significant bearing on the results, since most comprehensibility issues were not determined by archaic or obsolete words. In most cases, the obstacles to comprehension were due to an inadequate link between the phrase or sentence being translated and its wider context. This gave rise to semantic, syntactic and grammatical issues, as well as outright mistranslations that hindered reading and comprehension of some passages of the target text.

Notwithstanding its shortcomings, which could be expected given that it is a work in progress, MT should not be ignored as a tool for research from a CL perspective. As long as expectations are not too high and objectives are set to realistic levels, it can give researchers access to texts in languages that were hitherto inaccessible to them. In the case study described above, the researcher had two options: to keep aloof from Kruse's drama or to try MT and see if he could work with its output. The result was useful and could help one gain insights on the way that Kruse dealt with his subject matter, which could then be compared with strategies used by other writers. Translation technology is not a tool that is often looked upon favourably by literary scholars, but in certain cases it may be useful to overcome the language barriers that have limited the reach of researchers in CL for a long time.

Notes

1 No English translations have been found in the catalogues of the British Library and the Library of Congress.

2 Back translations and post-editing consider the context of the passage where the relevant words, phrases or sentences are found.

References

Apter, Emily. 2006. *The Translation Zone: A new comparative literature*. Princeton, NJ: Princeton University Press.

Bassnett, Susan. 1993. *Comparative Literature: A critical introduction*. Oxford: Blackwell.

Bassnett, Susan, and André Lefevere, eds. 1990. *Translation, History and Culture*. London: Cassell.

Bermann, Sandra. 2009. 'Working in the And Zone: Comparative literature and translation'. *Comparative Literature* 61: 432–46.

Bernheimer, Charles, ed. 1995. *Comparative Literature in the Age of Multiculturalism*. Baltimore, MD: Johns Hopkins University Press.

Besacier, Laurent. 2014. 'Traduction automatisée d'une oeuvre littéraire: une étude pilote'. In *21ème Traitement Automatique des Langues Naturelles*, Association for Computer Linguistics, 389–94.

Castilho, Sheila, Joss Moorkens, Federico Gaspari, Iacer Calixto, John Tinsley, and Andy Way. 2017. 'Is neural machine translation the new state of the art?' *Prague Bulletin of Mathematical Linguistics* 108: 109–20.

Castilho, Sheila, and Natália Resende. 2022. 'Post-editese in literary translations', *Information* 13, no. 2: #66. https:// doi.org/10.3390/info13020066.

Daems, Joke, Sonia Vandepitte, Robert J. Hartsuiker, and Lieve Macken. 2017. 'Identifying the machine translation error types with the greatest impact on post-editing effort', *Front Psychol* 8: #1282. https://doi.org/10.3389/fpsyg.2017.01282.

D'hulst, Lieven. 2007. 'Comparative literature versus translation studies: Close encounters of the third kind?' *European Review* 15, no. 1: 95–104. https://doi.org/10.1017/S1062798707000099.

Even-Zohar, Itamar. 1990. 'The position of translated literature within the literary polysystem', *Poetics Today* 11, no. 1: 45–51. https://doi.org/10.2307/1772668.

Genzel, Dmitriy, Jakob Uszkoreit, and Franz Och. 2010. '"Poetic" statistical machine translation: Rhyme and meter'. In *Proceedings of the 2010 Conference on Empirical Methods in Natural Language Processing*, edited by Hang Li and Lluís Màrquez, 158–66. Cambridge, MA: Association for Computational Linguistics.

Greene, Erica, Tugba Bodrumlu, and Kevin Knight. 2010. 'Automatic analysis of rhythmic poetry with applications to generation and translation'. In *Proceedings of the 2010 Conference on Empirical Methods in Natural Language Processing*, edited by Hang Li and Lluís Màrquez, 524–33. Cambridge, MA: Association for Computational Linguistics.

Hermans, Theo, ed. 1985. *The Manipulation of Literature: Studies in literary translation*. London: Croom Helm.

Jones, Ruth, and Ann Irvine. 2013. 'The (un)faithful machine translator'. In *Proceedings of the 7th Workshop on Language Technology for Cultural Heritage, Social Sciences, and Humanities*, 96–101. Sofia: Association for Computational Linguistics.

Kenny, Dorothy, and Marion Winters. 2020. 'Machine translation, ethics and the literary translator's voice', *Translation Spaces* 9, no. 1: 123–49. https://doi.org/10.1075/ts.00024.ken.

Kruse, Heinrich. 1876. *Marino Faliero: Trauerspiel in fünf Aufzügen*. Leipzig: S. Hirzel.

Kruse-Jarres, Jürgen D. 2008. *Heinrich Kruse: Journalist und Schriftsteller Ein Kämpfer für den Liberalismus im 19. Jahrhundert*. Düsseldorf: Grupello Verlag.

Lefevere, André. 1982. 'Mother courage's cucumbers: Text, system and refraction in a theory of literature', *Modern Language Studies* 12, no. 4: 3–20. https://doi.org/10.2307/3194526.

Lefevere, André. 1992. *Translation, Rewriting and the Manipulation of Literary Fame*. London: Routledge.

Lefevere, André. 1995. 'Introduction: Comparative literature and translation', *Comparative Literature* 47, no. 1: 1–10.

Moorkens, Joss, Antonio Toral, Sheila Castilho, and Andy Way. 2018. 'Translators' perceptions of literary post-editing using statistical and neural machine translation', *Translation Spaces* 7, no. 2: 240–62. https://doi.org/10.1075/ts.18014.moo.

Ning, Wang, and César Domínguez. 2016. 'Comparative literature and translation: A cross-cultural and interdisciplinary perspective'. In *Border Crossings: Translation studies and other disciplines*, edited by Yves Gambier and Luc van Doorslaer, 287–308. Amsterdam: John Benjamins.

Popović, Maja. 2018. 'Error classification and analysis for machine translation quality assessment'. In *Translation Quality Assessment: From principles to practice*, edited by Joss Moorkens, Sheila Castilho, Federico Gaspari, and Stephen Doherty, 129–58. Cham: Springer.

Savenkov, Konstantin. 2019. 'State of the machine translation', Intento blog, 19 June 2019. Accessed 3 April 2024. https://blog.inten.to/state-of-the-machine-translation-june-2019-e3ffb457b76c.

Taivalkoski-Shilov, Kristiina. 2019. 'Ethical issues regarding machine(-assisted) translation of literary texts', *Perspectives* 27, no. 5: 689–703. https://doi.org/10.1080/0907676X.2018.1520907.

Tee, Carlos G. 2012. 'Towards a new and more constructive partnership: The changing role of translation in comparative literature', *Fu Jen Studies: Literature and Linguistics* 45: 1–21.

Toral, Antonio, and Andy Way. 2015. 'Translating literary text between related languages using SMT'. In *Proceedings of NAACL-HLT Fourth Workshop on Computational Linguistics for Literature*, edited by Anna Feldman, Anna Kazantseva, Stan Szpakowicz, and Corina Koolen, 123–32. Denver, CO: Association for Computational Linguistics.

Toral, Antonio, and Andy Way. 2018. 'What level of quality can neural machine translation attain on literary text?' In *Translation Quality Assessment: From principles to practice*, edited by Joss Moorkens, Sheila Castilho, Federico Gaspari, and Stephen Doherty, 263–87. Cham: Springer.

Toral, Antonio, Martijn Wieling, and Andy Way. 2018. 'Post-editing effort of a novel with statistical and neural machine translation', *Frontiers in Digital Humanities* 5: #9. https://doi.org/10.3389/fdigh.2018.00009.

Venuti, Lawrence. 2008. *The Translator's Invisibility: A history of translation*. 2nd ed. London: Routledge.

Zanettin, Federico. 2017. 'Issues in computer-assisted literary translation studies', *inTRAlinea*, Special Issue: Corpora and Literary Translation, edited by Titika Dimitroulia and Dionysis Goutsos. Accessed 3 April 2024. https://www.intralinea.org/specials/article/2254.

3

Learning foreign languages through telecollaboration: embedding didactic audiovisual translation in the language classroom

Alejandro Bolaños García-Escribano
Beatriz Cerezo Merchán

Introduction

In today's globalised world, international collaboration, primarily fuelled by the internet and new communication technologies, is increasingly present in higher education. Nowadays, interaction between people from different linguistic and cultural backgrounds is a widespread reality, and work environments have changed considerably in the light of new modes of remote communication. There are, for instance, a greater number of professionals working in cross-cultural teams and communicating with each other via digital platforms and videoconferencing tools. To stay in tune with these systemic changes affecting work patterns, future professionals, such as linguists and translators, need to acquire twenty-first-century soft skills. For example, they ought to be capable of working in multilingual and multicultural teams, be they face to face or remote, and of managing and leading projects involving international members. The COVID-19 pandemic has enhanced off-site work, making remote and flexible work and international collaboration key aspects for businesses to succeed worldwide.

Higher education has been no exception to these substantial changes. In a very short space of time, particularly as a result of the lockdowns imposed in many countries across the globe in early 2020, universities had to embrace new communication systems and adapt their workflows to continue providing education with the use of remote technologies such as videoconferencing and online learning platforms, or learning management systems (LMSs). In blended learning – a learning approach that combines face-to-face classroom instruction with online activities and materials – online platforms such as Blackboard or Moodle have traditionally proved to be useful, albeit limited, for learning and teaching synchronous lessons online. Communication pathways among students are often insufficient in these systems, which are designed as online repositories fully controlled by instructors. Despite the evident disadvantages of abruptly switching to online teaching, the globality of lockdowns also created opportunities for learners to interact with each other online in a similar fashion to telecollaboration teaching approaches (Huertas-Abril 2020; Beecroft and Bauer 2022). Telecollaboration, herein understood as a form of virtual mobility (O'Dowd 2013), existed well before the eruption of the pandemic (see, for instance, Belz 2003; Dooly and O'Dowd 2018). As a matter of fact, telecollaboration had previously been adopted by university educators in Europe and elsewhere in projects involving students from a wide variety of schools and universities, and it is claimed to foster twenty-first-century competences, including linguistic, intercultural, digital and teamwork skills (Sevilla-Pavón 2020). In light of increasing scholarly interest in embedding telecollaboration in translator education (Marczak 2023), this chapter examines the application of telecollaboration practices in the teaching of a foreign language (FL) for the development of communicative competences.

There is an abundance of language-related literature that demonstrates the utility of telecollaboration for international interaction between students, which enables them to communicate using their FL skills. This chapter presents a telecollaboration project proposal focused on using didactic audiovisual translation (AVT) in language learning settings (see Chapter 4 by Ogea-Pozo and Talaván in this book). In particular, we discuss how to embed telecollaboration in an English-language module for student translators offered at the University of Valencia (UV), Spain, and a Spanish-language module for linguists in training from UCL in the UK. The discussion builds on teaching experiences from pre-pandemic times, in which students were exposed to innovative tasks that they completed in international teams. We hereby propose a number of synchronous and asynchronous activities, as well as the use of online tools and platforms, for English- and Spanish-speaking students to work collaboratively in international teams. The students study, analyse, compare, translate and revise video clips, which include topics such as gender, feminism, media accessibility and LGBTQI+ identities. This confirms the project's commitment to enhancing equality, diversity and inclusion (EDI). This chapter ultimately explores how telecollaboration can positively impact language training, not only for linguists and translators in training but also for language learners from other areas in higher education. Telecollaboration tools can also be affordable alternatives to language exchange programmes involving international travel, and it is therefore our belief that this methodology serves a twofold purpose. We ultimately claim that didactic AVT represents a pedagogically challenging, and rewarding, experience for language instructors wishing to challenge the physical boundaries of their classrooms and to embrace diversity.

Pedagogical translation in foreign language education

Translation, broadly understood as the linguistic and cultural transfer between two texts across languages, has traditionally featured in most FL teaching theories and methodologies (Pintado Gutiérrez 2012). The very understanding of (pedagogical) translation, alongside its usefulness for FL learning and teaching, has experienced fluctuations, which have been directly affected by mainstream language teaching methods, notably communicative approaches. Against the backdrop of new communicative theories, interlingual translation is oftentimes considered a type of cross-lingual activity pertaining to the faded grammar translation method (Thornbury 2011). Indeed, translation was virtually banished from FL classrooms for a long time, as it was associated with this method (Atkinson 1987; Carreres 2014), which was inherited from Greek and Latin language-teaching techniques that delved into the study of grammar and rhetoric through rule-memorisation activities and direct and reverse translation exercises of decontextualised sentences (Richards and Rodgers 2003), while ignoring the development of oral skills (Cook 2010, 10). At around the same time, translation scholars started to lose interest in the role of translation in language teaching following the development of dedicated professional translation programmes (Pym 2018).

Leading translation scholars such as Holmes (1972/2000) considered the two fields irreconcilable, but the relationship started to change with the advent of communicative approaches in language education. House (1977) summarised the ongoing debates between translation scholars and language educators. One of the key ideas from those debates was that translation was the 'fifth skill' in language learning, alongside speaking, writing, reading and listening. However, new light was shed on translation with Lavault's (1985) works and Duff's (1989) seminal book about sense-for-sense translation theory, which emphasises text-to-text language-transfer activities for the honing of FL skills. Several decades later, three official documents published by the Council of Europe – the *Common European Framework of Reference for Languages* (CEFR) (2001), its *Companion Volume* (2018) and the *Framework of Reference for Pluralistic Approaches to Languages and Cultures* (2013) – recognised translation as a necessary skill to activate communicative, plurilingual and pluricultural skills, which are basic skills if we want to train polyglot intercultural citizens. This recognition of translation as a communicative mediation tool reinforces the benefits of its use as a pedagogical tool in FL education.

Moving away from grammar-based approaches and drawing on communication-focused approaches, action-oriented theory gives mediation a pivotal role in language learning. The language learner thus becomes a social agent enabling knowledge while mediating texts and communications with other speakers (Piccardo and North 2019). In designing language tasks and utilising authentic resources, mediation becomes an increasingly important skill. Mediation emphasises 'the two key notions of co-construction of meaning in interaction and constant movement between the individual and social level in language learning, mainly through its vision of the user/learner as a social agent' (Council of Europe 2018, 36). According to Navarrete (2021), mediation has to be conceptualised considering that it was marginally included in the CEFR (Council of Europe 2001) and its potential in language learning still remains to be further ascertained.

North and Piccardo (2016) proposed mediation descriptors, according to which the interlingual translation of a given text is also considered a textual mediation activity in its own right. Such publications are indicative of a growing interest in pedagogical translation in language learning environments. However, as Pym (2018) points out, this recent interest in the role of translation in the language classroom calls for a necessary dialogue between translation and FL education theories. As argued by Pym (2018, 219), language educators have to put translation 'into the right kind of learning situations and encourage the full range of things that can be done in translation', including the fact that students ought to be able to produce and discuss different translations for the same input, thus learning to mediate a text depending on the communication context.

Contextualising language teaching and embedding telecollaboration

Understandings of language teaching, let alone the average student profile, can differ enormously between courses offered by British and Spanish universities. To understand how pedagogical translation is embedded in British curricula, we first analyse two compulsory language modules offered at UCL. These modules feature in the first two years of an undergraduate degree with Spanish and are worth 15 credits (that is, 30 credits in the European Credit Transfer System [ECTS]) each. This constitutes a total of 40 contact hours (across 10 weeks) besides independent work and office hours as well as additional oral-language seminars. Each module comprises three main components (Grammar and Communicative Skills, Translation from and into Spanish, and Additional Contents and Skills) and covers different varieties of Spanish as well as translation tasks that prepare students for a future Year Abroad programme. The module is taken by students majoring in any discipline offered at UCL's Joint Faculty of Arts and Humanities and Social and Historical Sciences, including not only other languages but also Business Administration, Political Sciences, History and many other disciplines. The students' backgrounds are therefore diverse and the student mixture is rich, which in turn means that the module must be generic enough to cater for students who are planning to become linguists or translators but also contain specific content for those who are learning Spanish for specific purposes. Additionally, the module must cater for students who will take a mandatory Year Abroad course as part of their degree course, thereby enhancing their language and intercultural skills and international experience. These modules differ from optional language courses offered by language centres.

The teaching of English as an FL in Spain can take multiple forms. In Spain, the training of translators and interpreters in tertiary public institutions officially began in 1974 with the creation of the Instituto Universitario de Lenguas Modernas y Traductores at the Universidad Complutense de Madrid (Muñoz Raya 2004, 14). Multiple separate institutions for the training of translators and interpreters were established shortly after, including the specialist schools at the universities of Granada and Barcelona in the 1970s and 1980s. At the time of writing, in 2023, there were almost 40 undergraduate programmes for the training of translators and more than 80 language-specific undergraduate programmes, according to Spain's Registry of Universities, Centres and Degrees (Registro de Universidades, Centros y

Títulos). This means that translator training is provided in the form of dedicated translation and interpreting degrees, and that the training of linguists takes place in language-specific undergraduate programmes. In the latter, however, translation is not generally part of the curriculum and is an optional tool at the disposal of the teacher. A case in point is UV, which offers a module entitled English Language, taught to students in language degrees as well as to those in a specialised translation degree. It is worth 6 ECTS credits, which constitutes a total of 60 contact hours (across 15 weeks) besides independent work and office hours as well as additional speaking seminars. For language degrees, the subject focuses on developing speaking, listening, writing and reading skills according to a textbook, which contains very few mediation or translation tasks. The teacher can choose to offer additional activities involving mediation or translation, but these are not part of the syllabus. In contrast, in the translation degree, the same textbook is used, but the aim is for students to learn grammar and develop communicative competences in English up to a B2 CEFR level, so that they can apply those skills to carry out translation and mediation professionally. To achieve this aim, many teachers employ pedagogical translation tasks, which can take the form of additional tasks or projects, including AVT tasks as further discussed in this chapter.

Considering the element of EDI in FL education, some clear differences can be observed between the average student profiles at UCL and UV. Being a bilingual region of Spain, Valencia tends to have a student body comprised of speakers of Spanish and Valencian. Another difference is that students are not formally required to complete a one-year exchange programme abroad and seminar groups tend to be large (30–35 students per group). As UCL is a London-based university, seminars (usually involving up to 12 students) are plurilingual spaces, because many students are not native English speakers, and language courses involve a mandatory, credit-bearing Year Abroad programme. In light of the different experiences of these cohorts, we envisage that telecollaboration programmes can bridge important gaps, such as enhancing the international aspect of the studies and bringing plurilingualism into the classroom.

Using audiovisual translation to teach foreign languages

When it comes to fostering mediation skills in the language classroom, special attention must be paid not only to linguistic competences, as described in the *Common European Framework of Reference for Languages*

(Council of Europe 2001), but also to plurilingual and pluricultural competences, as suggested in its *Companion Volume* (Council of Europe 2018) and the *Framework of Reference for Pluralistic Approaches to Languages and Cultures* (Council of Europe 2013).

Recent approaches to didactic translation have also shed light on the uses of AVT practices (for instance dubbing and subtitling) in the FL classroom (Lertola 2019; Talaván 2019a). Interlingual translation of video material requires translators to have expert knowledge of the languages and cultures involved, as well as a special sensitivity towards language and multimodal information. Students may struggle to analyse, interpret and ultimately comprehend the different layers of meaning entangled in an audiovisual text (Zabalbeascoa 2001), not least because text analysis in an FL poses additional challenges that are directly dependent on the student's proficiency. Just like with other creative works, such as literature, students may struggle to recompose and rewrite the source texts (that is, dialogues and narrations from video clips) if their linguistic and rhetorical resources in the FL are limited. To tackle this common issue, AVT scholars have conducted studies focusing on dubbing and on subtitling for didactic purposes (Incalcaterra McLoughlin and Lertola 2011; Lertola 2012; Talaván 2013; Borghetti and Lertola 2014; Talaván and Ávila-Cabrera 2015; Sánchez-Requena 2016; Talaván and Costal 2017; Lertola and Mariotti 2017; Sánchez-Requena 2018; Talaván 2019a) and on media accessibility practices, such as audio description and subtitles for the deaf and hard-of-hearing (SDH) (Ibáñez and Vermeulen 2013; Ibáñez et al. 2016; Calduch and Talaván 2017; Navarrete 2018; Talaván 2019b).

In the last two decades, research projects on internet-based learning applications with a focus on AVT have laid the foundation for further research on AVT as a tool to develop linguistic, plurilingual and pluricultural skills across international borders. One of these projects was LeViS (Learning via Subtitling), funded by the European Commission (Socrates/Lingua), from 2006 to 2008. Within the framework of this project, the first specific tool for making subtitles in a language learning environment was created, and activities in six different languages were designed and tested. According to the LeViS final surveys, learners not only consolidated and improved their language skills, but were also enthusiastic about the innovative nature of the subtitling activities (Sokoli et al. 2011). ClipFlair (http://clipflair.net), also funded by the European Commission, was developed from 2011 until 2014, and its main aim was to use interactive revoicing (including dubbing, audio description, karaoke singing and reciting) and captioning (including subtitling and video annotations) to teach FLs. The resulting online platform has ready-made exercises and an AVT system to create and complete revoicing and subtitling exercises. This platform was perceived as pedagogically useful for FL teaching purposes after being piloted by 1,213 learners with the help of 37 tutors in 12 different languages (Baños and Sokoli 2015). Alongside the LeViS and ClipFlair projects, other smaller-scale research projects have endeavoured to further examine the pedagogical benefits of AVT, including Babelium (2013–2015) and SubLanLearn (2009–2012).

More recent research projects with a strong focus on AVT are PluriTAV, funded by the Spanish government and the European Regional Development Fund, and TRADILEX (Audiovisual Translation as a Didactic Resource in Foreign Language Education), funded by the Ministry of Science and Innovation of Spain.[1] PluriTAV was carried out from 2017 to 2019 and its main aim was to explore the benefits of mediation activities following the Council of Europe's frameworks with a focus on plurilingual and pluricultural competences. The project consisted of designing and testing a set of didactic sequences involving the active use of different modes of AVT in higher education FL teaching. The results of the project (see, for example, Cerezo Merchán and Reverter Oliver 2022; Torralba et al. 2022) show an encouraging development of plurilingual and pluricultural competences among the students who participated in the pedagogical experiments. TRADILEX took place between 2020 and 2023. The main aim was to produce an ad hoc online learning tool to include ready-made didactic sequences with hands-on AVT exercises. The platform offered differentiated teacher and student access, allowing the language learning process to be fully monitored by educators. Similarly to PluriTAV, the results (Talaván and Lertola 2022) are promising and show that didactic AVT tasks have a positive effect on the honing of written and oral skills, thus confirming the findings of previous work in this field (Lertola 2019).

Telecollaboration in foreign language education environments: discussing a previous experience

Telecollaboration can take multiple forms. They can be academic, when they mostly take place in educational settings, or professional, when stakeholders from beyond academia are involved. In this chapter, we follow a user-centred approach and limit the application of telecollaboration to purely academic scenarios with particular emphasis placed on FL settings.

In the words of Dooly, telecollaboration can be defined as:

> the process of communicating and working together with other people or groups from different locations through online or digital communication tools (e.g., computers, tablets, cellphones) to co-produce a desired work output. Telecollaboration can be carried out in a variety of settings (classroom, home, workplace, laboratory) and can be synchronous or asynchronous. In education, telecollaboration combines all of these components with a focus on learning, social interaction, dialogue, intercultural exchange and communication all of which are especially important aspects of telecollaboration in language education. (2017, 169–170)

Telecollaboration has the potential to promote social interaction, dialogue, intercultural exchange, debate and communication, all essential in (foreign) language education. According to Dooly and O'Dowd (2018), there is a solid body of literature on telecollaboration nowadays; indeed, it is sufficiently vast to allow for multiple definitions and terms to define online collaborative initiatives (for instance virtual exchanges, social connections and tandem activities, among others). Groundbreaking technological advances in our internetised society, such as real-time videoconferencing tools, and particularly their democratisation, have been fundamental in enabling remote exchanges by means of telecollaboration.

Global interest in telecollaboration has grown significantly in recent years, and several regional, state and European projects have been financed to explore this exciting field. Many of these projects involve university students, such as the EU-funded project INTENT (Integrating Telecollaborative Networks into Foreign Language Higher Education, 2011–2014), the main output of which was the development of an online platform (www.unicollaboration.org) where educators can find the resources and training materials necessary to set up telecollaborative exchanges in higher education. Another two important projects are TILA (Telecollaboration for Intercultural Language Acquisition, 2013–2015) and TeCoLa (Telecollaboration and Gaming for Intercultural and Content Integrated Language Teaching, 2016–2019), funded by the European Commission, with the main aim of using gamified telecollaboration technologies to enhance FL teaching and learning by supporting online pedagogical exchanges between secondary school students throughout Europe. Additionally, international commercial initiatives, including but not limited to

Conversify and Tandem, were often marketed among higher education institutions as providing FL students with (paid) environments in which they could practise their oral skills.

Following the 2020 lockdowns, many universities had to adapt their teaching through the use of remote technologies such as videoconferencing and online learning tools. Existing blended learning tools, such as Blackboard or Moodle, proved useful albeit limited for online education. Communication among students often falls short in these systems, and even the use of live sessions through videoconferencing tools is far from ideal, as interaction becomes artificial in a virtual environment where students can stop sharing access to their camera and/or microphone and disengage more easily. As mentioned earlier, despite the evident disadvantages of swiftly switching to online teaching, the widespread lockdowns also created opportunities for learners to interact with each other online in a similar fashion to telecollaboration teaching approaches (Huertas-Abril 2020; Beecroft and Bauer 2022). Telecollaboration practices, however, existed long before the outbreak of the pandemic (Belz 2003; Dooly and O'Dowd 2018). Furthermore, from an EDI point of view, it is paramount to acknowledge that, during the pandemic, for many students the only chance to have an international experience and to gain fluency in their language of study was through a telecollaboration programme.

Irrespective of whether the teaching is done in person or online, collaboration is an essential component when it comes to embedding translation in the classroom; it thus constitutes the core of user-centred approaches to FL education. Contrary to transmissionist perspectives, whereby the learner is a passive listener and consumer of knowledge, socioconstructivism sees learning as 'a personal, holistic, intrinsically motivating and socially effectuated construction process' (Kiraly 2000, 23). Learning is not transmitted from the teacher to the students, but rather proactively constructed and transformed in collaborative learning processes. Coincidentally, this is also advocated by curriculum decolonisation efforts, which endeavour to enhance student–teacher collaborations by putting the learner at the centre of the learning experience.

Following the above principles, a telecollaboration project was carried out between two higher education institutions, namely UCL and UV. In the 2018–2019 academic year, a term-long telecollaboration project was conducted between 91 first-year students (divided into 8 seminar groups) of Spanish as an FL at UCL, and 66 second-year students (divided into 2 groups) of English as an FL at UV. Our main goal was to enhance the development of students' cultural awareness and language competences, by fostering their motivation to learn. The participating students, who were intermediate users of their corresponding FL, furthered their linguistic and communicative competences and fostered generic skills, such as media literacy, teamwork and problem-solving, by carrying out tasks in international teams. More specifically, an emphasis was put on intercultural communicative competence (that is, being able to interact with speakers of other languages and cultures in a seamless manner) and language competence (that is, being able to understand, produce and interact in the FL fluently) following the CEFR's descriptors (Council of Europe 2018). In addition to the main competences outlined above, by setting up an international rapport with fellow students, we were contributing to a friendly and safe learning space in a blended ecosystem, thereby enhancing the students' understanding of learning contexts other than their local ones and stimulating authenticity through student-centred and collaborative learning.

This term-long telecollaboration project, which encompassed synchronous and asynchronous tasks, was designed so that students had to communicate with each other in the classroom (face-to-face interaction) but also remotely with their international counterparts in a blended learning environment. A Padlet visual board was utilised for teachers and students to share content. To communicate and complete the asynchronous tasks, Padlet and Google tools were used, although most students (72.29 per cent) reported having mainly used their institutional email. Skype was encouraged for setting up regular meetings with fellow international students, because it offers licence-free group meetings (39.16 per cent used it). Tasks were intertwined with the existing curriculum and ranged from digital stories to oral presentations, promotional videos and online questionnaires, among other activities. Following the existing lesson plans, these new tasks promoted reflection on a range of topics as well as on written and oral production; the added international component allowed students to practise and receive feedback from their peers, thus further justifying the usefulness of the activities at hand.

To better understand the learners' perspective on this telecollaboration experience, pre- and post-questionnaires were handed out. The pre-questionnaire (N=145) was filled in by 57 UV students and 88 UCL students, whereas the post-questionnaire (N=88) was filled in by 21 UV students and 67 UCL students. Overall, the experience yielded excellent results, but only 22 respondents (25 per cent) wished to repeat it, compared to 22 (25 per cent) who did not and 44 (50 per cent) who were unsure or preferred not to say.

Engagement and motivation levels were not always shared equally among team members; in fact, 10 participants (11 per cent) reported not having enjoyed working with other students (compared to 57, that is, 65 per cent, who enjoyed it very much) and 21 participants (25 per cent) reported low levels of motivation upon project completion (compared to 46, that is, 52 per cent, with a higher degree of motivation). Surprisingly, 32 students (27 per cent) would have preferred to work on their own, rather than in groups, during their language classes. National, social and cultural factors also led to incompatible schedules – indeed, over 54 students (51 per cent) reported that it had not been easy to communicate with fellow students via telecollaboration, with many noting that different times and lifestyles affected the ways in which they worked together towards their learning goals. Having said that, only seven students (9 per cent) considered that cultural misunderstandings had hampered teamwork altogether.

Alongside the questionnaires, in-class observations were carried out, and some students shared their experiences in writing on the Moodle learning platforms used. Some of the main bottlenecks that had impacted the project to a considerable extent were identified. The aims and learning outcomes varied between the two universities and across groups, and so did students' understanding of the purpose of studying an FL, which affected their engagement with the activities. These drawbacks informed a new proposal for the teaching of AVT practices by means of telecollaboration in which language students can take advantage of working in international teams and collaborate towards common learning goals. Among the lessons learnt, we identified that group sizes had an effect on how effectively and regularly students communicated with their international counterparts, and it was established that closer monitoring – for instance through regular reports or forum posts to discuss work progress – were key to ensure students remain motivated and do not discontinue their participation. As Dooly and O'Dowd (2018, 25) claimed, 'telecollaborative projects require teacher know-how to coherently sequence the activities (both in and out of class)'; in our below proposal we discuss telecollaboration sequencing in further detail.

A proposal for telecollaboration: an international didactic audiovisual translation experience

Drawing on our previous telecollaboration experience, as well as on the many fruits yielded by previous AVT-focused projects, though especially PluriTAV and TRADILEX, this chapter introduces a methodological proposal for incorporating telecollaboration into the teaching of didactic AVT practices in the FL classroom for prospective linguists and translators.

Our pedagogical proposal for collaborative work using didactic AVT activities revolves around four main modes: dubbing, subtitling, SDH and audio description. It involves undergraduate students who are taking Spanish as a core subject at UCL and students from the undergraduate degree in Translation and Intercultural Mediation at UV who are studying English as an FL. The below proposal is for language modules that take place in the first year of these degrees, that aim to develop students' communication skills up to an intermediate level (B2) and that include interlingual translation as an essential component of their syllabi. The synchronous and asynchronous activities prompt English- and Spanish-speaking students to work collaboratively in international teams in order to study, analyse, compare, translate and revise audiovisual texts that touch on the representation of social minorities (BAME-BIPOC and LGBTQI+), disability and gender, with the ultimate objective of making teaching materials more diverse and inclusive. Additionally, tasks are designed to be developed in international teams so that students in mostly homogenous, monolingual environments can fully benefit from the experience.

Our didactic proposal would be suitable for a telecollaboration lasting approximately 20 hours, which we have divided into 6 sessions of 1 hour each, in class, plus 14 hours of independent work ('after class' activities) over a period of approximately 12 weeks (depending on term duration). This sequencing can, however, easily be adapted to other educational contexts by tweaking the methodology and replacing the video materials.

Throughout the proposal, there is a wide variety of activities in terms of reasoning (inductive and deductive), agency (individual, in pairs and in groups), learning setting (in class or at home), assessment (self-evaluation, peer review and tutor-marked), tools (a dedicated online platform, file-sharing tools, video-editing systems and subtitling editors) and resources (written and audiovisual materials). In terms of competences, communicative and plurilingual competences are predominantly addressed, but we would also like to help students to develop digital literacy, teamwork and creativity and to increase their motivation.

Following a task-based approach, and drawing on the PluriTAV and TRADILEX methodologies, as well as Baños's (2021) structure for AVT tasks, the project's phases are discussed in the sections that follow.

Phase 1: introduction to the project

Aims:

- To introduce students to telecollaboration in language learning settings
- To foster intercultural communication skills in higher education settings
- To raise awareness about the importance of diversity and an inclusive curriculum in FL education

Grouping: Individual, in pairs and in international teams
Approximate duration: 120 minutes (60 minutes in class and 60 minutes after class)
Materials: Initial questionnaire

Steps:
In class:

1. Students fill in an initial questionnaire to report any previous experiences in telecollaboration projects, translation tasks, learning technologies or audiovisual content.
2. Each educator explains the rationale behind the telecollaboration project, emphasising the importance of meeting deadlines and staying in touch with team members regularly. The first lesson is devoted to discussing UCL's Liberating the Curriculum initiative and foregrounding the use of EDI materials in translation classroom to address the development of a more inclusive curriculum in language and translation programmes.
3. International teams are formed by the teachers, based on timetables and other requirements that students may have (such as reasonable learning adjustments, including for learning disabilities). Every team should be composed of at least one member from each university (ideally two, depending on group sizes). Teams of more than four students should be avoided.
4. Students in each team set up their own communication channel and file-sharing tool, such as Google Drive, and identify a suitable time

slot to meet, at least once a week, using a videoconferencing tool of their choice. In addition, students choose a team leader, who will communicate with other teams and the teachers involved in the project in case any problems arise.

After class:

5. Students join a dedicated online platform (for instance MS Teams, Padlet or any other learning tool that the teacher has selected). Each student produces and uploads an introductory one-minute video in the FL, to introduce themselves to their team and the rest of the cohort.

Assessment: Students submit two deliverables: a questionnaire and an introductory video about themselves, in their FL.

Phase 2: pre-translation activities

Aims:

- To analyse and interpret audiovisual texts through observation
- To discuss media content, after examination, with peers
- To identify, discuss and engage with EDI-related issues in video clips

Grouping: Individual, in pairs, in groups and in international teams
Approximate duration: 120 minutes (60 minutes in class and 60 minutes after class)
Materials:

- *In a Heartbeat* (Bravo and David 2017); 4 minutes, 5 seconds
- *Phenomenal Woman* (Masucci 2015); 4 minutes, 44 seconds
- *Cuerdas* (Solís García 2014); 10 minutes, 53 seconds

Steps:
In class:

1. First, the teacher explains to the students that in this second session they will discuss and engage with EDI-related issues in video clips. Then, in small groups, they are asked to think of two series or films that deal with these issues. English-language programmes can include the likes of *Pride* (Warchus 2014), *Green*

Book (Farrelly 2018), *POSE* (Murphy et al. 2018–2021) and *Atypical* (Rashid 2017–2021). As for Spanish-language programmes, *Vis a Vis* (Escobar et al. 2015–2019), *Todo sobre mi madre* (Almodóvar 2019), *Campeones* (Fesser 2018) and *Roma* (Cuarón 2018) could be considered. Students select one film or series, read the synopsis in their FL – using an online film database such as Filmaffinity or IMDB – and write down three or four keywords. The keywords are then shared with the whole class, and the teacher writes them on the board to discuss the semantic similarities that there might be in the terminology produced by the students. Finally, students translate the keywords into their mother tongue, looking for as many synonyms as possible and paying attention to the context of each programme.

2. Students watch a short film about love and tolerance called *In a Heartbeat* (Bravo and David 2017). In pairs, students answer some comprehension questions, such as:

    - What happened in the story?
    - Who was your favourite character?
    - How are the red and the dark-haired boys feeling at the start of the short film?
    - What does the heart tell the red-haired boy to do? What is he afraid of?
    - What purpose was the short film intended to serve? Do you feel that it fulfilled its purpose?
    - What audiovisual resources were used to reinforce this purpose (visuals and music)?
    - How did the short film make you feel?

3. Finally, in pairs again, students write a dialogue for the short film in the FL, which can include dialogues between the red-haired boy and his heart and dialogues between the two boys. In class, students practise reading their dialogues aloud. Firstly, they read their dialogue aloud and make sure that they know how to pronounce all the words and that they give the sentences the correct intonation. Secondly, they read their dialogue aloud again while the video is playing and pretend they are voice actors recording their voices in a studio. In this second reading, students pay special attention to whether the text is too short or too long to be in sync with the image and sound of the video and make the appropriate changes. If there is enough time, the teacher can ask one or two pairs of students to

record the dialogue of the short film aloud with the video playing in the background without sound, allowing for a final reflection on the activity.

After class:

4. After class, Spanish-speaking students watch a short film in English and English-speaking students watch a short film in Spanish. The following are two examples of videos that could be used, one of which deals with women's empowerment and the other with disability, equality and solidarity:

    - *Phenomenal Woman* (Masucci 2015), in English
    - *Cuerdas* (Solís García 2014), in Spanish.

5. The team meets to discuss the following questions:

    - What was the short film about?
    - What purpose did the short film serve? In your opinion, is it successful?
    - What audiovisual resources were used to reinforce this purpose (visuals, music and sound effects)?
    - How did the short film make you feel?
    - In your opinion, how are minorities represented in the media nowadays?
    - Do you have any favourite short films or films on minority representations?

6. Finally, students write a report, individually, in the FL of about 300 words on the discussion and (dis)agreements in opinion among classmates.

Assessment: Students submit two deliverables: the dialogue in the FL for the short film *In a Heartbeat* and the 300-word report in the FL.

Phase 3: revoicing – dubbing

Aims:

- To become familiar with race-specific vocabulary while stimulating critical inquiry
- To develop an understanding of revoicing methods and the principles of dubbing
- To master revoicing software and manage a team

Grouping: In pairs and in international teams
Approximate duration: 240 minutes (60 minutes in class and 180 minutes after class)
Materials: *How Does It Feel to Be a Problem?* (Foreman 2019), narrated by William DeMeritt for *The Atlantic*; 2 minutes, 44 seconds; 383 words
Language combination: English into Spanish

Steps:
In class:

1. Students watch the video *How Does It Feel to Be a Problem?* (Foreman 2019) to prepare a discussion, moderated by the educator, on the (in)visibility of race and the alienation experienced by African Americans in the previous century as well as today. The discussion revolves around African American sociologist W. E. B. Du Bois's metaphor of 'the veil' (that is, a visual manifestation of the colour line that works as a social barrier and leads to race inequality), which students have to define using their own words in the FL.
2. Students are shown a transcript of the narrated video and are provided with a revoicing template to fill in. As illustrated by Table 3.1, the revoicing template can be a simple document containing a table with two main columns: on the left-hand side, names of characters or narrators, inserted manually by students; on the right-hand side, the Spanish translation of the original narration alongside the in and out time codes for each utterance. The principles of interlingual dubbing are explained, placing a particular emphasis on the importance of isochrony (that is, using in and out time codes in the translation to match the duration of the utterances) to follow the pace and content of the video.

Title of clip	
Character	**Translation (dubbing)**
Name of character or narrator	Please indicate the time codes (minutes and seconds) before each translation (e.g. 00.00 / 01.00). Your translation of dialogues, narrations and any other utterances should appear here.
...	...

Table 3.1 Sample revoicing template for inputting time codes and text

3. Before the students start translating the script, they answer some comprehension and pre-translation questions to confirm their understanding of the main ideas in the video. In order to provide a guided approach to this exercise, the teacher selects challenging passages from the script and asks students to translate them into Spanish. Then, the teacher suggests the maximum number of words each utterance should have, depending on the duration of the utterance and taking into consideration an expected speaking rate of approximately 150 words per minute in spoken Spanish.

After class:

4. Each team divides the narration into two main chunks of approximately 190 words and each team is split into two subgroups. Ideally, students work on their translations with a fellow student from the international partner university so that they can mediate the clip and hone their production skills while negotiating the work. During the translation process, the Spanish-speaking student(s) can add any annotations on the transcript if they fail to understand some of the concepts so that the English-speaking student(s) can help decode the text. Conversely, the English-speaking student(s) can add comments on any passages of their translation if they struggle to produce natural-sounding, idiomatic translations. Once the translations are finished, the team members merge the translations and provide feedback to each other. When the team meets to exchange feedback, comments and questions are addressed, and a final version of the translation is agreed upon by all team members.

5. Assuming that the final version of the translation has already been produced in writing, students now create a new audio track in Spanish. Students can use any free video-editing or screen-recording tool (for instance Screencastify) to watch the (muted) original video and voice their narration using the time codes they had previously fixed. Each member performs, in Spanish, a proportional chunk of the translation. The native Spanish speakers help their English-speaking fellow students with challenging passages and pronunciation-related queries.
6. As a follow-up activity, students can read Du Bois's article, entitled 'Strivings of the Negro People' (published in *The Atlantic* in 1897), on which the video was based. With or without having read said article, students produce, individually and in their FL, a 300-word reflection on their understanding of race in today's world.

Assessment: Students submit three deliverables:

1. the written translation, in Spanish, of the narration
2. the revoiced clip
3. the 300-word reflective commentary in the FL.

Since this is the first practical activity involving hands-on AVT practice, it is advised that the language instructors carefully monitor not only the process but also the outcome of the activities and provide feedback accordingly. Therefore, an assessment by the teacher is recommended shortly after submission of the revoiced clip and the written commentaries. Feedback can be offered in writing (through a submission slot or on each team's online platform) or shared verbally and collectively in class. Assessors should focus on isochrony, orality and naturalness, and how the resulting translation follows the pace of the video comfortably. If the narrations are either too slow or too rushed, the instructors can show examples of best practice and provide alternative translations that better match the video.

Phase 4: revoicing – audio description

Aims:

- To raise awareness about the importance of media accessibility
- To identify accessibility practices and their rationale
- To interpret visual information and produce verbal descriptions
- To develop translation skills by producing audio description scripts

Grouping: In international teams
Approximate duration: 240 minutes (60 minutes in class and 180 minutes after class)
Materials: *Hope* (Simoes 2022); 1 minute; 180 words
Language combination: Intralingual (English or Spanish)

Steps:
In class:

1. Teachers initiate a discussion on the concept of disability and the many physical and mental forms it can take. Students watch the Royal National Institute of Blind People's video entitled *What Is Audio Description?* (RNIB 2019) and are given a set of questions to answer in pairs. These questions relate to the nature of audio description as well as its uses and the target audience (blind and partially sighted viewers, in this case).
2. Students watch Southeastern Guide Dogs' short film entitled *Hope* (Simoes 2022) and examine the video in pairs using Fryer's (2016) recommendations on how to describe video content for the blind and partially sighted. More specifically, they have to indicate what and who they see in the clip and where and when the action is taking place; additionally, they can discuss how and why the action takes place. They compare their responses with a team sitting next to them to ascertain whether their interpretations of the clip are similar. At the end of the lesson, the teacher provides students with the English-language script and shows the video description. A comparison is established between the elements on which the describer focused in their description in contrast with the students' analysis of the visuals.

After class:

3. Each team is divided into two sub-teams at each institution. Students have access to the original clip and a revoicing template (see Phase 3: revoicing – dubbing). Students are prompted to insert the time codes themselves following basic audio description principles (for instance, create a new row after a pause of 3 seconds or more).
4. Students produce the description script in their FL using the relevant time codes in the template provided. Once the script has been finalised, each sub-team shares its written descriptions with its international counterpart to receive feedback. When peer reviewing the scripts, students can add comments with suggestions on how to pronounce challenging passages.

5. Once the feedback has been exchanged, each sub-team uses a tool of their choice to watch the (muted) original video and voice the descriptions using the amended script. Each member narrates, in the FL, a proportional chunk of the description. Figure 3.1 shows how students would voice a clip using the Screencastify plug-in on a browser (in this particular scene, students have to describe how the man is hanging decorations on his Christmas tree). The resulting video is shared with their fellow students to receive feedback on their performance in terms of oral skills, with an emphasis on not only fluency and prosody but also naturalness and idiomaticity. Depending on the feedback received, each sub-team may consider repeating the work and producing an improved version of the described clip.
6. Students submit their work in the form of two deliverables: the audio description script and the voiced video. The Spanish-speaking team provides the files in English, whereas their English-speaking counterparts produce the script and video in Spanish.
7. As a follow-up activity, the teacher shares the official audio description and the English-language script. Students check the official description against their own, and produce a 500-word report in their FL in which they discuss how their description of the clip compares to the one used by Southeastern Guide Dogs in English.

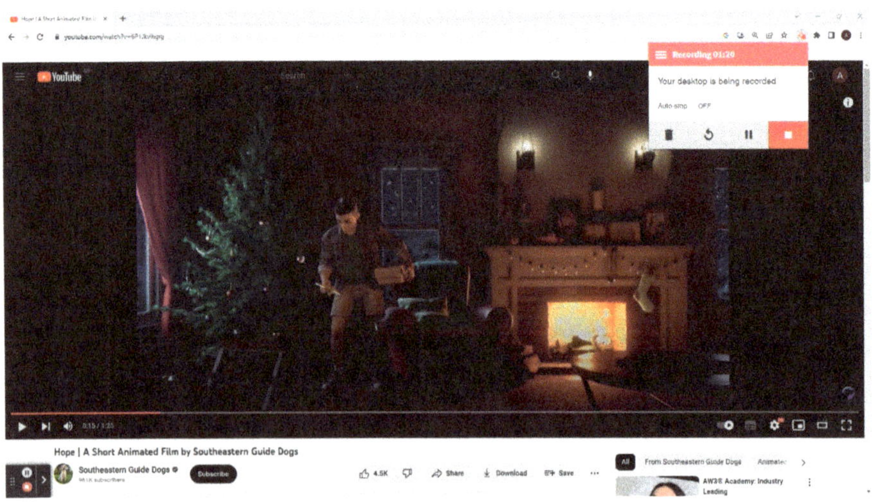

Figure 3.1 View of the screen-recording plug-in Screencastify, with a screenshot of the short film *Hope* (Simoes 2022). © Southeastern Guide Dogs.

Assessment: Students submit three deliverables: the script, the described clip and the 500-word reflection. Since this activity has already encompassed two peer-review phases within each team, it is advisable that the instructor assess each team's submissions and provide feedback accordingly.

Phase 5: subtitling – interlingual subtitling

Aims:

- To become familiar with LGBTQI+-related terms while stimulating critical inquiry
- To develop an understanding of subtitling techniques and the principles of subtitling
- To develop summarising and analytical skills, as well as soft skills such as empathy and understanding
- To produce subtitles using specialist software

Grouping: in pairs, in international teams
Approximate duration: 240 minutes (60 minutes in class and 180 minutes after class)
Materials: *Cocodrilo* (Yúdice 2019); 4 minutes, 54 seconds; 417 words
Language combination: Spanish into English

Steps:
In class

1. The activity in this phase revolves around the topic of communicating emotions between parents and children, especially when it comes to issues related to sexual preferences. Students watch *Cocodrilo* (Yúdice 2019), a short film that conveys a powerful message of reconciliation between Victor and his parents. Then, in pairs, they answer the following questions in their FL:

    - What seems to be the problem between Victor and his parents?
    - Why do you think Victor has not spoken to his parents for two years?
    - Why does the mother hide the screen when her husband comes into the house?
    - What purpose does this short film serve?
    - How did the ending make you feel?

2. In pairs, students write a summary of the short film, in no more than two lines and in Spanish. In doing so they put their summarising skills into practice, as these are essential in subtitling.
3. Students are provided with a transcription containing dialogue gaps. They watch the first half of the video again. Students fill in the gaps with the missing words and expressions, in Spanish, and then translate them into English.
4. The teacher introduces the principles of interlingual subtitling, putting a particular emphasis on the importance of synthesising information. Reduction and condensation techniques are presented, and students are briefed on the need to ensure that translations allow for comfortable reading by the viewer and that they sound natural and idiomatic. The instructor provides the students with the video file of the short film and a Spanish-language pre-timed subtitle template containing the first 40 subtitles approximately. Should the instructor be unable to produce a subtitle template with the in and out time codes and the corresponding transcriptions, an auto-generated subtitle file could be retrieved from commonly used streaming platforms such as Microsoft Stream or YouTube Studio. The template should have approximately 40 subtitles, corresponding to the first 2 minutes of the video. Finally, the teacher shows the students how to import the video and the Spanish subtitle template into a subtitle editor of their choice. If the teaching institution does not have a licence for professional commercial software, freeware such as Aegisub, Subtitle Edit or Subtitle Workshop can be used; these can easily be found on the internet. The teacher demonstrates how to translate the original subtitles using the software program and how to save and share their work (that is, producing and exporting an SRT file containing the subtitles). For more details on the software used, the teacher may consider providing access to a tutorial or sharing easy guides available on the internet.

After class:

5. Each team divides the template into two parts of approximately 20 Spanish-language subtitles each. Each international team is divided into two subgroups: Spanish-speaking students in one group and English-speaking students in the other. Each group translates 20 subtitles into English. Once the translations are finished, the team merges the translations and the two subgroups provide feedback to

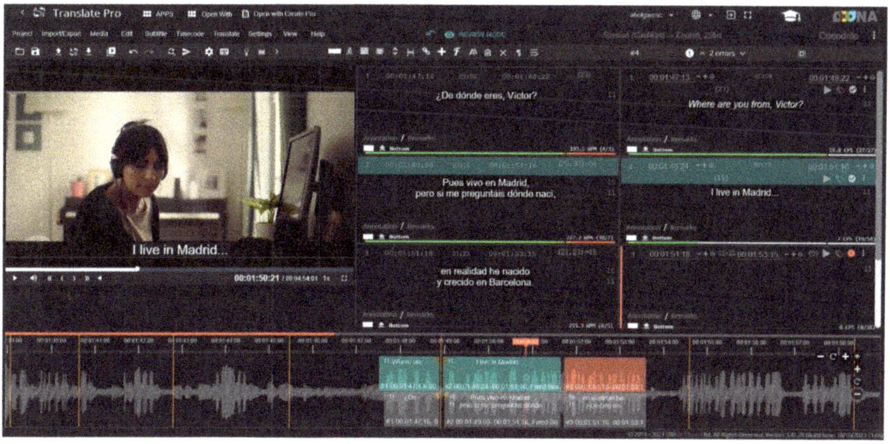

Figure 3.2 View of online subtitling tool OOONA Translate Pro, containing the source and target subtitles (with the relevant in and out time codes) for the short film *Cocodrilo*, directed by Jorge Yúdice (2019). © Jorge Yúdice for screenshot of *Cocodrilo*; © OOONA for screenshot of OOONA Edu (Translate Pro).

each other while discussing the experience on a videoconferencing tool of their choice or via any other communication channel of their choice. Students have to agree on a final version of the subtitle template and export the file in a shareable format using the subtitling editor (as per Figure 3.2).

6. As a follow-up activity, students write, individually and in their FL, a 300-word commentary on unspoken elements and how filmic language helps to construct the narrative. As special emphasis should be put on LGBTQI+-related issues, students are prompted to hypothesise on whether the protagonist's sexual orientation had anything to do with his family issues. The commentary can revolve around the audiovisual component of the clip and its triggers, including the boy's gaze, his tears and the representation of his father, among other visual elements.

Assessment: Students submit their work in the form of two deliverables: the subtitled file (to be peer reviewed by fellow students from different groups as well as ultimately assessed by the teacher) and the 300-word reflective commentary in the FL.

Phase 6: subtitling for the deaf and hard-of-hearing

Aims:

- To raise awareness about the importance of accessible subtitling
- To identify the needs of deaf and hard-of-hearing people
- To interpret acoustic information and produce accurate written descriptions
- To become familiar with (professional) standards of SDH

Grouping: In pairs, in international groups
Approximate timing: 240 minutes (60 minutes in class and 180 minutes after class)
Materials: *Hair Love* (Cherry 2019); 6 minutes, 47 seconds; 163 words
Language combination: Intralingual (English or Spanish)

Steps:
In class:

1. First, students watch the US National Deaf Center's video entitled *What Does Deaf Mean?* (NDC 2018). Assisted by the instructor, students discuss, in small groups, what it means to be deaf, different types of deafness and how deaf people communicate, as well as how deaf people can access media content.
2. Secondly, the teacher asks the students what they think deaf people may not perceive if they watch a programme subtitled for hearing people. Answers should include information about sound effects, music, intonation, character identification and other sound triggers that are plot-relevant.
3. The teacher then explains the basic guidelines and conventions of SDH. Guidelines tend to be nation-specific for national TV channels, so instructors can perhaps resort to Netflix's guidelines, for example, which are very similar for both English (Netflix 2015) and Spanish (Netflix 2016).
4. Students watch the short film entitled *Hair Love* (Cherry 2019), which deals with prejudice towards and stereotypes of Black people and childcare by using caring for natural Afro hair as a metaphor for family love. The film contains only a few utterances, in English. Students answer comprehension questions such as:

    - What is the short film about?
    - Why does the girl show excitement after waking up?

- What is the girl watching on her tablet?
- Why does her father want to cover her head with a hat?
- What message is this short film trying to convey?
- Do any relevant EDI-related issues feature prominently in this short film?

5. Finally, students watch the short film again and write down all the aspects that they would have to subtitle for deaf or hard-of-hearing people. They share their answers with the rest of the class and reflect on how they would indicate in subtitles the aspects they have noted down. Finally, these questions are shared with the class. Should the students be unable to identify appropriate sound triggers, the teacher can provide an answer sheet containing said triggers alongside approximate time codes of where they arise in the video.

After class:

6. Students from each country work in pairs. Spanish-speaking students do the SDH task of the short film in English, and English-speaking students complete the SDH task in Spanish. They produce subtitles using tags (that is, sound descriptions enclosed within brackets) to describe sound triggers while ignoring dialogue and other verbal information altogether. Students have to do the spotting (that is, inserting the input and output times of the subtitles with the subtitle editor software) of the subtitles alongside each sound tag (see Figure 3.3). Afterwards, the subtitle files are exchanged, and feedback is given both on the need to subtitle different elements and on how it has been done (formatting, positioning and reading speed).
7. As a follow-up activity, students read Shirley Campbell's (1994) poem *Rotundamente negra*. After having read said poem, students produce, individually and in their FL, a 300-word reflection on what the poem means to them and about the double discrimination against Black women – for being women and being Black – nowadays and in the past.

Assessment: Students submit their work in the form of two deliverables: the subtitled file and a commentary on Shirley Campbell's poem. The subtitle files are peer reviewed between the international teams, and the teacher reviews the commentary.

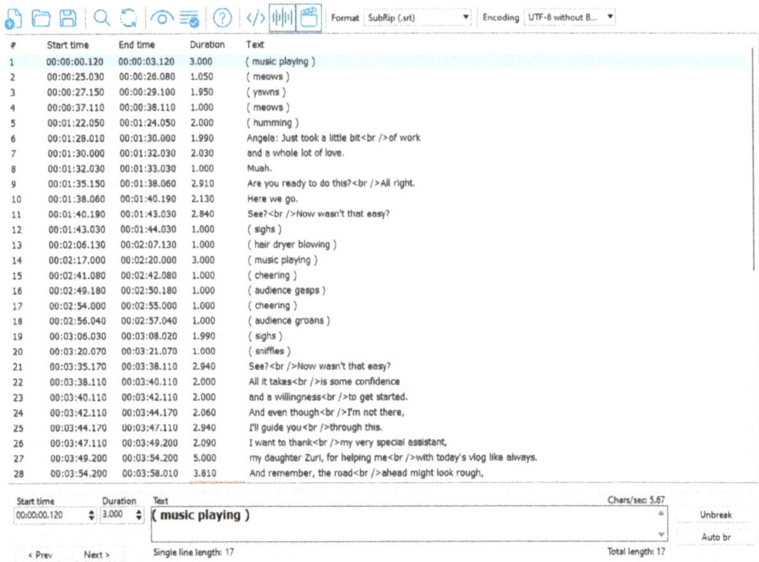

Figure 3.3 Representation of sound tags in Subtitle Edit, showing in and out times, durations and descriptions in brackets

Conclusion

This chapter has delved into the benefits of utilising didactic AVT tasks, more specifically the revoicing and subtitling of multimodal materials that deal with EDI issues, in telecollaboration settings. We have presented a task-based approach to hone FL skills using didactic AVT and have introduced the principles of a telecollaboration project involving international higher education institutions where English- and Spanish-speaking undergraduate students have to take English-to-Spanish and Spanish-to-English translation modules as part of their curricula. These principles were tested in a pre-pandemic initiative that was orchestrated by UCL and UV and that yielded positive results (Bolaños García-Escribano and Cerezo Merchán 2019).

For this purpose, a didactic sequence comprising six lesson plans has been designed, which covers four common AVT modes, namely intralingual SDH, interlingual subtitling, dubbing, and audio description for the blind and partially sighted. The lessons prompt the teacher and students to use specialist freeware programs to localise media content in international teams, with activities ranging from film analysis to timing texts and peer reviewing each other's revoiced clips. In doing these activities, students find numerous opportunities to mediate not only the clips (that is, the source materials for the translation activities) but also intercultural communication with fellow students and other teams. The ultimate aim of utilising didactic AVT tasks is to foster reception and production skills in the FL by exposing students to materials in a multimedia format, which they have to translate using relevant techniques and strategies. The use of pre- and post-translation activities allows for the discussion of EDI-related topics, with students being prompted to read seminal works on identity and other societal issues.

The ultimate aim of this pedagogical initiative is that students gain a greater understanding not only of the FL they study but also of the cultural nuances that exist when discussing EDI in different languages and educational settings. The use of audiovisual materials also allows for the liberation of the curriculum by giving further visibility to minorities such as African American and Black communities and LGBTQI+ networks, among others. Furthermore, following the impact of recent political changes in the teaching of FLs in higher education – notably the impact of Brexit on Erasmus+ and Turing schemes – telecollaborative initiatives mean students can continue to develop their plurilingual skills when international travel is unaffordable or unfeasible.

Note

1 See http://citrans.uv.es/pluritav and https://tradit.uned.es/en/proyecto-tradilex-2.

References

Atkinson, David. 1987. 'The mother tongue in the classroom: A neglected resource?', *ELT Journal: An International Journal for Teachers of English to Speakers of Other Languages* 41, no. 4: 241–7. https://doi.org/10.1093/elt/41.4.241.

Baños, Rocío. 2021. 'Creating credible and natural-sounding dialogue in dubbing: Can it be taught?', *The Interpreter and Translator Trainer* 15, no. 1: 13–33. https://doi.org/10.1080/1750399X.2021.1880262.

Baños, Rocío, and Stavroula Sokoli. 2015. 'Learning foreign languages with ClipFlair: Using captioning and revoicing activities to increase students' motivation and engagement'. In *10 Years of the LLAS Elearning Symposium: Case studies in good practice*, edited by Kate Borthwick, Erika Corradini and Alison Dickens, 203–13. Dublin: Research-Publishing.net.

Beecroft, Raphaelle, and Petra Bauer. 2022. *The Potential of a Telecollaborative Translation Course: Virtual exchange during the pandemic and beyond*. Hershey, PA: IGI Global.

Belz, Julie A. 2003. 'Linguistic perspectives on the development of intercultural competence in telecollaboration', *Language Learning and Technology* 7, no. 2: 68–117. https://doi.org/10125/25201.

Bolaños García-Escribano, Alejandro, and Beatriz Cerezo Merchán. 2019. 'Telecollaboration in the foreign language classroom: Interlingual competences'. In *Taking Stock of Recent Advances in Pedagogical Translation and Foreign Language Education*, edited by Soledad Díaz-Alarcón and Alejandro Bolaños García-Escribano, 12–13. Córdoba: UCOPress.

Borghetti, Cristina, and Jennifer Lertola. 2014. 'Interlingual subtitling for intercultural language education: A case study', *Language and Intercultural Communication* 14, no. 4: 423–40. https://doi.org/10.1080/14708477.2014.934380.

Calduch, Carmen, and Noa Talaván. 2017. 'Traducción audiovisual y aprendizaje del español como L2: el uso de la audiodescripción', *Journal of Spanish Language Teaching* 4, no. 2: 168–80. https://doi.org/10.1080/23247797.2017.1407173.

Campbell, Shirley. 1994. *Rotundamente negra.* San José: Arado.

Carreres, Ángeles. 2014. 'Translation as a means and as an end: Reassessing the divide', *The Interpreter and Translator Trainer* 8, no. 1: 123–35. https://doi.org/10.1080/1750399X.2014.908561.

Cerezo Merchán, Beatriz, and Beatriz Reverter Oliver. 2022. 'Proyecto de investigación PluriTAV: estudio cuasiexperimental de la aplicación de una secuencia didáctica centrada en el desarrollo de la competencia plurilingüe y pluricultural', *Revista de lenguas para fines específicos* 28, no. 2: 101–32. https://doi.org/10.20420/rlfe.2022.554.

Cook, Guy. 2010. *Translation in Language Teaching*. Oxford: Oxford University Press.

Council of Europe. 2001. *Common European Framework of Reference for Languages: Learning, Teaching, Assessment*. Strasbourg: Council of Europe.

Council of Europe. 2013. *A Framework of Reference for Pluralistic Approaches to Languages and Cultures: Competences and Resources*. Strasbourg: Council of Europe.

Council of Europe. 2018. *Common European Framework of Reference for Languages: Learning, Teaching, Assessment. Companion Volume with New Descriptors*. Strasbourg: Council of Europe.

Dooly, Melinda Ann. 2017. 'Telecollaboration'. In *The Handbook of Technology in Second Language Teaching and Learning*, edited by Carol A. Chapelle and Shannon Sauro, 169–83. Hoboken, NJ: Wiley-Blackwell.

Dooly, Melinda Ann, and Robert O'Dowd, eds. 2018. *In This Together: Teachers' Experiences with Transnational, Telecollaborative Language Learning Projects*. Bern: Peter Lang.

Du Bois, William Edward Burghardt. 1897. 'Strivings of the negro people'. *The Atlantic*, August 1897. Accessed 3 April 2024. https://www.theatlantic.com/magazine/archive/1897/08/strivings-of-the-negro-people/305446.

Duff, Alan. 1989. *Translation*. Oxford: Oxford University Press.

Fryer, Louise. 2016. *An Introduction to Audio Description: A Practical Guide*. London: Routledge.

Holmes, James S. 1972/2000. 'The name and nature of translation studies'. In *The Translation Studies Reader*, edited by Lawrence Venuti, 172–85. London: Routledge.

House, Juliane. 1977. *A Model of Translation Quality Assessment*. Tübingen: Gunter Narr.

Huertas-Abril, Cristina A. 2020. 'Telecollaboration in emergency remote language learning and teaching'. In *Sixth International Conference on E-Learning*, 87–91. https://doi.org/10.1109/econf51404.2020.9385425.

Ibáñez, Ana, and Anna Vermeulen. 2013. 'Audio description as a tool to improve lexical and phraseological competence in foreign language learning'. In *Translation in Language Teaching and Assessment*, edited by Dina Tsagari and Georgios Floros, 41–65. Newcastle-upon-Tyne: Cambridge Scholars.

Ibáñez, Ana, Anna Vermeulen, and María Jordano. 2016. 'Using audio description to improve FLL students' oral competence in MALL: Methodological preliminaries'. In *New Perspectives on Teaching and Working with Languages in the Digital Era*, edited by Antonio Pareja-Lora, Cristina Calle-Martínez, and Pilar Rodríguez-Arancón, 245–256. Dublin: Research-Publishing.net.

Incalcaterra McLoughlin, Laura, and Jennifer Lertola. 2011. 'Learn through subtitling: Subtitling as an aid to language learning'. In *Audiovisual Translation: Subtitles and Subtitling: Theory and Practice*, edited by Laura Incalcaterra McLoughlin, Marie Biscio, and Máire Áine Ní Mhainnín, 243–63. Bern: Peter Lang.

Kiraly, Donald C. 2000. *A Social Constructivist Approach to Translator Education: Empowering the translator.* Manchester: St Jerome.

Lavault, Elisabeth. 1985. *Fonctions de la traduction en didactique des langues: apprendre une langue en apprenant à traduire*. Paris: Didier Erudition.

Lertola, Jennifer. 2012. 'The effect of the subtitling task on vocabulary learning'. In *Translation Research Projects 4*, edited by Anthony Pym and David Orrego-Carmona, 61–70. Tarragona: Universitat Rovira i Virgili.

Lertola, Jennifer. 2019. *Audiovisual Translation in the Foreign Language Classroom: Applications in the Teaching of English and Other Foreign Languages*. Dublin: Research-publishing.net.

Lertola, Jennifer, and Cristina Mariotti. 2017. 'Reverse dubbing and subtitling: Raising pragmatic awareness in Italian ESL learners', *The Journal of Specialised Translation* 28: 103–21.

Marczak, Marcusz. 2023. *Telecollaboration in Translator Education: Implementing Telecollaborative Learning Modes in Translation Courses*. New York: Routledge.

Muñoz Raya, Eva, ed. 2004. *Libro Blanco:* Título de Grado en Traducción e Interpretación. Madrid: Agencia Nacional de Evaluación de la Calidad y Acreditación.

Navarrete, Marga. 2018. 'The use of audio description in foreign language education', *Translation and Translanguaging in Multilingual Contexts* 4, no. 1: 129–50. https://doi.org/10.1075/ttmc.00007.nav.

Navarrete, Marga. 2021. *Active Audio Description as a Didactic Resource to Improve Oral Skills in Foreign Language Learning*. Madrid: UNED.

Netflix. 2015. 'English timed text style guide'. Accessed 19 February 2023. https://partnerhelp.netflixstudios.com/hc/en-us/articles/217350977-English-Timed-Text-Style-Guide.

Netflix. 2016. 'Spanish (Latin America & Spain) timed text style guide'. Accessed 19 February 2023. https://partnerhelp.netflixstudios.com/hc/en-us/articles/217349997-Castilian-Latin-American-Spanish-Timed-Text-Style-Guide.

North, Brian, and Enrica Piccardo. 2016. *Developing Illustrative Descriptors of Aspects of Mediation for the CEFR*. Strasbourg: Council of Europe.

O'Dowd, Robert. 2013. 'The competences of a collaborative teacher', *The Language Learning Journal* 43, no. 2: 194–207. https://doi.org/10.1080/09571736.2013.853374.

Piccardo, Enrica, and Brian North. 2019. 'Broadening the scope of language education: Plurilingualism, mediation and collaborative learning', *Journal of e-Learning and Knowledge Society* 5, no. 1: 17–36. https://doi.org/10.20368/1971-8829/1612.

Pintado Gutiérrez, Lucía. 2012. 'Fundamentos de la traducción pedagógica: traducción, pedagogía y comunicación', *Sendebar* 23: 321–53. https://doi.org/10.30827/sendebar.v23i0.41.

Pym, Anthony. 2018. 'Where translation studies lost the plot: Relations with language teaching', *Translation and Translanguaging in Multilingual Contexts* 4, no. 2: 203–22. https://doi.org/10.1075/ttmc.00010.pym.

Richards, Jack C., and Theodore S. Rodgers. 2003. *Approaches and Methods in Language Teaching*. Cambridge: Cambridge University Press.

Sánchez-Requena, Alicia. 2016. 'Audiovisual translation in teaching foreign languages: Contributions of dubbing to develop fluency and pronunciation in spontaneous conversations', *Porta Linguarum* 26: 9–21.

Sánchez-Requena, Alicia. 2018. 'Intralingual dubbing as a tool for developing speaking skills', *Translation and Translanguaging in Multilingual Contexts* 4, no. 1: 102–28. https://doi.org/10.1075/bct.111.ttmc.00006.san.

Sevilla-Pavón, Ana. 2020. 'Aprendizaje lingüístico basado en problemas en el entorno telecolaborativo iTECLA'. In *Tecnologías integradas en la didáctica de las lenguas extranjeras (TIDLE)*, edited by Justine Martín, María Isabel Jiménez González, Alicia Fernández Barrera, and Claude Duée Zohgbi, 57–66. Madrid: Ministerio de Educación y Formación Profesional.

Sokoli, Stavroula, Patrick Zabalbeascoa, and Maria Fountana. 2011. 'Sub-titling activities for foreign language learning: What learners and teachers think'. In *Audiovisual Translation: Subtitles and subtitling: Theory and practice*, edited by Laura Incalcaterra McLoughlin, Marie Biscio, and Máire Áine Ní Mhainnín, 219–42. Bern: Peter Lang.

Talaván, Noa. 2013. *La subtitulación en el aprendizaje de lenguas extranjeras*. Madrid: Octaedro.

Talaván, Noa. 2019a. 'Creative audiovisual translation applied to foreign language education: A preliminary approach', *Journal of Audiovisual Translation* 2, no. 1: 53–74.

Talaván, Noa. 2019b. 'Using subtitles for the deaf and hard of hearing as an innovative pedagogical tool in the language class', *International Journal of English Studies* 19, no. 1: 21–40. https://doi.org/10.6018/ijes.338671.

Talaván, Noa, and José Javier Ávila-Cabrera. 2015. 'First insights into the combination of dubbing and subtitling as l2 didactic tools'. In *Subtitles and Language Learning*, edited by Yves Gambier, Annamaria Caimi, and Cristina Mariotti, 149–72. Bern: Peter Lang.

Talaván, Noa, and Tomás Costal. 2017. 'iDub – the potential of intralingual dubbing in foreign language learning: How to assess the task', *Language Value* 9: 62–88. https://doi.org/10.6035/languagev.2017.9.4.

Talaván, Noa, and Jennifer Lertola. 2022. 'Traducción audiovisual como recurso didáctico en el aprendizaje de lenguas extranjeras: una propuesta metodológica', *Encuentro* 30: 23–39. https://doi.org/10.37536/ej.2022.30.1931.

Thornbury, Scott. 2011. 'Language teaching methodology'. In *The Routledge Handbook of Applied Linguistics*, edited by James Simpson, 185–99. London: Routledge.

Torralba, Gloria, Rocío Baños, and Anna Marzà. 2022. 'Audio description and plurilingual competence: New allies in language learning?' *Revista de lenguas para fines específicos* 28, no. 2: 165–80. https://doi.org/10.20420/rlfe.2022.557.

Zabalbeascoa, Patrick. 2001. 'La traducción de textos audiovisuales y la investigación traductológica'. In *La traducción en los medios audiovisuales*, edited by Frederic Chaume and Rosa Agost, 49–56. Castelló de la Plana: Universitat Jaume I.

Filmography

Almodóvar, Pedro, dir. 2019. *Todo sobre mi madre* [Film]. El Deseo, Renn Productions, France 2 Cinema.

Bravo, Esteban, and Beth David, dirs. 2017. *In a Heartbeat* [Short film]. Ringling College of Art and Design.

Cherry, Matthew A., dir. 2019. *Hair Love* [Short film]. Lion Forge Animation, Matthew A. Cherry Entertainment, Six Point Harness, Sony Pictures Animation.

Cuarón, Alfonso, dir. 2018. *Roma* [Film]. Participant Media, Esperanto Filmoj.

Escobar, Iván et al., dirs. 2015–2019. *Vis a Vis* [TV series]. Globomedia.

Farrelly, Peter, dir. 2018. *Green Book* [Film]. Universal Pictures, Participant Media, DreamWorks SKG, Innisfree Pictures, Wessler Entertainment.

Fesser, Javier, dir. 2018. *Campeones* [Film]. Morena Films, Movistar Plus+, Películas Pendleton.

Foreman, Tynesha, dir. 2019. *How Does It Feel to Be a Problem?* [Short film]. The Atlantic.

Masucci, Elizabeth, dir. 2015. *Phenomenal Woman* [Short film]. Betty Henry Productions, Inc.

Murphy, Ryan et al., dirs. 2018–2021. *POSE* [TV series]. FX Productions, Color Force, Brad Falchuk Teley-Vision, Ryan Murphy Television, Fox 21 Television Studios, FX Network.

NDC (National Deaf Center). 2018. *What Does Deaf Mean?* [Short video]. NDC.

Rashid, Robia, dir. 2017–2021. *Atypical* [TV series]. Sony Pictures Television.

RNIB (Royal National Institute of Blind People). 2019. *What is Audio Description?* [Short video]. RNIB.

Simoes, Bruno, dir. 2022. *Hope* [Short film]. Southeastern Guide Dogs.

Solís García, Pedro, dir. 2014. *Cuerdas* [Short film]. La Fiesta Producciones.

Warchus, Matthew, dir. 2014. *Pride* [Film]. Calamity Films.

Yúdice, Jorge, dir. 2019. *Cocodrilo* [Short film]. Japonica Films. Interfilm Berlin Short Film Sales and Distribution.

4
Teaching languages for social and cooperation purposes: using didactic media accessibility in foreign language education

María del Mar Ogea Pozo
Noa Talaván

Introduction

In recent years, audiovisual media have become an essential part of most people's lives. A wide range of audiovisual genres and formats serve to entertain viewers and disseminate knowledge as well as rapidly spread news, raise awareness and provide information about key societal issues. In educational settings, audiovisual translation (AVT) practices have been employed as a didactic resource, proving to be excellent tools in the teaching of foreign languages (Nunan 1999; Incalcaterra McLoughlin and Lertola 2014; Alonso-Pérez and Sánchez-Requena 2018; Lertola 2019; Talaván 2020) as well as the acquisition-specific skills required for audiovisual and specialised translation (Herrero et al. 2017; Ogea Pozo 2018, 2020a, 2020b).

This chapter focuses on the pedagogical use of subtitling for the deaf and hard of hearing (SDH) – otherwise known as didactic SDH (Talaván et al. 2022) – and its main objective is to assess the impact of transferable content with an emphasis on gender-based violence (GBV). To that end, a lesson plan was designed for B2 learners of English from different higher education institutions and degrees, based on a short film entitled *The Mirror* (Reithmayr 2017) and following the methodological approach developed by Talaván and Lertola (2022). This didactic proposal prompts students to create Spanish-language subtitles (that is, interlingual SDH) from a video excerpt (originally in English) and to complete pre-viewing, viewing and post-viewing tasks. Students are expected to watch, analyse and ultimately localise audiovisual products with gender on the agenda. This implies exploring inequalities and types of violence (Barry 2017) within a pedagogical environment. The present chapter introduces media accessibility (MA) and describes its pedagogical applications, with a special focus on didactic SDH. It then explores how to introduce gender-focused audiovisual content in education to exemplify the potential of didactic MA through the analysis of a specific short-term classroom experience. A corpus consisting of SDH projects submitted by the 48 students who partook in this course has been used to assess students' language and personal skills when transferring gender-based linguistic load. The discussion revolves around how students create their own SDH by observing the interaction of the different channels and codes present in the audiovisual text and depicting the aural elements which are crucial to the story. This study is included within a wider and longer-term methodological proposal carried out within TRADILEX (Audiovisual Translation as a Didactic Resource in Foreign Language Education), a three-year project (2020–2023) sponsored by the Spanish Ministry of Science and Innovation.

Didactic media accessibility

Research and practice in the field of MA is paramount in today's world, particularly given the increasing awareness in society of the need to comply with regulations related to *design for all*. Prior to the beginning of this century various international laws and decrees had established a series of rights and regulations aimed at achieving real universal access for all, such as the UN's (1993) Standard Rules on the Equalization of Opportunities for Persons with Disabilities and the European Union's Directive 2019/882, also known as the European Accessibility Act (EU 2019). However, despite the progress as far as official regulations are concerned, accessibility to audiovisual materials still offers room for improvement. One of the greatest challenges in this regard is the lack of social awareness; in other words, it seems difficult for people to see the need for having every single existing audiovisual product accessible for any user regardless of their physical or cognitive characteristics (Romero-Fresco 2020). Fortunately, more recently the focus has also been placed on media access for any user (not only for people with specific challenges), given the wide scope this field is acquiring through the universalist view of MA as being relevant for all (Greco and Romero-Fresco 2023). This may hopefully help MA progress and generalise faster and more efficiently, promoting more inclusive and accessible classes and assessments in educational contexts.

Be that as it may, one of the contexts where the relevance of MA can and should be dealt with is education. The UN's 2030 Agenda for Sustainable Development includes a section on the role played by education in reducing inequalities, and that is why didactic MA can play a major role. Defined as the use of MA modes (including SDH) as resources in language education, didactic MA stems from didactic AVT (Talaván 2020), a discipline directly linked to the fields of language education and AVT which focuses on the use of revoicing and subtitling practices for language teaching purposes (see Bolaños García-Escribano and Díaz-Cintas 2019). Through a communicative task-based and action-oriented approach, learners are presented with didactic sequences comprised of lesson plans, focused on the localisation of pre-selected audiovisual texts, which students then use to produce new texts (or translations) in the foreign language (for instance, subtitles, dubs, descriptions). According to Lertola (2019), the main AVT and MA practices seen in the industry have been embedded in foreign language teaching to hone language and translation skills. More specifically, scholars started focusing on didactic subtitling (Williams and Thorne 2000; Talaván 2011; Lertola 2012) and didactic dubbing (Danan 2010; Chiu 2012; Sánchez-Requena 2016), but soon started researching MA practices as well. Didactic audio description has received increasing attention in this sense (Ibáñez and Vermeulen 2013; Ibáñez et al. 2015; Navarrete 2018), and the few studies on didactic SDH offer promising conclusions (see Talaván 2019; Talaván et al. 2022; Bolaños García-Escribano and Ogea Pozo 2023).

The potential benefits of didactic MA seem to outnumber those of didactic AVT. Learners exposed to didactic AVT benefit from the use of authentic video and specialised software, such as a subtitle editor or a video-editing program, as well as from the mediation skills that come into play in these types of tasks. The use of didactic MA adds to these benefits a more thorough mediation approach, through the combination of various codes (semiotic and linguistic) and channels (written and oral), and greater social projection based on the increase of MA awareness. Authentic audiovisual input and the use of technologies, such as subtitling editors, can provide realism, motivation and familiarity in educational settings. Mediation and transferable skills are a must in language education today, and learners producing new audiovisual output from a source audiovisual text in any form are building bridges of communication between two communicative contexts. As a result, didactic MA tasks are comprehensive and socially beneficial as far as they contribute to raising awareness about the importance of making audiovisual content accessible to all.

Didactic SDH capitalises on mediation while focusing on intersemiotic translation, since learners provide not only written information about what is being said (that is, dialogues), but also a verbal description of nonverbal information (for instance, character identification, tone, intention, dialect and idiolect, among other features) as well as any other relevant descriptions of sound triggers and music, if any. Intersemiotic mediation entails a more comprehensive and perhaps challenging pedagogical task as regards integrated skills enhancement in general (Talaván et al. 2022), and it could be argued that the need for concision and precision that SDH requires fosters the acquisition of vocabulary, as will be explained in this chapter.

Gender approaches in language education

Didactic MA is clearly linked to the educational approach known as English for social and cooperation purposes, which encourages the use of didactic materials that address issues of social impact, thereby improving the learning process (Huertas-Abril and Gómez Parra 2018; Tinedo-Rodríguez 2021). Tinedo-Rodríguez (2022a) argues that texts should be sufficiently complex to address topics seen in class and to stimulate critical thinking whilst providing creative opportunities. In this sense, gender inequality and GBV constitute major issues with a social impact that are worth including in curricula for the purpose of raising students' awareness and fostering their interest and commitment to the activity to be conducted in the classroom. Once this topic is included within a didactic resource of social relevance in itself, such as the use of didactic SDH, the potential benefits for learners may multiply.

The link between feminism and media studies has been in the spotlight since the 1960s (Von Flotow and Josephy-Hernández 2018; Von Flotow 2019). Some authors, such as Mulvey (1975), De Lauretis (1987) and Goodman (2019), have devoted their research to developing feminist criticisms of gender representations in films. In particular, authors such as Von Flotow and Josephy-Hernández (2018) and De Marco (2006) have pondered the role of gender in the study of translated audiovisual products. However, more research merging the study of gender issues and

AVT within an educational and awareness-raising approach is still needed. As mentioned at the beginning of this chapter, audiovisual contents have become an ideal instrument to shed light and initiate debate on topics of social interest, especially among young people, who tend to be highly familiar with multimedia environments. For this reason, the use of a video resource derived from a spot about GBV – such as the one used for the present study – may be a valuable asset in language education courses. In recent years, emotional advertising has become a major vehicle for change, the implementation of new values and sensitive education, for instance by involving society in the eradication of GBV, informing victims of their rights and alternatives for protection, and encouraging the rejection of abusers (Fernández Vázquez 2014). In the case of *The Mirror* (Reithmayr 2017), the clip forms part of a campaign with the objective of preventing GBV by raising awareness through direct and testimonial advertising that portrays a realistic picture of domestic violence.

GBV is defined as a form of violence – which may include sexual, physical, mental and economic harm – inflicted in public or in private against anyone because of their gender (UN Women n.d.). Violence against women and girls is one of the most widespread, persistent and devastating human rights violations in our world today. It is a major obstacle to the achievement of the 2030 Agenda for Sustainable Development and occurs across all generations, nationalities, communities and spheres of our societies, irrespective of age, ethnicity, disability or other background. Addressing GBV has become a major issue in societies striving to achieve gender equality, and research-led education remains a key tool for the eradication of sexist domination among the youth (UN Women n.d.). Several studies have shed light on the ideological nature of and role patterns associated with the cycle of GBV, facilitating intervention and prevention. In that respect, Expósito (2011) argues that each form of violence reinforces a pattern based on male dominance over women; she distinguishes five types of violence: physical violence, intimidation, emotional abuse, manipulation of children and isolation.

Regarding the representation of gender issues in fiction and the rise of women's voices in different cultures, visual images combined with words might enrich material as well as the learning process (Goodman 2013). Media products such as films constitute an excellent means to shed light on social issues like GBV. This is precisely the main goal of Reithmayr's *The Mirror* (2017), in which the cycle of violence, as described by Walker (2009), is vividly portrayed through visual and aural elements, as will be explained in the methodology section. The theory of the cycle of violence outlines a pattern of batterer behaviours and distinguishes three phases associated with a recurring battering cycle (Walker 2009):

1. Tension-building accompanied by a rising sense of danger. During this phase, the batterer expresses dissatisfaction and hostility through scorn, indifference and sarcasm.
2. The acute battering incident, which becomes 'inevitable without intervention' (Walker 2009, 94). The batterer unleashes a barrage of verbal and physical aggression that can leave the woman severely shaken and injured.
3. Loving contrition, also known as the 'honeymoon' phase, occurs when the batterer apologises, shows kindness and remorse, and offers the woman gifts and/or makes promises.

This three-phase model is a useful resource for analysing and grasping the storyline of *The Mirror* (Reithmayr 2017). Students identify the functions of the verbal and nonverbal elements that represent the escalating intensity of verbal and nonverbal violence endured by the female protagonist in the short film. When it comes to analysing the verbal items in the film, our understanding is that language and culture are intrinsically linked (Kramsch 1998; Gómez Parra 2018), so teaching a language involves teaching a culture (see Larrea-Espinar and Raigón-Rodríguez 2019). A translation activity inevitably involves cultural mediation, so it is crucial that any multimodal products used as class materials contain a rich amount of culture-specific information. From a feminist perspective, it is important to analyse the core elements of the systems to which students are exposed (Tinedo-Rodríguez 2022b), since they may depict a patriarchal cultural system (Bertens 2017). Following this approach, students can develop a better awareness of the relationship between language and culture that is gender-sensitive. To do so, and bearing in mind Barry's (2017) feminist criticism, students who carry out didactic MA tasks with gender-focused content can reflect not only on ways in which audiovisual texts portray women's experiences but also on how these products challenge the representation of women as the Other. By observing power relations and the representations of women on the screen, students can ultimately mediate the clip in producing subtitles that become political inasmuch as they reflect a gender-based approach to translation.

Methodology

This chapter uses a student-produced corpus to demonstrate the connection between didactic SDH tasks and their potential in raising gender awareness. To that end, 48 native-speaking Spanish students performed an interlingual English–Spanish translation task, producing Spanish SDH for the short movie *The Mirror* (Reithmayr 2017). It is worth mentioning that these students had limited experience in SDH, since they had received no prior training in MA other than two lesson plans previously conducted in the same course in which the SDH task discussed in this chapter was developed.

The data analysis processes used to carry out the search were:

1. Word sketch, which processes the word's collocates and other words in its surroundings and may be used to summarise the word's grammatical and collocational behaviour
2. Keywords (single words and terms), used to extract terminology employed in the target texts and to determine which words and terms (or multiword expressions) are typical of the corpus in question
3. Word sketch difference, to make comparisons by contrasting the most frequent words.

Sketch Engine (https://www.sketchengine.eu) allowed for the extraction of keywords and generated frequencies, which show the high density of terms related to GBV contained in the dialogues. The corpus was compiled with Sketch Engine and contains 48 subtitle files corresponding to the subtitles created by the students, who were asked to translate the original subtitles (in English) into Spanish and mediate the text according to SDH conventions. The corpus is comprised of 7,128 words in Spanish, including dialogues and different descriptors (for instance background sounds, music, paralinguistic features and other nonverbal information and sound triggers). It was expected that the corpus entries would help elucidate whether the students had translated the dialogues sensitively and would allow the students to explore further if they had correctly identified all the nonverbal elements that, in some way, could represent the different phases of the cycle of GBV.

To complement this data, two open-ended questions were included in the viewing phase, designed to assess the perceptions learners had derived from the video viewing experience. Their responses were reviewed to determine the learners' perceptions of the selected video and to ascertain whether the activity had enhanced their awareness of GBV and violence against women in general. The questions were as follows:

1. Write down three examples of threats or aggressive language found in the video.
2. What emotions did you experience while watching the video? Describe them in two or three sentences.

Resources: lesson plan and video

The main goal of the TRADILEX project was to prove the pedagogical benefits of didactic AVT and MA for the enhancement of integrated skills – productive and receptive, oral and written skills – with a special emphasis on mediation (Couto Cantero et al. 2021). As part of the TRADILEX project, 12 SDH-specific lesson plans of 60 minutes each were designed, six for each level of English proficiency incorporated into the project – B1 and B2 according to the *Common European Framework of Reference for Languages* (CEFR) (Council of Europe 2001).

The interlingual SDH lesson plan chosen for this study is as follows:

1. Warm-up (10 minutes): Students read a text about GBV and write a discussion on different forms of violence against women.
2. Video viewing (5 minutes): Students watch the English-language short film *The Mirror* (Reithmayr 2017) and answer two open-ended questions focusing on their comprehension of the verbal violence contained in the dialogues.
3. Didactic SDH (30 minutes): Students create SDH for the short film. For this particular lesson plan, the participants are given the original English subtitles in the form of a pre-timed template including the English subtitles. They have to translate the existing subtitles into Spanish, while also including descriptions for the nonverbal vocal elements and other paralinguistic features that have to be mediated to facilitate an understanding of the plot for deaf and hard-of-hearing viewers.
4. Post-AVT task (15 minutes): Students listen to a 2-minute audio excerpt extracted from an interview about gender equality in which British actress Emma Watson introduces HeforShe, a solidarity movement for the advancement of gender equality initiated by the United Nations (see www.heforshe.org). Students then write down their thoughts on the topic and record a 2-minute podcast.

When undertaking the SDH task proper, students are asked to take into consideration the following parameters:

- Character identification: In SDH, speakers need to be identified, especially in dialogues containing multiple speakers. Dashes must be used to identify characters when two or more characters are speaking. Alternatively, colours or name tags can be used before each character's intervention.
- Sound effects: Sound triggers need to be described within brackets. Nouns should be used wherever possible, for instance '(Cough)' instead of '*(He coughs)'. Descriptions must include the sound action only, not its reception, for instance '(Door slams)' instead of '*(We hear a door slamming)'.
- Paralinguistic information: Nonverbal information related to the mood, tone of voice and pitch of the characters needs to be included in brackets, in capital letters, preferably in a single word, for instance '(WHISPER) I miss you'. This should be placed right before the corresponding text that is affected by the feature being described.
- Music: When music is relevant for the plot, it should be included in the subtitles. The music genre should be described, for example '(Classical music)', or if the music is well known the name of the song should be specified, such as '(Sweet Child O' Mine by Guns N' Roses)'. If the subtitles include the lyrics of a song, a musical note (♪) or a hashtag (#) should be placed at the beginning and the end of the corresponding subtitles.

It should be noted that didactic SDH can be a complex task in itself. In the present case, students had to translate the pre-timed subtitles (from English into Spanish) and identify where and how to place the appropriate descriptors. None of the aforementioned SDH parameters (related to character identification, sound effects, paralinguistic information and music) was included in the pre-timed subtitle template, so students had to create new subtitles.

With regard to the audiovisual input selected for this lesson plan, *The Mirror* (Reithmayr 2017) is a short film produced by Go West Creative in association with YWCA (see www.ywcanashville.com), a non-profit organisation dedicated to women, girls and families and committed to working on issues of gender, women's empowerment and economic, social and racial justice. This video is filmed using point-of-view shots to portray the female protagonist's perspective. After an idyllic wedding, she experiences domestic violence and eventually decides to seek help by dialling the YWCA support helpline. The first frame of the short film shows her looking at herself in the mirror, with evident signs of physical violence and holding a phone in her hand. In the final scene, she dials the helpline number.

The duration of the excerpt chosen is compliant with the methodology used in the TRADILEX project (see Talaván and Lertola 2022). It was also deemed appropriate for B2-level English as a foreign language for Spanish speakers. As far as SDH is concerned, this video combines various visual and aural elements of particular interest, as the learner must pay attention to multiple sound and music effects and to paralinguistic, phonetic and utterance features. It is worth mentioning that learners were not informed of the harshness of the images, so as to avoid biasing their responses when asked about their feelings after viewing the short film. Moreover, this element of surprise allowed for an objective assessment of the awareness-raising effect of the task, based on their comments in the final questionnaire.

Aural elements play a major role in this audiovisual text. On the one hand, the constant ringing of the phone emphasises the importance of calling for help. On the other, the build-up of tension and the escalation of violence translates into the sound of sobs, crying and screams that must be addressed during the task-based action-oriented SDH task. In addition to this, linguistic elements play a key role, as the dialogues are in synchrony with the visual narrative and the progression of the cycle of violence. There are instances of emotional language, which eventually evolves into an intensifying verbal and physical violence. Through the examination of visual and aural, verbal and nonverbal elements, students are expected to not only produce subtitles which are consistent with the storyline, but also develop their emotional skills and become concerned about GBV, raising their social awareness of this issue.

Data analysis and results

The data selected and analysed in this study was obtained from a group of 48 students who completed this didactic interlingual SDH task (B2, according to the CEFR). On the one hand, the data derived from the SDH productions of the learners permitted us to obtain results regarding intersemiotic mediation, the description of the aural elements and the translation of emotionally intense dialogues. Additionally, students' perceptions on the topic addressed by the translated video were found to be complementary and significant for the objectives of the study.

Students' translations using a gender-sensitive approach

The first search carried out focused on linguistic aspects. To that end, the Wordlist tool from Sketch Engine was used to generate a frequency list of parts of speech and to classify words by grammar categories. The tool distinguished between lemmas, adjectives, adverbs, conjunctions, nouns, numerals, prepositions, pronouns, verbs and tags. The most significant results in this case were found for nouns and adjectives, as described below.

A total of 220 nouns were retrieved, and the 100 most frequently occurring nouns are displayed in Table 4.1. Among them, two types of nouns may be highlighted as being particularly relevant: those relating to gender and GBV specifically and those depicting aural elements framing the storyline.

It is worth noting the presence of nouns related to gender violence, since these lexical items may be used to build a narrative that is in line with the objectives of advertising campaigns promoting the eradication of violence against women, as stated by Fernández Vázquez (2014): to inform the victim about her rights and protection, to repulse the abuser and to eradicate violence. Hence, it is not surprising that the most frequent nouns are *teléfono* (1), *llamada* (2) and *mujer* (3) ('telephone', 'call' and 'woman'). Some of the most recurrent nouns portray violence; these are words that in some way represent verbal, psychological and physical forms of violence, such as *puta* (5), *prostituta* (92), *zorra* (100), *muerte* (6), *grito* (14), *golpe* (24), *abuso* (42) and *amenaza* (95), among others ('whore', 'prostitute', 'bitch', 'death', 'scream', 'hit', 'abuse' and 'threat'). Likewise, terms related to women's protection are prominent in the corpus – for instance *atención* (36), *ayuda* (38), *apoyo* (50), *derechos* (88) and *empoderamiento* (89), their back translations being 'care', 'help', 'support', 'rights' and 'empowerment'. Among the rest of the items, some emphasise the idea of calling for help, which is crucial from the beginning to the end of the video: *tono* (20), *vibración* (21), *móvil* (30) and *marcación* (63) (meaning 'tone', 'vibration', 'mobile', and 'dialling'), among others.

Other noteworthy nouns correspond to aural elements that frame the storyline and enhance the dramatic nature of the scenes, making them more realistic. The outcomes show that these nonverbal elements have been successfully identified and described in the subtitles by the students. Seven nouns could be linked to pleasant and subtly tense scenes, such as *risas* and *risa* (10 and 11), *carcajada* (61), *ternura* (65), *tensión* (64), *amenaza* (76) and *reproche* (84) ('laughter', 'guffaw', 'tenderness',

Noun	no.	Noun	no.	Noun	no.	Noun	no.
1. teléfono	73	26. fin	12	51. violencia	4	76. amenaza	1
2. llamada	66	27. latido	11	52. racismo	4	77. desesperación	1
3. mujer	55	28. hombre	10	53. zorro	4	78. gemidos	1
4. vida	46	29. latidos	9	54. bofetón	3	79. golpes	1
5. puta	43	30. móvil	9	55. jadeo	3	80. lloro	1
6. muerte	41	31. pitido	9	56. tintineo	3	81. pánico	1
7. resto	41	32. sollozos	9	57. cojón	3	82. pulso	1
8. hijo	39	33. llave	9	58. emergencia	3	83. quejidos	1
9. suerte	37	34. persona	9	59. llantos	3	84. reproche	1
10. risas	32	35. música	8	60. terror	3	85. acoso	1
11. risa	31	36. atención	8	61. carcajada	2	86. asistencia	1
12. llanto	28	37. tonos	7	62. ira	2	87. asociación	1
13. YWCA	27	38. ayuda	7	63. marcación	2	88. derechos	1
14. grito	25	39. bofetada	6	64. tensión	2	89. empoderamiento	1
15. casa	24	40. corazón	6	65. ternura	2	90. maltrato	1
16. vez	24	41. lloros	6	66. mujeres	2	91. miedo	1
17. bebé	23	42. abuso	6	67. crisis	2	92. prostituta	1
18. despertador	21	43. caso	6	68. culpa	2	93. chillido	1
19. alarma	20	44. chico	6	69. cura	2	94. beso	1
20. tono	20	45. respiración	5	70. género	2	95. amenaza	1
21. vibración	20	46. ruido	5	71. mirada	2	96. pulso	1
22. línea	20	47. pareja	5	72. número	2	97. guantazo	1
23. sollozo	15	48. verdad	5	73. toque	2	98. chillido	1
24. golpe	13	49. gritos	4	74. víctima	2	99. suspiro	1
25. tío	13	50. apoyo	4	75. voz	2	100. zorra	1

Table 4.1 Word list of the 100 most frequently occurring nouns, with frequencies

Adjective	no.	Adjective	no.	Adjective	no.	Adjective	no.
1. próximo	33	14. maldito	3	27. inquisitivo	2	40. severo	1
2. molesto	13	15. cariñoso	3	28. doméstico	2	41. amenazador	1
3. amenazante	10	16. hostil	3	29. entrante	2	42. triste	1
4. serio	10	17. saliente	3	30. intermitente	21	43. arrogante	1
5. furioso	10	18. telefónico	3	31. intrusivo	1	44. amable	1
6. rápido	7	19. curioso	2	32. ansioso	1	45. confuso	1
7. nervioso	5	20. juguetón	2	33. burlón	1	46. tranquilo	1
8. agresivo	5	21. pasional	2	34. emotivo	1	47. inquieto	1
9. tenso	5	22. tierno	2	35. altivo	1	48. victimista	1
10. feliz	4	23. firme	2	36. sospechoso	1	49. inseguro	1
11. contento	3	24. palpitante	2	37. afectuoso	1	50. tonto	1
12. alegre	3	25. fuerte	2	38. irónico	1		
13. desgarrador	3	26. celoso	2	39. deseperada	1		

Table 4.2 Word list for the 50 most frequently occurring adjectives, with frequencies

‘tension’, ‘threat’ and ‘reproach’). These terms seem to belong to the first phase of the cycle of violence. Moreover, a total of 23 nouns have been found to describe aural elements portraying explicit physical violence, among which the most frequent terms are *llanto* (12), *grito* (14), *sollozo* (23), *golpe* (24), *latido* (27), *respiración* (45) and *jadeo* (55) (‘crying’, ‘scream’, ‘sobbing’, ‘hit’, ‘heartbeat’, ‘breath’ and ‘gasping’).

The corpus was also filtered by adjectives and a total of 68 items were found, the first 50 of which are displayed in Table 4.2. Some of these adjectives constitute part of the dialogues, whereas most of them correspond to the descriptions of paralinguistic features perceived by the students. These are particularly interesting for this study as they demonstrate the degree of students’ implication and attentiveness to the signs of violence in the oral discourse.

Among the 68 adjectives in the corpus there are 42 adjectives that describe paralinguistic features or other aural components uttered during scenes of violence. These adjectives could be related to a particular phase of the cycle of violence, since the storyline constructs an audiovisual representation of the escalation of violence. Accordingly, the adjectives have been grouped depending on the phases of violence to which they are connected and taking into account both their semantic load and the visual and aural information they describe. Interestingly, several adjectives such as *alegre* (12), *firme* (23) and *nervioso* (7) (‘cheerful’, ‘assertive’, ‘nervous’) were employed by the students to describe scenes corresponding to at least two different phases of the cycle of violence. Table 4.3. exemplifies the verbal portrayal of the cycle of violence, based on the adjectives used by the students to describe the paralinguistic information (linked to the characters’ emotions and behaviours) in their SDH. The adjectives have been listed by order of frequency (high to low) and translated into English for the purposes of this chapter.

A third search for keywords was carried out, this time delving into multiword expressions. According to the information provided in the Sketch Engine website, these are expressions which appear more frequently in the focus corpus than in the reference corpus. A total of 354 items were collected, resulting in 84 lexical units. The 50 most frequently occurring ones are shown in Table 4.4.

Yet again, the results drawn from the corpus analysis show two major topics among the terms: information provided to the victim about the importance and reachability of help, and the description of aural elements which are connected to verbal and physical violence. Accordingly, among the 84 results of this search, a total of 34 lexical constructions refer to the helpline – for example, entries number 8,

Tension building	Battering incident	Loving contrition
Joyful	Assertive	Loving
Emotional	Tense	Hostile
Annoyed	Threatening	Sad
Happy	Aggressive	Arrogant
Affectionate	Heart-breaking	Kind
Cheerful	Damn	Confused
Curious	Throbbing	Calm
Passionate	Hard	Uneasy
Tender	Jealous	Victimhood
Playful	Inquisitive	Insecure
Nervous	Ironic	Nervous
Serious	Desperate	Cheerful
Assertive	Harsh	
Arrogant		
Intrusive		
Suspicious		
Anxious		
Derisive		
Threatening		

Table 4.3 Cycle of GBV represented by the adjectives found in the corpus (shown in order of appearance)

21 and 25 are *ayuda YWCA*, *emergencia YWCA* and *línea telefónica de ayuda* ('help YWCA', 'emergency YWCA', 'telephone helpline') – and the permanent sound of a ringtone: *llamada en espera* (11), *llamada saliente* (12) and *tono de llamada* (4, 19, 20), meaning 'call waiting', 'outgoing call' and 'ringtone'. The purpose of the phone line advertised in the video corresponds to *atención a la violencia doméstica* (26) ('domestic violence support'). In addition, 23 collocations address GBV in a direct way: some of them describe aural elements which were not part of the original subtitles and were perceived by the students as relevant when it came to portraying nonverbal violence – for instance, *grito desgarrador* (14), *llanto angustiado* (38) and *chilla desesperada* (41) ('wrenching scream', 'anguished cry' and 'screams desperately') – while others are part of the original English dialogues and were translated maintaining the same degree of intensity and emotional charge, such as *ropa de puta* (40) or *puta zorra* (43) (for the originals 'whore clothes' and 'bitch' respectively).

	Multiword expression	no.		Multiword expression	no.		Multiword expression	no.
1.	próxima vez	24	20.	tono de una llamada	1	35.	línea de ayuda	1
2.	sola llamada	16	21.	emergencia YWCA	1	36.	llamada entrante	1
3.	simple llamada	5	22.	línea de ayuda YWCA	1	37.	llamada telefónica	1
4.	tono de llamada	4	23.	tono de una llamada saliente	1	38.	llanto angustiado	1
5.	latido de corazón	3	24.	vibración de llamada	1	39.	abuso por parte de su pareja	1
6.	toque del móvil	2	25.	línea telefónica de ayuda	1	40.	ropa de puta	1
7.	espera intermitente	2	26.	atención a la violencia doméstica	1	41.	chilla desesperada	1
8.	ayuda YWCA	2	27.	tono de teléfono	1	42.	pitido de oídos	1
9.	tono de espera	2	28.	línea telefónica	1	43.	puta zorra	1
10.	única llamada	2	29.	línea de emergencias	1	44.	abuso a manos	1
11.	llamada en espera	2	30.	atención a la violencia	1	45.	grito fuerte	1
12.	llamada saliente	2	31.	red de ayuda	1	46.	pulso rápido	1
13.	llamada de teléfono	2	32.	número de atención	1	47.	acoso por parte	1
14.	grito desgarrador	2	33.	red de ayuda	1	48.	respiración agitada	1
15.	abuso por parte	2	34.	número de atención	1	49.	puta vida	1
16.	violencia doméstica	2				50.	víctima de violencia de género	1
17.	víctima de violencia	2						
18.	música tensa	2						
19.	tono de llamada saliente	1						

Table 4.4 Most frequent multiword expressions, with frequencies

Finally, the word sketch was used to contrast the collocations of the term *mujer* ('woman') – which was considered key to this video due to the fact that this informative campaign is primarily targeted at female audiences – and of the word *puta* ('whore'), which was considered most derogatory as well as triggering the escalation of violence in the story. In both cases, the terms were combined with verbs associated with forms of physical and verbal violence: *mujer* is frequently used with verbs implying physical violence, such as *maltratar* ('to mistreat'), *agredir* ('to attack') and *abusar* ('to abuse'), in contrast to *puta*, which is used in the dialogue to denote verbal violence through the expression *parecer una puta* ('to look like a whore').

With the help of the word sketch function, it is also possible to visualise all the collocations in which the word *mujer* is used within the corpus. A total of 45 collocations were detected, containing *mujer* as a subject, alongside action verbs such as *sufrir* and *llorar* ('to suffer' and 'to cry'); as the object of the sentence, used with verbs such as *maltratar, agredir, abusar* ('to batter', 'to attack' and 'to abuse'); and as the main word in prepositional phrases, such as lexical units that contain either *llantos* or *risa* ('cries' and 'laughs').

Concerning the other major issue addressed in this video spot (which is the existence of a telephone helpline), it is interesting to take a closer look at the results obtained regarding the collocational behaviour of the words *teléfono* ('phone') and *llamada* ('call'). Although the comparison between the two terms does not provide relevant data beyond the repeated presence of the phone ringing throughout the clip, it is worth noting that the collocations of *llamada* provide an interesting variety of uses of this term within the corpus, in which a total of 59 collocations were encountered.

These collocations include the word *llamada* as part of prepositional phrases, as the main subject and as an object in conjunction with verbs such as *hacer* ('to make') and *amar* and *querer* (both being terms translated as 'to love'). The presence of the latter two may be explained by the final statement of the video, uttered by a voice-over female narrator: 'Every day, 24,000 women are abused by someone they love.' Likewise, it is particularly interesting to draw attention to some modifiers accompanying keywords, such as *simple* ('simple'), *solo* ('only') and *único* ('single'), which emphasise the ease of access to and availability of the helpline and provide information to encourage women who need to know more about this service.

Students' perceptions

In order to find out whether this method successfully raised the students' awareness on GBV, the answers to the viewing task were reviewed. This section comprised two questions, regarding the forms of threats or aggressive language found in the video and the emotions that students experienced while watching it. Regarding the first question ('Write down three examples of threats or aggressive language found in the video'), most of the students underlined the controlling attitude of the man over the woman's clothes, phone and movements, recognising this behaviour as a form of passive violence. Thus, the visual narrative was pivotal in enabling students to draw their own conclusions from nonverbal elements. Verbal elements are no less important in the short film, and many of the students were able to extract at least three excerpts portraying verbal violence. As a sample, one of the students discussed the escalation of violence represented in the spot through a comment that undoubtedly recalls the cycle of violence described in previous sections:

> The man has been passive aggressive with her almost from the start. He criticised the clothes she used to go out and insulted her. He also tries to control where she goes or with whom she talks. [Even before halfway through] the video, he gets physically aggressive with the woman.

As for the second question ('What emotions did you experience while watching the video? Describe them in two or three sentences'), different types of reactions were acknowledged. According to the comments received, the prevailing feeling among both female and male students was anger, followed by fear and anxiety, as manifested by the following comments: 'I felt anger and pain watching this video. I am a man, but I put myself in the situation of that woman and I would really feel upset. I imagine a constant feeling of fear inside her'; 'I was scared when the screen went black and the woman shouted out loud, because she is probably being beaten by him. I also felt impotence, because the way the man behaved was so unfair but there is nothing the viewer can do to stop it.' The feeling of impotence was included in a notable number of responses. The point of view from which the storyline is framed (subjective shot) may have contributed to boosting viewers' feelings of impotence, empathy and anguish, as may be concluded from these responses: 'It is like I am the person living these situations. These emotions made me feel worried, vulnerable and really small'; 'It looked like I was part of the situations and that made me afraid'; 'When I watched the video, I felt anxiety. It looked like I was part of the situations and that scared me.'

Some positive feelings were also mentioned, such as relief and hope, related to the woman's ultimate decision to seek help: 'I felt relieved when I saw that the woman decided to call and asked for help'; 'In the end, I was relieved because the woman was going to ask for help'; 'I felt so anxious while watching the video. I felt extremely angry watching him treat his wife this way – verbally and physically abusing her. I was so worried about the woman and was relieved when she made that call.'

In light of the above accounts, this video seems to be both successfully informative and inspiring. The ultimate purpose – developing learners' emotional skills and raising their awareness of GBV and the importance of providing support to vulnerable women – was achieved. Moreover, it is remarkable that some students recognised early signs of gender-based abuse as well as the escalation of violence. For example, one student wrote: 'I believe [the video] does a great job showcasing the two sides of gender violence: possessiveness viewed as romantic gestures that turn into threatening and dangerous behaviour.' Another student wrote: 'I felt really shocked watching the video; at the beginning it seems to be the start of any other relationship, and then some passive-aggressive comments or attitudes start showing.' A third student claimed: 'When the woman was smacked while she was just playing, I had a bad feeling about him. But the red flag began to wave brightly when he insulted her just for what she was wearing. I felt quite mad about the situation.' Other comments show that the students were also able to distinguish different forms of violence (verbal and physical), such as the following account, also mentioned earlier: 'I felt extremely angry watching him treating his wife this way – verbally and physically abusing her.'

Conclusion

Nowadays, audiovisual content is ever-more present in everyone's lives, and yet it is still necessary to make media content accessible for all. This is even more important when audiovisual content, such as the short film *The Mirror* (Reithmayr 2017), serves to raise awareness of relevant social issues such as GBV. Previous studies on didactic AVT and MA have already stressed the benefits of this methodology, not only to foster integrated language skills in foreign language education but also to make learners aware of the importance of accessibility for all – that is, the urgent need to produce audiovisual products that are accessible for users with disabilities. The study described in this chapter has focused on didactic interlingual SDH and has explored the potential of exposing students to materials on GBV.

The corpus analysed, which contained a substantial number of verbal items related to GBV, showed that the task met the main objectives in terms of social issues – that is, to inform viewers on victims' rights and alternatives for protection, to raise awareness about the signs of verbal and nonverbal abuse and, lastly, to illustrate the cycle of violence. The results obtained from the translations made by the students and analysed through Sketch Engine show that the creation of SDH triggered their awareness of GBV, as they identified and duly described all signs of violence in their subtitles and used self-conscious and visibility-enhancing vocabulary.

Additionally, the responses shared after the video-viewing phase indicated a reaction of shock among the students, who mainly felt empathy and concern. Students seemed to have felt relieved by an encouraging ending, in which the woman finds the support needed to face her abuser. Many students were able to detect early signs of GBV implicit in both verbal and nonverbal elements, which proves that their awareness and understanding of the topic was appropriate. Furthermore, some students noted in their comments that their concerns regarding GBV had increased after the completion of this action-oriented task.

This experiment has shown that didactic MA can easily be used in conjunction with novel approaches that emphasise inclusion in education, such as English for social and cooperation purposes. The use of audiovisual materials that explore GBV contributed to raising students' awareness while the use of active translation tasks involving multimedia products and specialist tools improved the language learning experience. This multidisciplinary proposal combines didactic MA methodologies and language learning to approach GBV while enhancing foreign language communicative skills within an inclusive educational framework.

Funding

This research is part of the R&D&i TRADILEX Project (Universidad Nacional de Educación a Distancia [UNED]) (https://tradit.uned.es/en/proyecto-tradilex-2), funded by the Spanish Ministry of Science and Innovation (Gobierno de España, Ministerio de Ciencia e Innovación). Reference: PID2019-107362GA I00/AEI/10.13039/501100011033.

This research is part of the TRADISUB Teaching Innovation Project, funded by the IUED (Instituto Universitario de Educación a Distancia, UNED) and implemented in the academic year 2022–2023.

References

Alonso-Pérez, Rosa, and Alicia Sánchez-Requena. 2018. 'Teaching foreign languages through audiovisual translation resources', *Applied Language Learning* 28, no. 2: 1–24.

Barry, Peter. 2017. *Beginning Theory: An introduction to literary and cultural theory.* Manchester: Manchester University Press.

Bertens, Hans. 2017. *Literary Theory: The basics*. London: Routledge.

Bolaños García-Escribano, Alejandro, and Jorge Díaz-Cintas. 2019. 'Audiovisual translation: Subtitling and revocing'. In *The Routledge Handbook of Translation and Education*, edited by Sara Laviosa and Maria González-Davies, 207–25. London: Routledge. https://doi.org/10.4324/9780367854850-14.

Bolaños García-Escribano, Alejandro, and María del Mar Ogea Pozo. 2023. 'Didactic audiovisual translation: Interlingual SDH in the foreign language classroom', *Translation and Translanguaging in Multilingual Contexts* 9, no. 2: 187–215. https://doi.org/10.1075/TTMC.00108.BOL.

Chiu, Yi-hui. 2012. 'Can film dubbing projects facilitate EFL learners' acquisition of English pronunciation?', *British Journal of Educational Technology* 43, no. 1: 24–7.

Council of Europe. 2001. *Common European Framework of Reference for Languages: Learning, teaching, assessment*. Strasbourg: Council of Europe.

Couto Cantero, Pilar, Mariona Sabaté Carrové, and María del Carmen Gómez Pérez. 2021. 'Preliminary design of an initial test of integrated skills within TRADILEX: An ongoing project on the validity of audiovisual translation tools in teaching English', *Research in Education and Learning Innovation Archives* 27: 73–88. https://doi.org/10.7203/realia.27.20634.

Danan, Martine. 2010. 'Dubbing projects for the language learner: A framework for integrating audiovisual translation into task-based instruction', *Computer Assisted Language Learning* 23, no. 5: 441–56. https://doi.org/10.1080/09588221.2010.522528.

De Lauretis, Teresa. 1987. *Technologies of Gender: Essays on theory, film, and fiction*. Bloomington, IN: Indiana University Press.

De Marco, Marcella. 2006. 'Audiovisual translation from a gender perspective', *Journal of Specialised Translation* 6: 167–84.

EU (European Union). 2019. *'Directive (EU) 2019/882 of the European Parliament and of the Council of 17 April 2019 on the accessibility requirements for products and services (Text with EEA relevance)'*. Accessed 26 March 2024. http://data.europa.eu/eli/dir/2019/882/oj.

Expósito, Francisca. 2011. 'Violencia de género', *Mente y Cerebro* 48: 20–25.

Fernández Vázquez, Jessica. 2014. 'Análisis y evolución de las campañas publicitarias promovidas por el Gobierno', *Pensar la Publicidad: Revista Internacional de Investigaciones Publicitarias* 7, no. 2: 409–24. https://doi.org/10.5209/rev_pepu.2013.v7.n2.46184.

Gómez Parra, Elena M. 2018. 'Bilingual and intercultural education (BIE): Meeting 21st-century educational demands', *Theoria et Historia Scientiarum* XV: 85–99. https://doi.org/10.12775/ths.2018.006.

Goodman, Lizbeth. 2013. *Literature and Gender*. London: Routledge.

Goodman, Robin. T. 2019. *The Bloomsbury Handbook of 21st-Century Feminist Theory*. London: Bloomsbury Academic.

Greco, Gian Maria, and Pablo Romero-Fresco. 2023. 'Universalist, user-centred and proactive approaches in media accessibility: The way forward', *Journal of Specialised Translation* 39: 140–64.

Herrero, Carmen, Alicia Sánchez-Requena, and Manuela Escobar. 2017. 'Una propuesta triple: Análisis fílmico, traducción audiovisual y enseñanza de lenguas extranjeras', *inTRAlinea Special Issue: Building Bridges between Film Studies and Translation Studies*, 2245. Accessed 26 March 2024. http://www.intralinea.org/specials/article/2245.

Huertas-Abril, C. and Elena M. Gómez Parra, eds. 2018. *Inglés para fines sociales y de cooperación*. Barcelona: Graó.

Ibáñez, Ana, María Jordano, and Anna Vermeulen. 2015. 'Diseño y evaluación de VISP, una aplicación móvil para la práctica de la competencia oral', *Revista Iberoamericana de Educación a Distancia* 19, no. 1: 63–81. https://doi.org/10.5944/ried.19.1.14580.

Ibáñez, Ana, and Anna Vermeulen. 2013. 'Audio description as a tool to improve lexical and phraseological competence in foreign language learning'. In *Translation in Language Teaching and Assessment*, edited by Dina Tsagari and Georgios Floros, 41–65. Cambridge: Cambridge Scholars.

Incalcaterra McLoughlin, Laura, and Jenifer Lertola. 2014. 'Audiovisual translation in second language acquisition: Integrating subtitling in the foreign-language curriculum', *The Interpreter and Translator Trainer* 8, no. 1: 70–83. https://doi.org/10.1080/1750399X.2014.908558.

Kramsch, Claire. 1998. *Language and Culture*. Oxford: Oxford University Press.

Larrea-Espinar, Ángela, and Antonio Raigón-Rodríguez. 2019. 'Sitcoms as a tool for cultural learning in the EFL classroom', *Pixel-Bit* 56: 33–50. https://doi.org/10.12795/pixelbit.2019.i56.02.

Lertola, Jennifer. 2012. 'The effect of the subtitling task on vocabulary learning'. In *Translation Research Projects* 4, edited by Anthony Pym and David Orrego-Carmona, 61–70. Tarragona: Intercultural Studies Group.

Lertola, Jennifer. 2019. *Audiovisual Translation in the Foreign Language Classroom: Applications in the teaching of English and other foreign languages*. Dublin: Research-publishing.net.

Mulvey, Laura. 1975. 'Visual pleasure and narrative cinema', *Screen* 16, no. 3: 803–16. https://doi.org/10.1093/screen/16.3.6.

Navarrete, Marga. 2018. 'The use of audio description in foreign language education', *Translation and Translanguaging in Multilingual Contexts* 4, no. 1: 129–50. https://doi.org/10.1075/ttmc.00007.nav.

Nunan, David. 1999. *Second Language Teaching and Learning*. Michigan: Heinle and Heinle.

Ogea Pozo, María del Mar. 2018. *Subtitulado del género documental: de la traducción audiovisual a la traducción especializada*. Madrid: Sindéresis.

Ogea Pozo, María del Mar. 2020a. 'Subtitling documentaries: A learning tool for enhancing scientific translation skills', *Current Trends in Translation Teaching and Learning E* 7: 445–78.

Ogea Pozo, María del Mar. 2020b. *La traducción audiovisual desde una dimensión interdisciplinar y didáctica*. Madrid: Sindéresis.

Romero-Fresco, Pablo. 2020. 'The accessible filmmaker and the global film', *Monografías de Traducción e Interpretación* 12: 381–417. https://doi.org/10.6035/MonTI.2020.12.13.

Sánchez-Requena, Alicia. 2016. 'Audiovisual translation in teaching foreign languages: Contributions of dubbing to develop fluency and pronunciation in spontaneous conversations', *Porta Linguarum* 26: 9–21.

Talaván, Noa. 2011. 'A quasi-experimental research project on subtitling and foreign language acquisition'. In *Audiovisual Translation: Subtitles and subtitling: Theory and practice*, edited by Laura Incalcaterra McLoughlin, Marie Biscio, and Máire A. Ní Mhainnín, 197–218. Oxford: Peter Lang.

Talaván, Noa. 2019. 'Using subtitles for the deaf and hard of hearing as an innovative pedagogical tool in the language class', *International Journal of English Studies* 19, no. 1: 21–40. https://doi.org/10.6018/ijes.338671.

Talaván, Noa. 2020. 'The didactic value of AVT in foreign language education'. In *The Palgrave Handbook of Audiovisual Translation and Media Accessibility*, edited by Łukasz Bogucki and Mikołaj Deckert, 567–91. London: Palgrave Macmillan. https://doi.org/10.1007/978-3-030-42105-2_28.

Talaván, Noa, and Jennifer Lertola. 2022. 'Audiovisual translation as a didactic resource in foreign language education: A methodological proposal', *Encuentro* 30: 23–39. https://doi.org/10.37536/ej.2022.30.1931.

Talaván, Noa, Jennifer Lertola, and Ana Ibáñez. 2022. 'Audio description and subtitling for the deaf and hard of hearing: Media accessibility in foreign language learning', *Translation and Translanguaging in Multilingual Contexts* 8, no. 1: 1–29. https://doi.org/10.1075/ttmc.00082.tal.

Tinedo-Rodríguez, Antonio J. 2021. 'La perspectiva de género, la competencia multicultural y la mejora de la competencia comunicativa a través de los textos: Propuesta pedagógica basada en "The Yellow Wallpaper"'. In *Lenguaje, textos y cultura: perspectivas de análisis y transmisión*, edited by Francisco J. Perea Siller, Clara E. Peragón López, Alicia Vara López, Lucía Cabrera Romero, and Estrella Ramírez Quesada, 117–36. Barcelona: Octaedro.

Tinedo-Rodríguez, Antonio J. 2022a. *La enseñanza del inglés en el siglo XXI: una mirada integradora y multimodal*. Madrid: Sindéresis.
Tinedo-Rodríguez, Antonio J. 2022b. 'Producción fílmica y traducción audiovisual didáctica (TAD) para la enseñanza integrada de contenidos y lenguas (AICLE)', *DIGILEC: Revista Internacional de Lenguas y Culturas* 9: 140–61. https://doi.org/10.17979/digilec.2022.9.0.9155.
UN (United Nations). 1993. *Standard Rules on the Equalization of Opportunities for Persons with Disabilities*. Adopted by the United Nations General Assembly, forty-eighth session, resolution 48/96, annex, of 20 December 1993. Accessed 26 March 2024. https://www.un.org/esa/socdev/enable/dissre00.htm.
UN Women. n.d. 'Frequently asked questions: Types of violence against women and girls'. Accessed 4 March 2023. https://www.unwomen.org/en/what-we-do/ending-violence-against-women/faqs/types-of-violence.
Von Flotow, Luise 2019. 'Gender in audiovisual translation studies: Advocating for gender awareness'. In *The Bloomsbury Handbook of Feminist Theories for the 20th Century*, edited by Robin Truth Goodman, 229–44. London: Bloomsbury Academic.
Von Flotow, Luise, and Daniel Josephy-Hernández. 2018. 'Gender in audiovisual translation studies: Advocating for gender awareness'. In *The Routledge Handbook of Audiovisual Translation*, edited by Luis Pérez-González, 296–311. London: Routledge. https://doi.org/10.4324/9781315717166-19.
Walker, Lenore E. 2009. *The Battered Woman Syndrome*. New York: Springer.
Williams, Helen, and David Thorne. 2000. 'The value of teletext subtitling as a medium for language learning', *System* 28, no. 2: 217–28. https://doi.org/10.1016/S0346-251X(00)00008-7.

Filmography

Reithmayr, Matthew, dir. 2017. *The Mirror*. Go West Creative [Producer].

Part II
Transmedia

5 Synergising literature and film in the French literary translation classroom: a focus on gender equality

Soledad Díaz Alarcón

Introduction

Living in an equal society implies fully exercising citizenship, enjoying every right and undertaking the inherent duties of a sociopolitically democratic structure. However, throughout history worth has been assigned arbitrarily to people and the abilities and value of women have been disregarded, resulting in an asymmetric collective construction. Despite significant advances in work and the public sphere (see Bahous 2021), effective equality between genders is far from being a reality in our time. One of the main components of this disparity is the unjustified distribution of roles based on deep-rooted cultural traditions. These deliberate role allocations have shaped gender stereotypes, which are prejudices created by a dominant, predetermined social group that qualify the masculine and the feminine. And as Menéndez Menéndez (2008, 50; my translation) points out, 'from the stereotypical construction of the masculine and the feminine, as is obvious, the norms of behaviour, behaviours and attitudes that society allows and promotes for both sexes are established, censoring the transgression of the role'. This social, political, economic and cultural inequality is preserved through forms of domination (Díaz Gorfinkiel and Elizalde San Miguel 2019) that perpetuate the idea that this disparity is natural.

Educators ought to integrate students whilst promoting social and civic abilities and creating a diverse, equal and critical learning environment. It is essential to ensure that education is focused on more than just specialised knowledge and skills. In this way, students are enabled to understand their reality, be aware of gender-based differences (for instance, between men and women), and assume their responsibilities and exercise their rights in a tolerant, cooperative and supportive manner. These skills enable them to practise dialogue, defend human rights and promote equal treatment of and opportunities for different genders, rejecting any form of discrimination based on gender or other personal or social conditions.

In the literary translation classroom, this civic and cultural education is delivered through multidisciplinary educational focuses, like the one presented in this work. The main objective of the initiative explored in this chapter is the acquisition of the skills needed to complete an optimal translation, from French into Spanish, of a selection of texts from the novel *Les Liaisons Dangereuses* by Choderlos de Laclos (1782/1913), a classic story of French literature that depicts the aristocratic society of the eighteenth century with stark irony. Nevertheless, the intention transcends the linguistic scope. It integrates both a multimodal dimension, through the combined use of the novel and its cinematographic adaptation, and an intersectional dimension (Crenshaw 1989) after considering classifiers like age and social class. Further, Crenshaw (1989) states that the concept of intersectionality refers to marginalisation and structural disadvantages in the intersection of gender with other identities and social rankings – like age, economic status, race, ethnicity, religion, disabilities and abilities – supported or exacerbated by the colonial legacy of power relations.

The decision to use audiovisual texts in the literary translation classroom was driven by the evident proliferation of audiovisual tools since the end of the twentieth century, the accessibility of audiovisual media and their usage and consumption in our daily lives. Educators are obliged to integrate audiovisual material into academic work because our society is immersed in what Marzal Felici (2007, 64) designates as 'the era of multi-screens', in which students are now accustomed to thinking audiovisually. Undoubtedly, the close relationship between film and literature cannot be ignored. As Lamoure (2005) claimed, 'la littérature et le cinéma sont deux arts n'utilisant pas les mêmes outils mais ayant un même but: créer une émotion pour mieux transmettre un message'. [Literature and cinema are two distinct art forms using different tools to one another but having the same aim—that of creating an emotion to better convey a message.] Based on the arguments presented above, the following actions were carried out using Laclos's novel.

Firstly, a study of the selected narrative texts (letters II and IV) was conducted to obtain the necessary discursive, linguistic and historical-cultural content. This preliminary study was done in preparation for the combined analysis of two artistic expressions: the novel and a film adaptation. The second step was therefore to explore both the literary work and a French-dubbed film adaptation based on the English-language film adaptation *Dangerous Liaisons* (1988), directed by Stephen Frears. Using images and sound provides a quick and effective contextualisation, which is indeed crucial to understanding the written text and its subsequent translation. Additionally, it facilitates a contrastive analysis between the written text and the audiovisual text that paves the way for the subsequent translation of the French-language script of the sequences that recreate the actions described in the letters. The students acquire linguistic, discursive and translation skills through analysing and comparing both artistic expressions. The third stage of the didactic proposal focuses on the analysis of the sociocultural roles assigned to women in the texts. These roles reveal a social hierarchy marked by stereotypes. By reflecting social reality, literature and film offer tangible examples of how these roles and stereotypes influence collective perceptions over time. Thus, the contrastive study of the novel and its film adaptation, in the same way, invites critical reflection on the representation of gender and the evolution of societal roles, allowing students to acquire cultural analysis and critical thinking skills.

In short, this multidisciplinary educational proposal, which encompasses discourse and translation analysis and multimedia materials alongside a social focus, embraces an approach that furthers equality, diversity and inclusion (EDI) by providing an educational experience that not only focuses on curricular content but is also concerned with the integral development of students as informed citizens. Through actively promoting social justice, bridges are built between disciplines, cultures and generations, and students are ultimately empowered to act as agents of change in a global and complex society. In the digital age, catering to different learning styles can be achieved through audiovisual materials.

The upcoming sections detail the didactic proposal, focusing on the methodological phases. These include setting objectives, choosing appropriate materials, understanding student characteristics, conducting descriptive and contrastive studies of texts, analysing stereotypes and, ultimately, presenting conclusions.

Materials, aims and methods of the case study

The principal aim of the case study was that students would translate several excerpts from Choderlos de Laclos's novel *Les Liaisons Dangereuses* (1782/1913) from French into Spanish. To prepare for this task, the main activity undertaken by students was to view and subsequently analyse selected sequences from the French-dubbed version of the American film *Dangerous Liaisons* (released in 1988). The French-language film was released on 22 March 1992 and the English-language original is an adaptation of the French-language novel.

The publication of *Les Liaisons Dangereuses* dates back to 1782; for reference, students utilised the Bibliotheque des Curieux edition from 1913. The texts under study were letters II and IV, which largely correspond to the sequences in the film between 00:06:22 and 00:11:50. The actors appearing in these sequences are Glenn Close (Madame de Merteuil, a marchioness), John Malkovich (the Viscount of Valmont), Swoosie Kurtz (Madame de Volanges) and Uma Thurman (Cécile de Volanges).

Although the audiovisual text used is not itself an original version, which would have been the ideal scenario, the film was awarded the Oscar for Best Adapted Screenplay in 1988 (by Christopher Hampton) and for Best Costume Design (by James Acheson) and Best Production Design (by Stuart Craig and Gérard James). I consider that these multiple acknowledgements by the Academy of Motion Picture Arts and Sciences in the US, together with the recognition and prestige that the actors in the film enjoy globally, support the usage of the American film for a lesser-known French production. It is also worth mentioning that the American film has been the subject of study in numerous scholarly analyses, which have approached the text from different angles. In many of these studies, faithfulness to the novel is commended; however, the originality of the present exercise lies in the sequences chosen, their relationship and link with Laclos's literary text, and the overarching translation studies perspective from which the texts are analysed, the latter being the final goal of the exercise. These elements of originality underpin the desire to share this innovative teaching proposal for literary translation.

As concerns the selection of sequences linked to the chosen texts, Aumont and Marie (1988, 89) posit that it is possible to conduct an analysis from a partial perspective by using sequences, as film segments condense the film's meaning considerably. Nevertheless, the following criteria should also be met:

- The fragments selected for analysis should be defined (that is, they should correspond to segments or subsegments of the film).
- The sequences should be consistent and coherent in a stand-alone fashion, having a sufficiently explicit internal organisation.
- The sequences should be representative of the film as a whole.

Insofar as this case study is concerned, all three criteria are met. As regards the first criterion, the segments are delineated, beginning at the start of a scene and finishing at its close. During the clip in question, Madame de Merteuil receives the Viscount of Valmont in one of the reception rooms at her home and proposes a ploy to him. At the end of the conversation, Valmont leaves (by walking downstairs) and the scene concludes. The second criterion is fulfilled because the segment takes place around the marchioness's speech: first, her confidant is placed in the background, the different characters are introduced, and details about her character are revealed, as are the intentions of the various characters at play. Merteuil then unveils her project for revenge, along with the personal and social gains she expects to gain from the plan. Finally, she explains his role in the scheme to the Viscount and gloats about the rewards to come. Valmont accepts, but states his conditions and demands a higher form of payment. The scene closes as the two enter an agreement. As for the third condition, the chosen scene lays the foundations upon which the literary work and, therefore, the film are built. This sequence in the film is thus crucial to understanding the core narrative of the text.

The literary translation class frequently includes a diverse group of students, with a higher proportion of women than men. Usually, the majority of students are of Spanish nationality, with a small number of international students, including French-speaking students. Regarding training, both the Spanish- and French-speaking students tend to lack experience in the discipline of literary translation, so this would be their first approach to this speciality. On the other hand, the Spanish students' linguistic competence in French tends to be solid, at least enough for them to approach the texts confidently. French-speaking students generally face a more significant challenge, because they need to perform reverse translation rather than translating into their native language. However, their understanding of the texts is likely to be superior to the Spanish students' knowledge of classical French culture and literature. The level of Spanish varies among French-speaking students. The understanding of texts and cultural knowledge generally varies between the two groups, providing opportunities for collaboration and learning from each other's strengths and weaknesses.

Aims

The aims underpinning this study are the following:

- Linguistic aim: To carry out an evaluative comparison of the linguistic resources of morphosyntactic, lexical and semantic nature present in both the audiovisual and written texts.
- Literary aim: To enable the detection of discursive structures, stylistic features, symbolism and symmetries present in both texts and that can be recreated in the target text.
- Sociocultural and communicative objective: To provide the necessary knowledge of and contextualisation surrounding these literary and audiovisual texts.

Likewise, the transfer of the novel to a second language makes it possible to reflect on current gender imbalances. In this sense, university students become aware of the various forms of aggression (manipulation, humiliation or abuse) women continue to face in contemporary society. The translation process becomes a means to examine how language plays a role in the perpetuation of exclusionary attitudes and individual and social control.

Method

The methodological model applied in this teaching experiment is described below, with the different steps outlined. These are a pre-translation phase and a translation phase, in line with the methodology set forth by Nord (2018) for approaching audiovisual and written texts. Regarding the first, Nord (2018, 14) demonstrates a model of pre-translational analysis of the original text that is structured according to extratextual factors, intertextual factors and communicative effect. Following Nord's (2018, 14) definition, this analysis 'is designed to identify the function-relevant elements in both the existing source text and the prospective target text, as defined by the translation brief'. The challenges detected when translating the original text into a second language are addressed in the subsequent translation phase. Nord (2018, 59–63) calls these challenges 'translation problems' and classifies them, according to their nature, into pragmatic, cultural, linguistic and extralinguistic problems. An additional phase has been included in the form of a pre-viewing step, which precedes the pre-translation phase and involves preparatory activities.

Regarding the study of stereotypes, which is carried out after the translation phase has been completed and corrected in class, an analysis sheet was created based on the character characterisation model of Galán Fajardo (2006) and Lozano (2020). The students use this to evaluate stereotypes about women in the letters they have analysed, according to their physical, social and psychological dimensions. The instrument for measuring stereotypes by Colás Bravo and Villaciervos Moreno (2007), based on the assessment of parameters such as sexuality, social behaviour, skills and abilities, emotional expression and social responsibility, is also used. (The analysis sheet is shown in Table 5.5 later on in this chapter.)

The pre-viewing phase

In this phase, some preparatory activities are carried out. The first consists of anticipating the possible meanings of the novel's title, *Les Liaisons Dangereuses*. A liaison ties two things or people together. Such a union may be romantic (between lovers), social (an agreement) or material (a letter) in nature. *Dangereuses* ('dangerous') implies an element of risk, harm or criminality. These three notions are fitting descriptions of the modus operandi shared by the protagonists. Students are asked to reflect on the sense of the terms in groups, to express their proposals freely and to predict the novel's plot.

The second activity is an online questionnaire designed to evaluate the prior knowledge of the students and spark their interest. The questionnaire consists of 15 multiple-choice questions which students can complete individually or in small groups. If they do not know the correct answer, they may consult the internet. The answers are revised as a class, and students may volunteer their responses.

The pre-translation phase

Next, the pre-translation analysis of the two letters and the corresponding film scenes is carried out. As established by Nord's (2018) functional method, the extratextual factors encompass aspects like the sender, intention, receiver, medium, time, space, motive and textual function. Intertextual factors include theme, content, presuppositions, composition, nonverbal elements, lexicon, syntax and suprasegmental characteristics. Finally, the communicative effect is the realisation of the text's communicative intention.

To carry out the pre-translation analysis, the students are provided with a link to the Bibliothèque Nationale de France (see www.bnf.fr), where the digitised, copyright-free novel is located, as well as the video material, which was previously hosted on the module's virtual learning platform. The first activity consists of extracting some of the extratextual data (sender, medium, time and place) from both documents so that students can complete the extratextual analysis sheet, as shown in Table 5.1. The rest of the factors have to be researched on the internet, in French. This way, the Spanish-speaking students exercise their comprehension skills in French, whereas the international (French-speaking) students are instructed to complete the worksheet in Spanish, so that they fulfil the requirements for written expression competence in their L2.

Students are divided into groups for the activity. Collaborative work can be more efficient thanks to the distribution of tasks, and it can help establish bonds between classmates. One or several French-speaking students should be placed in each group in order to facilitate their integration in the class. This also promotes a linguistic and cultural exchange that enriches perspectives, clarifies doubts and enables active learning. The data is discussed as a class once all the groups have completed the worksheet shown in Table 5.1. All groups are encouraged to participate, either voluntarily or as directed by the teacher. For revision purposes, the extracts from the original texts (novel and film) are shared in class. Once the students have filled in the table using internet resources, they share their answers and the correct answers are discussed as a group. Students then check their answers against the corrections given in class. Table 5.2 shows an example of what the completed worksheet could contain.

Elements	**Literary text (novel)**	**Audiovisual text (film)**
Sender		
Intention		
Receiver		
Medium		
Place		
Time		
Motive		
Textual function		

Table 5.1 Worksheet for identifying extratextual factors (based on Nord 2018) in excerpts from the novel *Les Liaisons Dangereuses* (Laclos 1782/1913) and scenes from the French-dubbed film *Les Liaisons Dangereuses* (Frears 1992)

Elements	Literary text (novel)	Audiovisual text (film)
Sender	*Choderlos de Laclos*	Stephen Frears (director)
Intention	Critique of the aristocratic French society of the eighteenth century. Literature as entertainment and reflection of power dynamics and human nature.	Coincides with the intention of the literary text.
Receiver	Adult audience interested in satirical, social and psychological literature.	Adult audience interested in classic and historical cinema.
Medium	Digitised book with 12 illustrations.	Colour feature film, dubbed into French from English.
Place	Space and setting in eighteenth-century aristocratic Paris.	Internal space equal to that of the literary text.
Time	Internal time: 17 August The publication date of the edition is 1913.	Internal time equal to that of the novel. English-language film released in 1988 and French-dubbed film released in 1992.
Reason	Satirical criticism of the aristocratic society of its time, exploring themes of morality, power and manipulation and the dissonance between appearances and the truth.	Similar to that of the literary text.
Textual function	Expressive function	Equal to that of the literary text.

Table 5.2 Sample completed worksheet for analysis of extratextual factors (based on Nord 2018) in excerpts from the novel *Les Liaisons Dangereuses* (Laclos 1782/1913) and scenes from the French-dubbed film *Les Liaisons Dangereuses* (Frears 1992)

Before beginning the analysis of the intertextual factors of the texts, the plot is briefly summarised. Given that the students have read information about the plot, they are invited to participate in the discussion. This epistolary novel, framed in the eighteenth century, presents a non-linear structure (sometimes the reader has to wait several dozen pages to read, in another letter, that an announced event has come to pass) and then follows a chronological sequence. The protagonists, who belong to the aristocracy, personify antagonistic ethical poles: the honourable and the libertine. Madame de Merteuil, a distinguished noblewoman, conceals a vengeful misandry under a mask of honourability. The Viscount of Valmont displays an insatiable power of seduction. Both characters conceive double-scope plots: the marchioness seeks revenge against an ex-lover, while Valmont seeks to seduce the righteous Madam President of Tourvel and corrupt the innocent Cécile. The story unfolds through epistolary exchanges between Merteuil, Valmont, their confidants and their victims.

Regarding the theme, the novel showcases the tensions between appearance and reality through letters and plots, being a satirical critique of the aristocracy of the eighteenth century. It encompasses themes like power and manipulation, morality, the subversion of societal standards because of personal interests, human relationships and the fragility of virtue. In the first studied letter (letter II), the marchioness, in a confidential tone, confesses to the viscount the betrayal by her lover, the Comte de Gercourt, and communicates her desire to take revenge. She proposes to Valmont that he seduces Cécile, Gercourt's fiancée, to humiliate him. Therefore, it is assumed that the relationship between the marchioness and the viscount is close and complicit, as Valmont is the only one who knows of the betrayal of Gercourt and is an active participant. It is evident that Merteuil and Valmont have a shared history. The marchioness openly expresses her feelings and makes it clear that she dominates the relationship, which is sustained by a shared objective: harming another and gaining the maximum benefits in respect of their interests. She knows the viscount very well and knows how to persuade him to do whatever she wants. This letter therefore serves to introduce readers to the main characters. Letter IV is the viscount's response to the marchioness. He rejects her proposal and confides in her his plans to seduce Madame de Tourvel. This seduction project constitutes the second intrigue of the novel. In this letter, the power game between Merteuil and Valmont is evident – it is a competitive relationship in which Valmont intends to outdo and surpass Merteuil.

The literary text underwent an adaptation, or rather a metamorphosis, in being adapted to the medium of audiovisual expression. The transition from the written to the oral word implies a direct communicative exchange, which translates into bidirectional communication (instead of unidirectional, as the format of the letters dictates) as well as a lightening of style. For example, the issuer of letter II is Madame de Merteuil and she directs it to Valmont, while letter IV is Valmont's response to the marchioness; however, in the film sequences the two characters converse face to face at the marchioness's house. The film, to bring across the effect of the epistolary exchange, incorporates scenes that recreate moments where personal notes are exchanged and uses voice-over to inform the viewer of the information necessary to understand the plot.

On the other hand, in the film the constant play of images, whose semiotic function is to display a substantial volume of information, takes the place of the descriptions in the written text (such as the description that Valmont makes of Cécile and Madame de Tourvel in letter IV). It also makes visible the pragmatic function of the communicative act by uncovering implicit meanings through facial gestures, tone and register, and body movements that denote tension, trust or complicity. For example, in the film, Cécile and Madame de Volanges feel uncomfortable in Valmont's presence; his posture is rigid and they do not look him in the face. Valmont, for his part, shows impudence when he gives Cécile's behind a surreptitious slap or when he kisses Madame de Merteuil's cleavage when saying goodbye to her. Finally, the images facilitate the viewer's understanding of the plot and do not require the recipient to make an intellectual effort like that required of the reader of the written text due to the connotative complexity of the literary language in the novel.

Furthermore, in the film the plot has been simplified. It focuses on the aims of the two main characters: the marchioness's desire for vengeance and Valmont's efforts to charm Madame de Tourvel. To achieve this, the scriptwriter has had to carry out significant cross-checks, jumping from one letter to the next to find the plot lines and link them and shorten the time. For example, letters II and IV are written between 4 and 5 August; in the film, they are summarised in the first five minutes. During the translation phase of the exercise proposed in this chapter, the linguistic-discursive elements that are part of the intertextual factors should be studied.

Lastly, communicative effect is addressed. This concept refers to the extent to which the target text transmits the same impact on the reader or audience as the original text did on its target audience. It consists of visualising the hypocrisy of high society, criticising moral conventions and commenting on the manipulation of emotions of others in the quest for power. The communicative effect of the cinematographic adaptation coincides significantly with that of the novel, thanks to the high level of fidelity to the source. The film captures the novel's tone and atmosphere, transmits emotions through the artistic interpretation of history and the characters and emphasises the intention of the writer to put the focus on the central themes. The set and costumes also offer an accurate image of the decadence of French high society before the French Revolution.

The translation phase

Despite the changes made in order to adapt the novel for film, the scriptwriter has successfully preserved not only the novel's essence but also the wording used. In the translation phase, the changes that the written discourse has undergone in the audiovisual adaptation are attended to. To make these changes more evident and more accessible for students to understand and analyse, passages from the letters that correspond to the film sequences are selected. Students are provided with a table containing the passage from each letter (Table 5.3 shows some illustrative examples) and then, in groups, they identify their equivalents in the film sequences. They then compare both discourses from a linguistic point of view and translate the letters and the script of the sequences into Spanish. Finally, the students debate the challenges that different segments present and categorise the translation challenges posed in this phase, following Nord's (2018, 59–63) taxonomy. Table 5.4 presents, as an example, the textual correlations and the linguistic observations extracted from the contrastive analysis.

Letter II segment	Sequence	Observations
[…] Que faites-vous, que pouvez-vous faire chez une vieille tante dont tous les biens vous sont substitués?		
Letter IV segment	**Sequence**	**Observations**
[…] une jeune fille qui n'a rien vu, ne connaît rien; qui, pour ainsi dire, me serait livrée sans défense; qu'un premier hommage ne manquera pas d'énivrer, et que la curiosité mènera peut-être plus vite que l'amour. Vingt autres peuvent y réussir comme moi.		

Table 5.3 Analysis sheet for extracts from letters from *Les Liaisons Dangereuses* (Laclos 1782/1913) and the equivalent scenes from the French-dubbed film *Les Liaisons Dangereuses* (Frears 1992)

Letter II segment	**Sequence**	**Observations**
[…] Que faites-vous, que pouvez-vous faire chez une vieille tante dont tous les biens vous sont substitués?	00:06:30–00:06:35 *M.: Votre tante?* *V.: C'est exact.* *M.: Ne vous a-t-elle déjà légué par testament toute sa fortune?*	The polite and formal register of the written text is simpler and less ceremonious in the film, like the reflective tone that transitions to a clear and direct style. Subordinate syntax is simplified to clear, syncopated sentences. Legal terms such as *biens* or *substitués* are generalised.
Letter IV segment	**Sequence**	**Observations**
[…] une jeune fille qui n'a rien vu, ne connaît rien; qui, pour ainsi dire, me serait livrée sans défense; qu'un premier hommage ne manquera pas d'énivrer, et que la curiosité mènera peut-être plus vite que l'amour. Vingt autres peuvent y réussir comme moi.	00:08:25–00:08:39 *V.: elle n'a rien vu … elle ne connaît rien, et par simple curiosité, elle ne voudra pas me résister … et cèdera dès mon premier assaut … Ah, cette affaire … vingt autres que moi triompheraient d'elle.*	The text from the novel has a more complex structure and is narrated in the third person. The film script has a more dramatic, theatrical and direct tone. It alternates between third- and first-person singular. The subordination of the extract from the novel has been transformed into simple sentences in direct speech. Implicatures are included through ellipses that denote the shared information, and emphatic statements are used. The literary lexicon of the text from the novel (*énivrer*, *hommage*) is trivialised and emphasised through a passionate tone in the film script (*me résister*, *cèdera*). In the film script the passionate and persuasive tone clearly shows a seductive approach intent on conquest.

Table 5.4 An example of a completed analysis sheet for extracts from letters from *Les Liaisons Dangereuses* (Laclos 1782/1913) and the equivalent scenes from the French-dubbed film *Les Liaisons Dangereuses* (Frears 1992)

Regarding the translation issues posed by the different texts, students were instructed to classify them (for instance pragmatic, cultural, linguistic or extralinguistic) and explain what they consist of. The students then had to determine the most appropriate translation technique for each segment, and explain their motivations. A few examples are discussed below.

> Il m'est venu une excellente idée, et je veux bien vous en confier l'exécution.
>
> He tenido una excelente idea y estoy dispuesta a confiaros su ejecución.
>
> I've had an excellent idea and I am willing to entrust its execution to you.

In French, the expression *je veux bien* can express disposition or consent. This can create pragmatic ambiguity in Spanish, since it could be understood either as a desire to do something or as a statement that it will be done. To adapt the text chronologically, the reverential *voseo* – or use of the pronoun *vos* – was adopted for the second-person singular or plural, which, as indicated by the Royal Spanish Academy's (n.d.) *Diccionario panhispánico de dudas*, persists in literature set in ancient times and in ritual formulas.

> Vous connaissez ses ridicules préventions pour les éducations cloîtrées.
> Conocéis sus ridículos perjuicios sobre las educaciones conventuales.
> You know his foolish prepossessions in favour of conventual education.

In French, the expression *éducations cloîtrées* refers to education in a convent or monastery in the sense of a person who has entered as a religious adherent; this is therefore culturally specific. In Spanish, the translation should preferably not convey the cultural and religious nuance of the original term, but instead refer to the training of a layperson in a religious institution.

> Le Président est en Bourgogne à la suite d'un grand procès.
> El magistrado está en Borgoña inmerso en un gran juicio.
> The magistrate is in Burgundy immersed in a great trial.

The French term *le Président* refers to a magistrate who directs one of the chambers of the courts of justice (since the seventeenth century), as stated by the Centre National de Resources Textuelles et Lexicales (see www.cnrtl.fr). In Spanish, particularisation in the legal field facilitates understanding of this term. Likewise, the place name Bourgogne refers to the east central region of France. The decision can be made to translate it into Spanish through adaptation or it can be maintained in French through transliteration.

> […] et cèdera dès mon premier assaut.
> Y cederá en el primer ataque.
> And she will give in at the first attack.

The military lexicon that makes up the simile that Valmont establishes between the conquest of territory on the battlefield and the love conquest of Madame de Tourvel ought to be respected in the Spanish text through coined equivalents.

Analysis of stereotypes

After concluding the translation phase and the translation analysis of the letters and the script, students conduct a study of the two main characters, Madame de Merteuil and the Viscount of Valmont, and the secondary character Cécile, who ultimately is the vehicle of Madame de Merteuil's revenge. The analysis is done following the structure of the worksheet in Table 5.5. Students determine to what extent Cécile fits the stereotype of the naïve and innocent young woman whose life is destined to bring honour and prestige to her family through an arranged marriage in which she will fulfil the role of a model wife. The marchioness, on the other hand, contradicts the stereotype of a virtuous, devout, beneficent woman concerned with the interests of others, typical of the aristocratic woman of the eighteenth century. Valmont does depart somewhat from the stereotype of the aristocratic young man due to his more libertine and hedonic outlook, but he nevertheless represents the stereotype of a dominant, corrupt man who views women as objects of pleasure at the service of his sexual needs.

Students can use written documents, letters and sequences to configure the parameters to analyse the stereotypes. In order to justify their decisions, they must provide examples taken from the film dialogues. Tables 5.6, 5.7 and 5.8 demonstrate how students might complete the activity for Madame de Merteuil, Cécile and Valmont, respectively. This activity also serves as a revision tool; this can be done through a class discussion to encourage debate and to enrich the students' knowledge through the sharing of all the groups' proposals.

Physical description (Age and physical appearance)	**Social dimensions**	**Psychological dimensions (Personality, feelings, objectives and social relationships)**
Sexuality This includes beauty and physical attractiveness. Women must meet beauty standards to please men and fulfil their traditional roles. A woman's physical expression is limited by what is expected of her.	Social behaviour Behaviours and abilities are learnt within the family and the sociocultural group to which one belongs, through social interactions and imitation.	Skills and abilities Men's interest in perpetuating discrimination against women is based, in part, on the arbitrary assignment of skills, competencies and capacities – which men establish – in which gender-based prejudices prevail over the intellectual capacities and education of individuals.
	Social responsibility In eighteenth-century French aristocratic society, the public space was dominated by men, with women being merely accessories.	Affective expression In eighteenth-century French aristocratic society, it was expected of a woman to take a passive role in relationships, in which she was not permitted to express her desires. She was not allowed to act as a participating and active subject (which would have created greater emotional balance).

Table 5.5 Worksheet for analysing stereotypes about women, based on the instruments developed by Colás Bravo and Villaciervos Moreno (2007: 43–51)

To conclude the unit, students carry out a final activity in which they identify examples of the objectification of women, as well as acts of misogyny or sexism, in the news and on social networks and through talking with their friends and acquaintances. This is so that, considering the parameters studied for the characters in the novel, students can extract concrete and tangible instances of socioculturally accepted behaviours – in areas such as politics, justice, economy, work, culture or sport – that undervalue women or result in them being manipulated or harassed. Students discuss real-life scenarios from an array of areas, which can be easily researched online and in the media. These could include well-known French-language scandals in areas such as politics (for instance Éric Zemmour's 2014 interview on French BFMTV, in which he argued that femininity is incompatible with power), economy (for instance comparing salary gaps across Europe, with a particular emphasis on Spain's gender gap), culture (for instance sexist lyrics from well-known, controversial songs such as *Je ne dirai rien* by Black M and *Copine de b...* by Keen'V) and sports (for instance, French sports commentators making sexual comments about sportswomen, such as Philippe Candeloro's infamous comments about skater Valentina Marchei during the Winter Olympics in Sochi, 2014).

Lastly, all materials selected by the students are compiled and shown to the class in thematic segments. Each group presents their examples, explaining and justifying their choices. An in-class debate allows the teacher to encourage reflection on 'mansplaining' and outright sexism as well as on the internalisation of reproduced and assumed social stereotypes that preclude women's personal and professional development. As a unique task, it is proposed that students meet with groups outside of the classroom and present suggestions and recommendations on how to eliminate the behaviours identified in the thematic segments discussed and how to implement change in society.

Assessment and reflection

Once students have finished the pre-translation and translation phases, they are given a control questionnaire to evaluate the learning about the chosen literary work. The questionnaire consists of 10 open-ended questions related to the content of the texts (context, symbolism, literary resources and linguistic characteristics). Upon completing the questionnaire, the students exchange their answers with their peers. The teacher gives out sample correct answers, and the students correct and suggest a grade for each other's written assessments.

Madame de Merteuil	**Example**
Sexuality She uses her physical attractiveness as a weapon to manipulate men. She is conscious of her beauty and uses it strategically to meet her objectives.	She critiques social prejudices in terms of women's physical appearance: *[…] la retenue des blondes* *[…] si elle eût été brune, ou si elle n'eût pas été au Couvent.*
Social behaviour She is a master of societal norms and etiquette. She moves in high society with ease and knows the social conventions of the era. Despite this, her behaviour is also subversive and manipulative, as she secretly challenges these norms to reach her goals.	She positions herself as against the socially acceptable female education (i.e. convent education and social etiquette): *[…] sotte présomption* *[…] ridicules préventions* *[…] préjugé plus ridicule encore*
Social responsibility She lacks a traditional sense of social responsibility. Her only objectives are to obtain power and pleasure. She is selfish and manipulative, which contrasts with the stereotype of aristocratic women as benefactors in society.	Her desire for vengeance leads her to destroy the honourability of a magistrate: *Prouvons-lui qu'il n'est qu'un sot*
Skills and abilities She is very intelligent. She has learnt through observation and the psychological analysis of others, and she has built up her own identity and character and acquired the skills to become a strong, independent and free woman. She has great knowledge of music, art and literature. Her capacity to manipulate people around her shows her skills in social strategising and her ability to plan and execute complicated schemes. She plays with social norms and adapts them for her own benefit.	Dominating (orders and imperatives): *[…] j'exige* *Partez-sur-le-champ* *Prendre mes ordres à genoux* Strategising: *Je veux donc bien vous instruire de mes projets.* Manipulative: *Une rouerie digne d'un Héros*

Affective expression She hides her true feelings behind a mask of coldness and control. Very rarely does she show genuine emotion; she presents herself as a cold and calculating woman. This contrasts with the idea that aristocratic women should be emotive and expressive in their social behaviour.	Rage: *Qui m'aurait dit que je deviendrais la cousine de Gercourt? J'en suis dans une fureur…* Disdain: *L'importance que met Gercourt à la femme qu'il aura.* Self-control: *[…] vous voyez que l'amour ne m'aveugle pas*
Conclusion: Madame de Merteuil is a complicated character who challenges, to a great extent, the stereotype of an aristocratic woman in eighteenth-century France. Although she possesses some qualities associated with aristocratic women, like physical attractiveness and the ability to navigate through society, her manipulative behaviour, lack of responsibility and strategic intelligence distinguish her as a unique and powerful character in the plot. She challenges and subverts many gender expectations of the time, making her, in a way, timeless.	

Table 5.6 Example stereotype analysis sheet for Madame de Merteuil

Cécile de Volanges	**Examples**
Sexuality Cécile is presented as a beautiful and delicate young woman who exemplifies the ideal beauty standards of the time. Her physical attractiveness and virginity are central themes in the storyline.	*[…] vraiment jolie* *[…] certain regard langoureux*
Social behaviour She is a shy and obedient woman who adheres to social conventions and obeys her mother's will. She is submissive to figures of authority.	There are no examples of this in the letters. However, in the sequences of the film it is clear that Cécile is always in the background of the scene. She remains standing when the main characters are seated. She only speaks when her mother tells her to.
Social responsibility She lacks social responsibility. Her life revolves around pleasing her mother and marrying according to the expectations of society. Her lack of independence reinforces the stereotype of the young aristocratic woman who is passive and obedient.	*[…] l'héroïne de ce nouveau roman*
Skills and abilities Cécile does not possess skills or abilities beyond the tasks associated with women of her class (embroidery and playing the harpsichord). She is a naïve and inexperienced young woman.	*Cela n'a que quinze ans* *N'a rien vu, ne connaît rien.* *Vingt autres peuvent y réussir comme moi. Il n'en est pas ainsi de l'entreprise qui m'occupe.*

Affective expression Cécile shows genuine emotion; she is impulsive because of her lack of life experience.	There are no concrete examples in the letters, but in the film her gestures express great surprise when Valmont touches her bottom. She does not know how to dissimulate.
Conclusion: Cécile de Volanges embodies the stereotype of a young aristocratic woman in eighteenth-century France. Owing to her youth and her convent education, she is incapable of making her own decisions and believes her role in life is to make a favourable marriage. She will therefore shape her character to what her husband, family and society expect of her. Cécile is an example of how aristocratic society of the time moulded young women to embody a certain model of femininity and submission, making her an emblematic character in the novel.	

Table 5.7 Example stereotype analysis sheet for Cécile

Viscount of Valmont	**Examples**
Sexuality Valmont embodies bold sexuality and promiscuity. He is a seducer and uses his physical attractiveness and his skills in the art of seduction as a fundamental part of his personality.	His goal is to accumulate love affairs. He sets himself more and more difficult challenges and does not give up until he achieves them. *[…] j'y pense le jour, & j'y rêve la nuit. J'ai bien besoin d'avoir cette femme.*
Social behaviour He moves in high society with ease, but his behaviour is subversive and transgressive in comparison with the stereotype of a young aristocrat. He defies societal norms and plays an active role in the manipulation and destruction of the reputation of other members of high society.	He mocks women: *[…] femmes faciles* *[…] qui se défendent si mal* He pretends to be obedient and submissive in order to achieve his goals: *[…] nous prêchons* He is a flatterer: *[…] vous seriez un jour la Patronne […] au plus un Saint de village.*
Social responsibility He lacks a sense of social responsibility. His main objective is his own entertainment and personal satisfaction.	His exploits are in fact a collection of amorous conquests. *[…] vous servirez l'amour et la vengeance ; ce sera enfin une rouerie de plus à mettre dans vos mémoires.*

Skills and abilities Valmont is a master of manipulation and accomplishes his objectives through cleverness and deceit. These abilities are unusual in a young aristocratic man, whose stereotypical role would be to work at a court or in the military.	Wicked: *[...] Ce sera enfin une rouerie de plus à mettre dans vos Mémoires.* Calculating: *[...] Je lui en prépare de plus efficaces* *[...] Vous feriez chérir le despotisme* Frivolous: *Conquérir, défense, succès ataque, ennemi, gloire, couronne.* (Cultural reference to La Fontaine)
Affective expression Valmont is characterised by a lack of authenticity in his personal relationships. He rarely shows intimate emotions.	Love is merely pleasure and he mocks it: *Plaisirs, désirs, jouissance, ridicule.*
Conclusion: Valmont is a main character and an interesting counterpoint to the stereotype of the young aristocratic man in eighteenth-century France. Although he possesses qualities associated with the aristocracy (such as his capacity to move in high society), his daring sexual behaviour, lack of social responsibility and skill at manipulation make him a unique and subversive character in the plot. His role reflects the decadence and moral ambiguity of the aristocracy of the time.	

Table 5.8 Example stereotype analysis sheet for the Viscount of Valmont

In terms of the translation, students give their texts to the teacher, who assesses them based on the evaluation scale from Hurtado Albir (2001, 305–6), as seen in Table 5.9. This scale is used for its agility in evaluating shortcomings in the target text that can affect the comprehension of the meaning of the original and the written expression in the target text. It also rewards quality adaptations. This scale has an exhaustive taxonomy that is easy for students to understand. Once the assessments are returned to the students, the revised files and scores will allow them to understand their mistakes and adjust their work accordingly.

The delivery of the translation and its evaluation then give way to a reflection on the translation process, the difficulties involved and the resources the translator has to solve translation issues.

Phase	Type of mistake	Value	Result
Issues that impact understanding of the original text	Contradiction	−2/−3	
	False sense	−1.5	
	Nonsense	−2/−3	
	Unnecessary addition	−1/−1.5	
	Unnecessary suppression	−1/−1.5	
	Inadequacy of linguistic variation (register, style)	−1.5	
Issues that impact the proper expression of the target language	Orthography	−0.5	
	Grammar (morphology, syntax)	−1	
	Lexicon: Inappropriate term	−1	
	Lexicon: Wrong term	−1.5	
	Textual (incoherence, lack of sense)	−2	
Issues with functionality		−3	
Achievements	Commission, transmission of message, target language conventions	+1, 2, 3	
	TOTAL	100	

Table 5.9 Translation evaluation scale from Hurtado Albir (2001, 305–6)

Conclusion

This study led to various insights, as discussed in this section. The use of cinematographic adaptations in the teaching of literary translation involves advantages and challenges. On the one hand, there is a risk that film will replace the original source (for instance a novel), discouraging the reading of literature. Additionally, students could adopt the focuses and themes of the film without questioning them, which could lead to translation mistakes. In order to address this, it is suggested that the necessary sequences of the film be used to translate fragments of the novel.

Despite these challenges, I believe that incorporating cinematographic adaptations in teaching literary translation offers many advantages. Firstly, it actively involves the students, encourages research and teamwork, and constitutes an attractive alternative for learning. Furthermore, it improves cognitive skills, like the association of ideas, reflection, memorisation and interpersonal communication. On the other hand, adaptations provide essential contextual details, like settings and/or pragmatics, which are crucial to understanding and efficiently translating the message of the literary text. It is vital for the teacher to plan this focus carefully, leading the learning process and ensuring the reinforcement of knowledge after students have watched the film. Watching the sequences should be a proactive experience that develops students' attention and critical capacities.

Ultimately, I advocate for the combination of the audiovisual medium with literature in the classroom, given that students are immersed in a multimodal world. They regularly consume digital products, many of which are adaptations of literary works. It is therefore essential that educators modernise their methods and instruct students in linguistic, cultural and technological competences, preparing them to explore literary works as well as audiovisual fiction.

In addition, students' translations of fictional narrative into Spanish allows for open discussion and reflection in the classroom. It also encourages students to exercise critical judgement, enabling them to analyse situations as they occur in order to avoid perpetuating an unfair system.

In the context of EDI teaching methodology, this exercise presents an opportunity to reflect on the persistent gender inequality in society, a state that is learnt and imposed and not inherently human. A crucial part of tackling this inequality is the deconstruction of gender stereotypes rooted in culture. To achieve this, it is essential not only to educate but also to co-educate. This means that gender equality ought to be taught and promoted in the classroom so that students can develop skills without being limited by prejudicial gender roles.

To conclude, gender equality is not a distant ideal but rather a goal that can be reached through education. EDI methodology provides us with the opportunity to contribute to this change and work towards a more equal and diverse society in which everyone has the same opportunities to flourish, no matter their gender.

References

Aumont, Jacques, and Michel Marie. 1988. *L 'Analyse des films*. Paris: Nathan Université.

Bahous, Sima. 2021. *Annual Report of the Under Secretary-General/Executive Director on the Strategic Plan, 2014–2017*. Executive Board of the United Nations Entity for Gender Equality and the Empowerment of Women. Accessed 3 October 2023. https://www.unwomen.org/es/executive-board/documents/2018/annual-session-2018.

Colás Bravo, Pilar, and Patricia Villaciervos Moreno. 2007. 'La interiorización de los estereotipos de género en jóvenes y adolescentes', *Revista de Investigación Educativa* 25, no. 1: 35–8.

Crenshaw, Kimberle. 1989. 'Demarginalizing the intersection of race and sex: A black feminist critique of antidiscrimination doctrine, feminist theory, and antiracist politics', *University of Chicago Legal Forum* 1989, no. 1: 139–67.

de Laclos, Choderlos. 1782/1913. *Les Liaisons Dangereuses*. Paris: Bibliothèque des Curieux.

Díaz Gorfinkiel, Magdalena, and Begoña Elizalde San Miguel. 2019. 'Análisis sobre desigualdades de género en la sociedad actual'. *VIII Informe FOESSA*. Madrid: FOESSA Foundation.

Galán Fajardo, Elena. 2006. 'Personajes, estereotipos y representaciones sociales: una propuesta de estudio y análisis de la ficción televisiva', *ECO-PÓS* 9, no. 1: 58–81.

Hurtado Albir, Amparo. 2001. *Traducción y traductología: introducción a la traductología*. Madrid: Cátedra.

Lamoure, Alexandra. 2005. 'Les Liaisons Dangereuses: Laclos et Frears'. *La Page des Lettres.* Académie Versailles. Accessed 18 April 2024. https://bit.ly/2Fd53s4.

Lozano, Sandra. 2020. 'Mirada al pasado: estereotipos y arquetipos de género en series históricas españolas (2011–2018)', *Comunicación y Medios* 41: 67–79. https://doi.org/10.5354/0719-1529.2020.54276.

Marzal Felici, José Javier. 2007. 'El análisis fílmico en la era de las multipantallas', *Comunicar: Revista Científica de Comunicación y Educación* 29: 63–68. https://doi.org/10.3916/C29-2007-09.

Menéndez Menéndez, María Isabel. 2008. *Discursos de ficción y construcción de género en televisión*. Palma de Mallorca: UIB.

Nord, Christiane. 2018. *Translating as a Purposeful Activity: Functionalist approaches explained*. 2nd ed. London: Routledge.

Royal Spanish Academy. n.d. *Diccionario panhispánico de dudas*. Accessed 3 October 2023. https://www.rae.es/dpd.

Filmography

Frears, Stephen, dir. 1992. *Les Liaisons Dangereuses, Version Française*. Warner Bros. Entertainment.

6

Transmediation: pedagogical applications of film adaptation in modern foreign language education

Carmen Herrero
Isabelle Vanderschelden

Introduction

With the rapid development of 'convergence' culture (Jenkins 2006, 2), increased opportunities to work within the sector of intersemiotic translation have emerged. In the 1950s Roman Jakobson (1959, 233) identified different ways of transferring verbal signs through intersemiotic translation, defining said transfer as 'into another, nonverbal system of symbols'. Other types of adaptation and expansion have also been developed as educational tools in modern foreign language curricula. However, there remains a paucity of work that has critically explored the potential of transmediation as an effective approach to translation practice and training through a wider lens than purely linguistic transfer. This chapter presents how transmediation can enhance translation practices in the language classroom. It argues that the study of adaptation and transmedia storytelling allows (language) students to better understand how multimodal texts are interlinked in different ways of recycling stories. Working with different modes of transmediation implies recognising the multiple points of entry into literary and cultural translation processes. It is also an effective method for reflecting critically on the ways in which literary adaptation finds its place in language education through innovative exercises structured around transmediality.

The first part of the chapter briefly revisits concepts derived from traditional translation theory, such as intersemiotic translation and transmutation (Jakobson 1959) and the notion of an *invariant* core in translation (Bassnett 2002; Malmkjær 2011; Robin 2016). These help to redefine the notion of universals of translation to account for practices of transmediation, such as intermediality, adaptation and transmedia storytelling. In addition, it presents a critical model for media analysis structured around the concept of multimodality, developed in the twenty-first century for the social sciences (Cope and Kalantzis 2000). As we will show, this interdisciplinary model constitutes a useful toolkit for film analysis but also for the other types of texts and communication practices – including adaptation and translation – that learners encounter in the real world.

The second part presents possible applications of our pedagogical model, which promotes an interdisciplinary approach (intermedial, transmedia and translation studies) for discussing and critically evaluating the intersemiotic and transmedia translation of media and literary texts. It comments upon some strategies of adaptation and transmedia extension, as well as the processes involved in intersemiotic translation that could be explored pedagogically in language classes. This chapter makes use of two examples: one French and one Spanish. The first case study is a transnational and multilingual French animation film, *Josep* (Aurel 2020b), based on the biography of the artist Josep Bartoli and his published drawings retracing the detention camps in France for refugees during the Spanish civil war. The second case study is a graphic novel (Rey 2016) and a film (Zambrano 2019), both based on the Spanish novel *Intemperie* (2013) (translated into English as *Out in the Open* in 2016) by Jesús Carrasco.[1]

These works lend themselves to a comparative analysis focusing on transmediation, hereby understood as the processes involved in the translation of meaning from one mode (written text or a visual image) to multiple modes (a film or a graphic novel). Both case studies show how, through this new prism, the discussion of adaptation practices can form the basis of language exercises that enhance learners' translation skills in a broader sense. The framework we propose is represented via four tables (see Tables 6.1 to 6.4) that can be used and adapted as worksheets. They are designed to help teachers to engage their students with the critical analysis of the processes and strategies involved in intermedial adaptation, cross-media and trans-genre storytelling and narrative expansion. The materials can be easily adapted and tailored to other contemporary multimodal texts and cross-media extensions for use in secondary and higher education.

Revisiting translation theory

The invariant core in translation

Two areas within translation studies – the invariant core and universals of translation – are used to contextualise our claim that analysing intersemiotic and transmediation adaptation processes can help to develop critical analysis in modern language teaching and engage learners with innovative pedagogical applications of transmedia practice adapted to the new media of the twenty-first century. In translation studies, the invariant core refers to the elements that remain unchanged in the process of translation. Identifying an invariant core presupposes a comparative approach before and after translation (or adaptation) of texts, even though, from the 1990s onwards, descriptive approaches in translation studies based on empirical research focused on 'the transfer operations and the shifts that occur as a result of translators' decisions' (Toury 1995, 31). The notion of an invariant core helped to identify general laws of translation known as universals of translation, which then led to establishing 'universals of translational behaviour' (Toury 1995, 81). The universals of translation therefore describe factors and qualities that distinguish translations from source texts; they can be defined as 'linguistic features which typically occur in translated rather than original texts and are thought to be independent of the influence of the specific language pairs involved in the process of translation distinctive distribution of lexical items' (Baker 1993, 243).

Putting these theoretical principles into practice, our materials extend the notion of universal features beyond the field of interlingual transition to embrace broader universal cognitive phenomena that affect intermedial and intersemiotic adaptation processes. The cognitive dimensions of this transfer process are important, for example, in the context of films that have been adapted from literary sources. Audiovisual adaptation is not just a verbal or visual process, but one that can also include the transfer of affect. The cognitive nature of choices and behaviour guiding intermedial adaptation also start from an invariant core, which can take various forms and be associated with specific modes of transfer. Clüver's work (2007), for example, as we will see below, expands on the diachronic and synchronic dynamics of culture, which also have a place in adaptation modes in different periods and cultural contexts.

Multimodal literacy

Several scholars have acknowledged the need to account for the multiple dimensions of literacy practices and discourses in digital and non-digital contexts. In their pioneering work, the New London Group (1996, 63) coined the term 'multiliteracies' and proposed a new pedagogy of literacy. The prefix *multi-* refers to the 'enormous and significant differences in contexts and patterns of communication and the "multi-" of multimodality' (Cope and Kalantzis 2015, 3). The multiliteracies instructional approach formulated by the New London Group includes four knowledge processes: situated practice, overt instruction, critical framing and transformed practice (Cope and Kalantzis 2009, 166). In their application to curriculum design, Kalantzis et al. (2016, 75) reframed these terms into words that students could recognise. Situated practices (*experiencing*) focus on the connections between meaning-making processes in real-world situations and educational spaces, using everyday experiences. Overt instruction (*conceptualising*) involves learners developing an explicit metalanguage to describe the concepts and their connections. Critical framing (*analysing*) entails the capacity to critically analyse text functions and to interpret the power relationships involved in communicative actions. Transformed practice (*applying*) implies that learners become creators of texts in real communicative contexts.

Multimodal forms of representation and communication have expanded due to the technological advances taking place in the current digital age. Different theoretical and analytical frameworks have been proposed to conceptualise multimodal phenomena, drawing from social semiotic theories (Kress and van Leeuwen 1996) and systemic functional theories (Serafini 2014; Jewitt et al. 2016; Lim 2018). The 'multimodal turn' (Jewitt 2009, 4) acknowledges that multimodal texts, or 'ensembles', use a range of semiotic resources to represent and communicate meaning (Serafini 2014). In these theories, a *mode* is defined as 'a set of socially and culturally shaped resources for making meaning' with 'distinct affordances, such as colour, typography, font and frames' (Bezemer and Jewitt 2018, 291), and the term *semiotic resource* refers to the linguistic, visual and cultural tools that are capable of representing and communicating meaning (Kress 2003). In addition to written language, other multimodal resources available are music, still images (painting, photography, drawing) and moving images (video, film). After all, as Kress (2003, 48) notes, the spread of digital technologies has given more importance to the 'logic of the screen'.

Shifts in communication practices require learners to acquire new skills to decode, interpret and create meaning with multimodal texts in different sociocultural contexts (Lankshear and Knobel 2003). As Lim (2018, 2) remarks, multimodal literacy 'is about understanding the affordances, that is the potentials and limitations, of the different meaning-making resources, as well as how they work together to produce a coherent and cohesive multimodal text'. Moreover, a 'critical multimodal curriculum framework' should engage with the 'range of artistic and design elements used across multimodal texts' and involve comparing multimodal texts through different strategies across social contexts and cultural practices (Serafini 2023, 27).

Intermediality and transmediality

In recent years, with the advent of the new media age, intersemiotic translation has been seen as a 'bridge concept between translation, adaptation, and by default semiotics' (Giannakopoulou 2019, 201). This has opened new theoretical discussions within translation studies that call for interdisciplinary research on the transmedia adaptation praxis. As the expansion of digital media opens up new artistic and cultural practices, intermediality and transmedia have become key concepts in cross-disciplinary academic research on cultural and commercial practices; they are central to the pedagogical applications that we propose.

Intermediality is used 'to describe a huge range of cultural phenomena which involve more than one medium' (Rippl 2015, 1), including different types of cultural creations, such as literature, art and media. Since the turn of the century, intermedial studies have tried to comprehend the various aspects of the 'intermedial turn' across comparative literature, media, film, cultural and communication studies (Wolf 2011, 2). Bruhn and Schirrmacher (2022, 6) claim that intermedial studies are the best way to describe, study and compare different media products: analysing 'translations and transformations that exist not between languages but between different media types', investigating the way some elements of the narrative are altered in film adaptations or comparing multimodal communication in different media products in order to understand 'how medial choices shape, form and support what is communicated'.

Looking at the specificities of different intermedial articulations, Rajewsky (2005, 46–51) proposes three subcategories of intermediality that can support the analysis of texts and media products:

1. Intermediality as 'medial transposition' (such as film adaptations and novelisations) refers to the 'transformation of a given media product (such as literature and film) or of its substratum into another medium' (Rajewsky 2005, 51).
2. Intermediality as 'media combination' includes opera, theatre and comics.
3. Intermediality as 'intermedial references' describes how a given media product is the result of imitation and transposition techniques across media.

Clüver (2007) also argues that adaptation is a form of transformation that may involve intersemiotic transposition. Transmediation thus describes the repeated mediation of equivalent sensory configurations by another technical medium (Elleström 2019, 4–5). This broadens the notion of intermedial transformation processes to account for new combinations of media transformations now taking place in media cultures, and this broader conceptualisation can be applied in the language classroom to expand the use and creation of multimodal texts.

Against this backdrop of participatory creative and knowledge cultures, transmedia studies have gained scholarly relevance since the turn of the century (Freeman and Gambarato 2019). As introduced by Kinder (1991), transmedia refers to the intertextual processes present in films, animation, TV series and toys. Jenkins (2003) thereafter coined the term 'transmedia storytelling', which he defines as a process where fictional elements get dispersed to create a new unified entertainment experience. Transmedia storytelling involves narrating stories across the media spectrum (films and television series, social media, literature, websites, fan videos and video games), thereby benefiting from the affordances provided by each media channel or platform. This offers creative opportunities in four areas: backstory, mapping the world, displaying other characters' perspectives on the action and expanding audience engagement (Jenkins 2011). Transmedia storytelling has been successfully exploited by popular existing franchises such as *Harry Potter*.

Transmedia scholars and practitioners tend to disagree on the relationship between adaptation and transmedia storytelling. For some (Jenkins 2011; Scolari 2013; Pratten 2015), adaptations are not part of the transmedia phenomenon, as they are not shared across multiple media platforms, are redundant (story retelling) and lack co-creativity. On this, Long (2007, 22) considers that 'retelling a story in a different medi[um] is *adaptation*, while using multiple media types to craft a single story is transmediation'. For others (Baetens and Sánchez-Mesa Martínez

2015; Elleström 2019), adaptation is part of the transmedia process. We support Dena's (2019, 204) argument that transmedia adaptations and extensions could be exploited further to engage students creatively with popular products.

Pedagogical applications of transmedia in language education

Intermediality is at the centre of common adaptation practices to translate stories and other artistic productions into films. In the context of cinema production in French and Spanish, it has taken many forms, from the adaptation of classic texts (plays, novels, stories, *bandes dessinées*) to more derivative self-standing works (*pastiche* and parody). Transmediation, as discussed by Elleström (2019, 2), takes place both diachronically and synchronically and reveals an invariant core derived from a source text, consisting of the common formal, narrative and linguistic elements retained from the source in film adaptations (broadly assimilated to target texts).

Transmediation provides a model for using multiple sign systems and semiosis experiences in language curricula. The notion of transmediation, 'which remains vital to understanding multimodalities' (Siegel 2006, 68), is particularly significant when developing a curriculum that does not privilege written and oral language over all other sign systems, thereby considering the multimodality inherently appearing in all texts and semiotic adaptations. The teaching materials that we present here for French- and Spanish-language classes follow a clear pedagogical rationale and showcase multimodal and transmedia practices (Herrero and Vanderschelden 2019; Herrero 2021; Herrero 2022; Herrero and Vanderschelden 2023; Herrero et al. 2023; see also www.transmediaineducation.com). In terms of linguistic content, the materials are designed to enhance the four key language skills (speaking, reading, writing and listening) using authentic visual and audiovisual sources. On the lexical level, they will expand students' critical metalanguage and specialist vocabulary in the foreign language on a range of topics (for instance character analysis, film language and critical terminology). They can be used for autonomous learning but are also designed to promote active participation with peers in collaborative tasks. Embracing sociocultural content, the learners are encouraged to communicate, transmit knowledge to their peers, express and value different opinions through discussions and engage actively in project planning and the distribution of tasks. They may also be asked to provide peer evaluation with a view to developing their constructive critical skills.

Building on new media literacies (Jenkins et al. 2009; Scolari 2018), the activities are also designed to help learners increase their understanding of film and visual artefacts as effective modes of communication. Some of the exercises are tailored to encourage learners to carry out their own multimedia projects around the materials proposed using creativity, digital resources and editing skills. For example, this may include the ability to think and respond creatively to a given multimedial input with an audiovisual translation project (Herrero et al. 2020) or to participate in a transmedia project (video essay, book trailer, digital review) (Herrero 2019).

We have designed four thematic tables – reproduced in Tables 6.1 to 6.4 – that can be used as worksheets and templates to provide a structured visual representation of intermedial analysis and critical thinking tasks. These tables can easily be adapted and tailored to different needs and pedagogical objectives. The sample analyses provided as guidance in Tables 6.5 and 6.6 are merely illustrations to guide teachers or independent learners if needed. We also provide indicative elements of critical analysis using the multimodal and transmedia principles established in the previous sections to encourage teachers to develop their own exercises. Table 6.1 places the emphasis on modes of meaning in multimodal theory of representation and communication.

In Table 6.2, we offer guidance on how to plan the critical analysis of a scene, extract or other multimedia artefact.

Table 6.3 will allow students to name the transfer processes which take place between the original text and the adaptation and transmedia extensions.

Table 6.4 provides a grid template for assessing learners' skills. It can help students to get a deeper understanding of the steps in the learning and creative strategies involved in the process of transmediation (cross-media and trans-genre storytelling and narrative expansions).

In the following section we present two case studies which can aid language teachers of French and Spanish to apply the pedagogical tables to the study of transmedia processes. We also offer information and brief indicative analytical comments that will help teachers to prepare their classes and adapt the materials to their needs. The examples from the case studies also show how our pedagogical approach facilitates the critical reading of texts and provides new opportunities to engage students in the critical reading of classical and modern literary texts and the transmission of history across different cultures.

	Relevant examples from the film studied Provide examples of how each mode is used in individual scenes, segments of the text studied (clip, graphic novel, film, animation).	**Meaning and effect produced** Critically analyse what effects the examples have on the audience.
Written mode Use of written text or subtitles		
Visual mode Use of still or moving images		
Visual style Colour and lighting		
Spatial meaning Indoor or outdoor location design (architecture, streetscapes, cityscapes and landscapes)		
Proxemic mode Positioning of characters (interpersonal distance, interactions)		
Gestural mode Body language, gestures, way of walking, costume, hairstyle		
Audio mode Music, sound and diegetic noises		
Linguistic mode Dialogue, monologue, speech, voice-over		

Table 6.1 Modes of meaning in multimodal theory of representation and communication (adapted from Kalantzis et al. 2016, 232)

Aspects to analyse	**Relevant examples from the film or extract studied** (how each element is used in scenes or extracts)
How to describe images Frame Type of shot Camera angles Composition	
How to discuss *mise en scène* **[visual]** Actors' positioning Costumes and accessories Use of space Location Light, colour, perspective Montage	
How to discuss *mise en scène* **(sound)** What are the main features of the dialogue? Is there a musical soundtrack? Are there sound effects?	
How is meaning created out of all the *mise en scène* elements? (emotions and sensory perceptions)	
What are the effects produced on audiences by the different *mise en scène* strategies deployed?	
Critical thinking activity: Build a solid argument and provide illustrations of your points using one of the aspects of the scene which you have identified above.	

Table 6.2 Planning the critical analysis of a scene or extract

Transfer process	From the original text to the graphic novel or film studied
Narrative and structure Features retained and changed in plot, storytelling chronology, characters, genre	
Visual style Colour, typography, visual texture, shape, form, space	
Aural mode Music, sound effects, silence, sound and spoken language (volume, tone of voice, accent), ambient noises	
Artistic features Art and visual references	
Communication priorities Relevant features and elements that are prioritised in the transfer of the story	
Target audience and language level	

Table 6.3 Transfer processes between two artefacts in the process of transmediation

	Aware	Familiar	Skilled	Expert
Visual literacy Ability to analyse and create images competently				
Multimodal literacy Ability to analyse, compare and create multimodal texts competently				
Transmedia literacy Ability to understand communication and articulation across multiple media Ability to create and consume multiple media				
Critical thinking skills Ability to argue, question, deduce and generate intelligent and convincing criticism				
Digital skills Ability to use digital tools to create artefacts				

Table 6.4 Grid to assess students' visual, multimodal and transmedia literacy and critical thinking and digital literacy skills

Case study 1: Josep – exploring transmediation in film animation

This case study focuses on the transmediation process from several pictorial sources to an animated video format designed for cinema. The animation film *Josep* (Aurel 2020b) is an experimental form of adaptation of the artist Josep Bartoli's (1910–1995) life.[2] He was a republican Catalan and an international artist who was exiled from Spain in 1939. The telling of his life story can be categorised as a media crossover and a point of translation transfer – and, more importantly, as the blending (and unification) of different forms of visual media to create another work of art. This type of transmedia adaptation process is unusual. The sources used include drawings and artworks as well as published biographical notes.

Josep (74 minutes) was produced with a budget of €2.7 million in 2019 and directed by Aurel, a French artist of the twenty-first century.[3] Released in 2020, *Josep* is the outcome of eight years of research and (pre)production, drawing on a range of resources and collaborators. The film illustrates how experimental arthouse animation films can represent innovative transmedia artefacts – underused in language education thus far – displaying specific strategies of translation of meaning and form. This process of transmedial adaptation follows Rajewsky's (2005) taxonomy by transposing carbon drawings onto animation images, combining different media in such a way that still and animated images imitate pictorial styles, mixing trends from different established art forms and periods. The animation film is a new, independent audiovisual work achieved through a 'union/fusion' process (Clüver 2007, 26), inspired by pre-existing artwork and reinterpreting its formal properties. By adapting and transferring Bartoli's drawings and Frida Kahlo's distinctive use of colour, Aurel pays tribute to these artists. He also displays his own creative talent and expresses his own agenda by mixing graphic forms: animated drawings recalling still drawings, iconic paintings blended into animated film frames and animated (occasionally satirical) figures with the traits of real-life characters. He recycles other textual sources (biography, letters, memoirs, interviews) to produce audiovisual animation.

The film portrays Barcelona-born Josep Bartoli, who worked as a press illustrator. A militant for the Catalan Communist Party in the 1930s, he fled the Franco regime in February 1939. He was immediately interned in a French refugee camp in Argelès-sur-Mer (Pyrénées-Orientales) after crossing the Pyrenees. He was detained for several months in dreadful conditions before escaping and being arrested again on several occasions by the authorities of Vichy France. Sent for deportation to a German concentration camp in Dachau, he jumped from the train and eventually fled to Mexico in 1943. There he became a lover of Frida Kahlo, a relationship which continued when he moved to New York in 1946. In New York, he worked as a set designer and magazine illustrator and was acquainted with artists such as Jackson Pollock and Franz Kline, under whose influence his art became more abstract. Art critics agree that his later work did not have as much impact as his early drawings.

These works, first published in *Campos de concentración (1939–194…)* (Bartoli and Molins i Fábrega 1944) and later by his own nephew, Georges Bartoli, in *La retirada* (Bartoli and Garcia 2009), were discovered by Aurel in 2010, by chance. He felt the urge 'to immerse' himself 'in this story, to take it over, digest it and then bring it back to life' (Aurel 2020a). By rearranging and bringing together little-known biographical accounts, Aurel pays tribute to fellow graphic artist Bartoli, adding his own historical, political and artistic commentary. His film targets new audiences and transmits history and culture in a way that students will be able to discuss and evaluate from different interdisciplinary perspectives. A wide range of exercises can be designed to explore the adaptation process, which involved transmedia translation of drawings and translating words into moving images, sound and sensorial elements. For example, the tasks summarised in Tables 6.1 and 6.3 aim to enhance critical and artistic appreciation within the linguistic and cultural contexts of modern languages programmes. Table 6.5 lists possible elements which could be discussed or proposed as feedback. The next paragraph also provides a few guidelines on the film's characters, narrative form and genre conventions to help educators prepare and tailor their sessions to their needs.

Josep draws on true events, but it also manipulates and interprets the primary sources left behind by Bartoli in several ways. Aurel's background is journalism, hence his comments on the real world using graphic form. During preproduction, he created a storyboard following a three-stage process of intersemiotic translation. The first step was decoding (in this case, the drawings as primary source testimonies); in a second step, he transposed the primary sources' invariant core into animated film images embracing a range of forms and media. Finally, to arrive at a more cohesive narrative form, he collaborated with an experienced screenwriter and storyteller, Jean-Louis Milesi, who developed a more fictional narrative and wrote the dialogue to complement the images: 'He knows how to handle intergenerational relations, politics, militant action, struggles, humanity … and humour, the politeness of despair' (Aurel 2020a).

Bartoli's story is transmediated into a twenty-first-century animation film that brings together historical facts and a fictional narrative by introducing two fictional characters: Valentin, a clumsy but talented drawer and street artist, and his grandfather. Using flashbacks to represent the fragmented memories of the old man, a new, more distanced perspective of Bartoli's story is given, filling some of the gaps in his adventurous life to complement his drawings. The grandfather's memories, which capture Valentin's imagination, recreate the figure of an empathetic gendarme, referred to as Serge, who was instrumental to Josep's survival in France and his escape from the camp (see Figure 6.1). In the confused old man's tale, Serge was a guard working in the camp who also witnessed the post-war journeys of Bartoli in Mexico and America. When the old man gives Valentin a torn drawing by Josep, representing his friend Helios – killed in the camp, a victim of the guards' cruelty as shown in the initial scenes of the film – we do not realise that this drawing will provide a moving, symbolic narrative closure for the film. The last scene shows an older Valentin travelling to a gallery in New York where Bartoli's work is being exhibited, and finding the other half of his drawing. By reuniting the two fragments anonymously, Valentin reunites two friends from the past, making his small contribution to the collective transmission of memory.

Through animation, Aurel increases the iconicity of his images, going beyond a naturalistic treatment of history to achieve a certain allegorical universality. One type of transmedia practice exercise is to engage with the merits of animation as a mode of communication of messages and effects. *Josep* presents some graphic challenges for the

Figure 6.1 Still from *Josep* (Aurel 2020b) representing Valentin and his grandfather. © *Josep* by Aurel, reproduced with permission from Les Films d'Ici Méditerranée.

animation artist, who sets out to let Bartoli's intentions and graphic moods shine through while putting his own graphic work at the service of history and expressing his own feelings about Bartoli's art (Aurel 2020a). His transmedia adaptation work produces a personal film while serving another artist. Animation is a medium that enables a director to capture and immediately editorialise an event, to highlight a flaw, a contradiction or an injustice and make it instantly clear to the viewer (see Aurel 2020a; Batalla 2020).

Through transmedial and intersemiotic transposition Aurel appropriates some of the thematic motifs and drawing techniques that define Bartoli's artistic signature. Critics have, for example, identified artistic visual influences found in Bartoli's drawings and retained by Aurel for his film, such as horrific, Goya-like drawings of prisoners' faces ravaged by disease and hunger, contorted with despair (Clarke 2021). Aurel then transfers some of these into animated images, adding movement, sound, music, breath and rhythm to the still images. To engage with this heterogeneous process of *mise en scène* in the film (or extract), learners could use Table 6.2 to identify the different visual styles, interpret still and moving images and highlight the heterogeneous use of colour. Through this they can ascertain the symbolic significance of these aspects and the effects produced on viewers. The colour schemes strategically indicate the different periods of Josep's life by using visual contrasts: bright colours illustrate his encounter with Frida Kahlo in the 1940s and with the New York abstract school of art in the 1960s. They stand out against the sepia or monochromic tones used to characterise the conditions of detention in the camps. Similarly, the rhythm and editing of the animated images convey different moods as, often, the image remains still and the characters' expressions static, 'like memories fixed in the brain after all these years' (Clarke 2021).

Also significant in the film's genesis are the audiovisual strategies used to convey sensorial effects, including the cold and lack of basic hygiene in the camps, illnesses and hunger. Drawing on his experience as a political cartoonist, Aurel sometimes enhances the allegorical dimension of Bartoli's drawings, resorting to caricature when he portrays the cruel guards as pig faced. The inclusion of pre-existing poetic texts for the songs used in the film (Miguel Hernández's poem 'Guerra' [War] inspired the film's credit song, 'Todas las madres del mundo' [All the Mothers of the World], written and performed by Silvia Pérez Cruz) and the indirect references to Federico García Lorca's work add extra intersemiotic dimensions. These features are summarised as effects produced by multimodality in *Josep* (see Table 6.5).

Another recurring motif in the film is the act of drawing as a political statement, a testimony, an act of transmission, a creative response to horror. Frida's words to Bartoli help us to better understand the communicative power of graphic art: 'You draw caricatures because what you've seen and remember scares you. And the day you finally let colour in, you'll have tamed your fear' (Aurel 2020b). It also shows how visual elements and dialogue complement one another. *Josep*'s multilingual soundtrack (Catalan, English, French, Spanish) enhances the multicultural dimension of the film and could be the base for a range of translation activities. The silences in the film are also telling, and learners could write interior dialogues, articulating the characters' thoughts in the film through the narrative device of voice-over.

In addition to its visual and verbal dimensions, the film represents diverse spatial and cultural environments and sensorial forms of expression: Valentin's character is constructed around rap music, licence plates of the Marseille and Aix en Provence region and the graffiti of Massilia (Latin for Marseille). If the audience identifies with Valentin's reactions, they will receive the intersemiotic messages transmitted by Serge and Bartoli. By returning the missing part of the drawing, Valentin also becomes a *passeur* of memory and history at the end of the film. His act symbolises the reinterpretation of the past: Serge's memories are reinterpreted by his grandson using first-hand accounts of the Spanish Civil War (Sorfa 2022).

Aurel resorts to intersemiotic resources that he recycles and adapts to communicate meaning. His film can be approached diachronically as

Figure 6.2 Shot from *Josep* (Aurel 2020b) representing the characters of Josep, Serge and Frida. © *Josep* by Aurel, reproduced with permission from Les Films d'Ici Méditerranée.

	Relevant examples from the film studied	**Meaning and effect produced**
Written mode Use of written text and subtitles	Several books of memoirs and biographical information used to prepare the screenplay and lyrics (Valentin)	Identifies documentary value and introduces some historical facts
Visual mode Use of still or moving images	Drawings (black, pencil carbon) Photos Posters Paintings Visual representation of memories	Differentiate between different periods and spatial contexts of the narrative Historical documents Iconic pastiche
Visual style Colour Lighting	Use of sepia Monochrome images Pale, cold light for camps Night Use of bright colours	Sepia to represent memory Political cartoons of Aurel or Bartoli Visual signal of Josep's distress and sense of danger Kahlo's style or Bartoli's US work
Spatial meaning Indoor or outdoor location design (architecture, streetscapes, cityscapes and landscapes)	Barbed wire, enclosed spaces, barracks Open spaces (Pyrenees, Catalan beaches) Mexico New York skyscrapers and galleries Marseille/Aix en Provence Serge's bedroom	Claustrophobic Open air but hostile climate Sun and colour, happy moments Stereotyped, simplified context Valentin's urban modern world Serge's end of life

Proxemic mode Positioning of characters (interpersonal distance, interactions)	Long shots of camp on the beach Contact between Serge and Valentin Camera placement for gendarmes and prisoners in camp	Isolation of Josep in camp Weakness and support Power, distress, submission
Gestural mode Body language, gestures, way of walking, costume and hairstyle	Quite static in camp More gestural (Kahlo) Serge immobilised in bed	Passive and helpless characters Danger associated with movement
Audio mode Music, sound and diegetic noises	Song 'Todas las madres del mundo' Offscreen noises and screams Use of silence	Expressing cultural and linguistic identities in songs Poetic effect Danger
Linguistic mode Dialogue, monologue, speech and voice-over	Voice-over (Serge) Reported speech Valentin's questions Dialogue, insults and jokes	Multilingual dialogue and internal monologues Narrator (subjective point of view) Investigator Expresses power, danger, authority

Table 6.5 Multimodal modes and their effects in *Josep* (Aurel 2020b)

Figure 6.3 Shot from *Josep* (Aurel 2020b), blending the animation character and drawings by Bartoli. © *Josep* by Aurel, reproduced with permission from Les Films d'Ici Méditerranée.

'a journey through the twentieth century of this character with a thousand lives, from the underbelly of Barcelona to New York, from the 1960s to the 1990s, including the Spanish Civil War, the Retirada, Mexico and Frida Kahlo' (Aurel 2020a). His transmediation, or adaptation, is diachronic in the sense that it updates Bartoli's graphic style into animated images (see Figure 6.2). From this perspective, Aurel's artistic journey makes provision for new audiences of the twenty-first century.

When it comes to the transmission of collective memory and history, the transmediation process allows for expression in various ways: artistically in its pictorial style; graphically, with the animation of pictorial images, visually, through the use of perspective; and verbally, through dialogue and song. Aurel's film demonstrates how multimodal film-making creates powerful and universal communication by translating into film elements of Bartoli's biographic and artistic legacy that will resonate for new generational audiences. By blending multimodal materials (see Figure 6.3), *Josep* therefore lends itself well to a range of transmedia pedagogical activities.

Table 6.5 offers a number of other examples of multimodal strategies used to promote language learning. This worksheet can support the discovery of transnational cultures and diverse forms of creative expression and highlight effects produced on the viewers that students can analyse.

Having considered in this first case study a transmedia process from pictorial format to animation film, we now move to our second case study, which brings together other forms of media adaptations.

Case study 2: Intemperie – exploring multiple forms of transmediation

This case study focuses on transmediation from a Spanish literary text – *Intemperie* (Carrasco 2013) – into two different multimodal artefacts: a graphic novel (Rey 2016) and a film (Zambrano 2019). This proposal is particularly useful for identifying multimodal representation and communication in different media (see Table 6.1). It can generate activities for the critical analysis of extracts from the graphic novel and scenes from the film (see Table 6.2). More crucially, it can help learners to familiarise themselves with the processes used in transmediation from a novel into a graphic novel and a film. These two multimodal texts provide effective ways of fostering a deeper understanding of the linguistic, cultural and intellectual dimensions of the original literary text in the language classroom. The use of cross-media comparisons and film and graphic-novel adaptations can stimulate the study of literature among students, help them to develop a multimodal approach to critical thinking, reinforce reception skills such as reading and integrate multimodal literacies in curricula (Puig 2019). The use of these adaptations can facilitate transmediation activities, such as visualisation, the use of online translation tools and resources and collaborative translation activities (see Whicker 2019).

Making use of three versions of *Intemperie*, this case study examines the strategies employed to transfer content and formal features from one semiotic system (the novel) into multimodal texts – that is, a graphic novel and a film. A closer look at the graphic novel and the film reveals how this literary text is transmediated into a range of modes beyond writing, such as still and moving images, speech, sound effects and music, among others. Table 6.6 contains a list of the transmedia processes that take place between the original source and the adaptations. It lists elements that could be discussed when critically analysing the transmediation processes. We also examine how the adaptations transfer the instances of invariant core of the original text into new multimodal products. As the understanding and awareness of the multimodal distribution of meaning in multimodal texts can be key for informing translational decisions, this case study can be a useful model for enhancing students' translation skills and integrating more multimodal texts into the language classroom.

Since its publication in 2013, Carrasco's first novel, *Intemperie*, has received numerous awards and has been translated from Spanish into over 20 languages.[4] As the writer himself has stated, *Intemperie* is a representation of the rural world in which he grew up. It is a tale of

Transfer process	Graphic novel adaptation	Film adaptation
Narrative and structure Features retained and changed in plot, storytelling chronology, characters, genre	Similar plot focusing on the relationship between the main characters Storytelling related to violence and lack of morality Retaining a vague reference to the characters, location and chronology From two sections (novel) to a prologue, three sections and epilogue	Similar plot focusing on the relationship between the main characters Storytelling related to violence and lack of morality via genre conventions (western, thriller and road movie) Providing a specific reference to the location and the chronology (post-Spanish Civil War in Andalusia, year 1946) and to the main characters (names and nicknames)
Visual style Colour, typography, visual texture, shape, form, space	Poetic style, with a minimalist composition Sketches Use of colours with many textures	Barren landscape = western and road movie
Aural mode Music, sound effects, silence, spoken language (volume, tone of voice, accent), ambient noises	Not applicable to this type of novel	From third-person narration and a few dialogues to a more extensive use of dialogues

Artistic features Art and visual references	Intertextual references to the *España negra* legend: Luis Buñuel's *Tierra sin pan* (1933) (*Land without Bread*) and Miguel Delibes's *Los santos inocentes* (1981) (*The Holy Innocents*)	Intertextual references to the *España negra* legend (poverty) Other intertextual references to Carlos Saura's *La caza* (1966) and Cormac McCarthy's *The Road* (2006)
Communication priorities Relevant features and elements that are prioritised in the transfer of the story	Both focus on the land and how characters interact within the barren wasteland Poetic tone of the story Violence and nightmares Final message: kindness, compassion and forgiveness	Both focus on the land and how characters interact within the barren wasteland Poetic tone of the story Violence and nightmares Final message: kindness, compassion and forgiveness
Target audience and language level	Undergraduate language students (level B2–C1) and master's-level translation students (C1–C2)	Undergraduate language students (level B2–C1) and master's-level translation students (C1–C2)

Table 6.6 Transmediation processes in *Intemperie* (2013 novel by Jesús Carrasco, 2016 graphic novel by Javi Rey and 2019 film adaptation by Benito Zambrano)

survival and personal growth. Situated in an indeterminate rural setting in Spain, it tells the story of a young boy fleeing from a drought-stricken land. It details the extreme violence of the abuse the boy suffers at the hands of the bailiff, the local authority, and his encounter with an old goatherd, which will change his fate. *Intemperie* is a universal story which can be interpreted as a metaphor for helplessness, lack of shelter/protection and the constant threat to the human condition due to the progressive damage to, and decline of, the environment (Pérez-Trujillo 2017).[5] With no specific geographical or historical references, the story focuses on the relationships between the characters, who are at the mercy of the elements. In this dystopian vision of the world, there is an explicit depiction of violence and the corruption and inhumanity of those in authority.

Javi Rey adapted *Intemperie* into a graphic novel published by Planeta Cómic in 2016. It was also translated into other languages (French, English and Italian).[6] For the graphic novel, Rey aimed to retain two fundamental features from the source text: first, the land and how characters interact within the barren wasteland and, secondly, the poetic tone of the story and how violence and a lack of morality are narrated. These two features will also guide our analysis of the transmediation processes. For example, the prologue of the graphic novel contextualises the hostile nature of the environment and introduces a narrative voice with the same poetic quality that characterises the original text. The first vignette presents a dead greyhound hanging from a tree (see Figure 6.4),

Figure 6.4 Vignette of a dead greyhound, representing the cruelty of the rural landscape. *Intemperie* by Javi Rey (based on Jesús Carrasco's [2013] novel). © Javi Rey, for the graphic novel (Planeta Cómic, 2016). © Jesús Carrasco for the novel (Seix Barral, 2013).

evoking the cruelty of the rural landscape. Below the image, the narrator compares the past and the present: 'The town was built on the bed of a broad gully down which water has flowed at some point. Now it was just a long hollow in the middle of an endless plain' (Rey 2018, 1). As Vigneron (2020, 4) notes, this image echoes the devastating imagery of an inhospitable landscape and human misery portrayed in Luis Buñuel's *Tierra sin pan* (1933) [*Land without Bread*] and the cruelty of the callous rural domain run by the local *cacique* in Miguel Delibes's *Los santos inocentes* (1981) [*The Holy Innocents*], turned into a film by Mario Camus in 1984.[7]

Carrasco's minimalist literary style creates a schematic fragmentation of suggestive impressions. For instance, the physical suffering of the characters is narrated in detail throughout the novel.[8] Rey opted to retain this poetic quality through the design of the images. In terms of graphic style, he chose a simple composition, with a few vignettes per page dedicated to a key episode of the story. In order to convey the tone of the story, he paid specific attention to the 'freshness of execution that the sketches have [...] to transmit the strength of the story' (Rey, in Jiménez 2016).

As noted by Laget (2018, 171), the sensorial quality of the verbal and visual representation of the landscape is central to "the quality of" the novel and the graphic adaptation. In Rey's work, images narrate the actions. After the prologue, the rest of the graphic novel is divided into three parts, each introduced by a silent image and an epilogue. The first part opens with a blue-tone image of an empty bowl and cup at the boy's feet; this explains, partly, why the young protagonist fled from the village and signals the care that he will later receive from the goatherd (see Figure 6.5). The second part focuses on his relationship with the goatherd in terms of mutual trust and solidarity. The vignette chosen is the Bible in the hand of the goatherd, referring to his religious beliefs and the spiritual lessons that the boy will learn from him. This section narrates the development of the friendship between the boy and the old man while they travel in search of pasture and water for the herd of goats. The third part is announced by an extreme close-up of a donkey's head; the donkey accompanies the young protagonist until the end of the story and epitomises the legacy left to him by the goatherd at the end of their journey.

Colour is used to highlight the iconicity of the images and Rey makes use of it as a way of translating the tone of the characters' emotions. In fact, the colour scheme is one of the most useful tools employed by Rey to transfer core invariant features of Carrasco's novel. To mark the

Figure 6.5 Vignette representing an empty bowl and cup at the feet of a child. *Intemperie* by Javi Rey (based on Jesús Carrasco's [2013] novel). © Javi Rey, for the graphic novel (Planeta Cómic, 2016). © Jesús Carrasco for the novel (Seix Barral, 2013).

significance of the dry landscape, Rey applies colour with many 'textures' to convey the perceptions and feelings associated with exposure to the inclemency and the weather. Shades of yellow and orange are employed to stress the scarcity of water and the heat that suffocates the characters in this harsh environment. Similarly, colour is applied to narrate the violence and lack of morality. For example, the use of colour visually enhances the boy's nightmares and trauma as the vignettes change colour – from yellow and brown to blue in the first nightmare in the first part of the story, and from dark blue to green and blue in the second part – while red and orange tones reinforce the bailiff's monstrous characterisation in the sequences relating to the nightmares (see Figure 6.6).

In 2019, the novel was adapted for cinema by Benito Zambrano, with a script written by Pablo Remón, Daniel Remón and Benito Zambrano.[9] The film adaptation uses different strategies to transfer aspects of the invariant core of the original text: the central role of space (*a la intemperie*) and the human side of the story – that is, the boy's transformative journey and the friendship between the goatherd and the boy. The film avoids the vague geographical reference of the novel. The plateau region of Granada – a dry land with canyons, badlands, ravines and valleys – conveys the leitmotif of a land without water. Similarly, the narrative of the film is set

Figure 6.6 Image of the boy's nightmare, illustrating that the bailiff is the real monster. *Intemperie* by Javi Rey (based on Jesús Carrasco's [2013] novel). © Javi Rey, for the graphic novel (Planeta Cómic, 2016). © Jesús Carrasco for the novel (Seix Barral, 2013).

in 1946. The specific historical setting contextualises the references to hunger and violence in the aftermath of the Spanish Civil War. Zambrano's (2019) film version is a story of *cortijos* (farmhouses) and peasants in a state of near-slavery due to caciquism and the prevalence of *latifundia* lands in Andalusia after 1939. Thus, the lower-class misery depicted in Carrasco's novel was one of the invariant core elements transferred to the film adaptation in the form of the poverty of the Andalusian landless peasant farmers, who suffered decades of brutality and abuses of power. These intertextual references can be associated with the archetypes of the *España negra* legend, characterised by the harshness and poverty of the rural areas (Bozal 2020; Esparza 2020).

In Carrasco's novel, the characters are unnamed and therefore represent archetypes. However, in the adaptation process, biographical characteristics have been added. For example, in the film adaptation the solitary old man is also known by the nickname *el Moro* ('the Moor'), suggesting a connection to the Rif War (II Moroccan War) (1922–1926), a cruel postcolonial conflict that brought the future Spanish dictator Francisco Franco to prominence. The foreman's knife with the swastika symbol is another example of anchoring a character in a specific historical context by connecting the Francoist and Nazi regimes and ideologies.

One more point to be added in connection with the transfer across modes and the recomposition of the novel into film is the lyric depiction of the characters' emotions through music and poetry. Inspired by Federico García Lorca's and Antonio Machado's poetry, Javier Ruibal's lullaby

'Intemperie' – interpreted by Silvia Pérez Cruz – transfers the story of the young boy and his suffering to music and verbal representation.

Another major strategy employed for adapting the literary text into a film is the use of specific genre conventions. *Intemperie* can be identified as a western in which the barren landscapes are symbolic of the marginal position of the characters. In the face of adversity the relationship between the old man and the young boy becomes something resembling a father–son relationship. The plot is reappropriated as a thriller, with the hunt being used as a narrative device to keep the attention of the audience through chases, action and revenge; the mystery of what is hidden by the boy's past is similarly employed. One can recognise references to Carlos Saura's *La caza* (1966) [*The Hunt*], whose allegorical setting evokes the cruelty and violence perpetrated during the Spanish Civil War. The film also uses the genre conventions associated with road movies, with clear similarities to Cormac McCarthy's novel *The Road* (2006) in the storyline. The goatherd's kindness and compassion transmit a pacifist message, which is reinforced by the note in the credits at the end of the film: *A todos los que enseñan a perdonar* ('To those who teach us to forgive'). This moral point reinforces intertextual references to other literary and film works that have reflected on the ongoing process of trauma and historical memory in contemporary Spain.[10]

Activities based on this case study could include the creation of a blog to compare literary works that have been transmediated into a film or a graphic novel, or a vlog to analyse the motivations of the character in each text. Digital storytelling can enhance students' media skills through, for example, the production of a short video that analyses a fragment of one of the works. Designing a new version of the book trailer or the film trailer can also be complemented with audiovisual translation tasks – subtitling or audio description, for example. Finally, we suggest exploring different booktuber or filmtuber genres – review, ranking, unboxing, (book)haul – and tags that could engage learners in finding associations with their own preferences for literary works, films or TV series.

Conclusion

This chapter has presented a framework to enhance secondary and higher education language students' translation skills by engaging them in a close analysis of the processes and strategies involved in intermedial adaptation, cross-media, trans-genre storytelling and narrative expansion. The model has been illustrated with two proposals that educators may find useful when integrating transmedia examples into language curricula.

From a pedagogical perspective, the film *Josep* can be used to develop learners' visual literacy and intersemiotic analysis skills as well as their language and critical thinking skills. Tables 6.1 to 6.4 provide a base for specific exercises. The activities can include the creation of derivative artefacts involving image analyses and narrative exercises adopting different points of view. The second case study draws on transmediation processes. A cross-media comparison of *Intemperie* (novel, graphic novel and film) can encourage learners to foster a deeper understanding of the linguistic, cultural and intellectual dimensions of the original literary text and of its adaptations. Understanding the strategies and techniques employed to transmediate the novel into multimodal texts will enhance language learners' critical analysis and translation skills. We have proposed a series of indicative activities that will support a multimodal, collaborative and interactive use of transmediation practices, based on examples similar to the case studies presented in this chapter.

Ultimately, what we have shown in this chapter is that translation, as an interdisciplinary pedagogical practice, offers a useful model for creating innovative activities for the language classroom, not just working at an interlingual level but also exploring intersemiotic transfers that lead to transmedia practices. This should encourage language educators to use more contemporary multimodal texts in their classrooms.

The participatory nature of popular culture is already transforming language learning in formal and informal settings. The examples presented in this chapter have demonstrated how transmedia popular texts can be adapted to students' needs and interests, increasing their motivation. Further research is required to evaluate the relationship between factors that can enhance the uptake and productive use of transmedia materials in the language classroom. Moreover, there is a need to undertake more research projects on the changing role of transmedia practices in language pedagogy to support educators in integrating these materials and activities into curricula.

Notes

1 This case study is part of the project Vessels of Communication (Rewriting and Story Transfer in the Hispanic World), led by Dr Carmen Herrero within the Film, Languages and Media in Education (FLAME) group at Manchester Metropolitan University. This project seeks to investigate literary, artistic and filmic intertextuality through the reflections of novelists,

playwrights, poets, film and television directors, creators of comics and video games. In collaboration with the Instituto Cervantes in Manchester, this project was launched with Jesús Carrasco as guest author in November 2022.

2 During the 2022 edition of the Beyond Babel Film Festival, *Josep* was screened as a Film Day event for Year 12 French and Spanish students in Manchester. The film was also used in a film literacy workshop organised for French classes (Year 10 equivalent) at the College Pierre Loti in Istanbul, Turkey, in March 2023.

3 Aurel was born in 1980 in the Ardèche region. He trained as a graphic artist and has been the cartoon illustrator of the political columns in *Le Monde*. For more detailed contextual information, see Aurel (2020a) and Batalla (2020).

4 Jesús Carrasco was born in Badajoz, Spain, in 1972. His family later moved to a village in Toledo. He has published four novels at the time of writing.

5 Some scholars have seen *Intemperie* as part of neoruralism (Champeau 2019), a literary trend that advocates a return to the so-called *España vacía* ('empty Spain'), which refers to the depopulation of the rural areas of inland Spain (Molino 2016).

6 Born in Brussels, Javi Rey is an illustrator and comic book artist. He studied at the Joso School in Barcelona and since then has worked in France and Spain.

7 Carrasco's narrative has been compared to Miguel Delibes's literary works. Most of Delibes's novels are set in a rural environment and his literary style has been commended for the richness and precision of the rural language. However, Carrasco has confessed his preference for Cormac McCarthy's aesthetics, which is characterised by the lyric depiction of places and characters' emotions.

8 To facilitate the reading, we use the English translation of Javi Rey's graphic novel adaptation (Rey 2018).

9 *Intemperie* stars Luis Tosar, Luis Callejo, Vicente Romero, Manolo Caro, Kándido Uranga and the young actor Jaime López.

10 The Pacto de Olvido ('Pact of Forgetting') was set up after Franco's death in 1975. Since then, the Ley de Memoria Histórica ('Historical Memory Law') was approved by the Spanish Government in 2007 to recognise and broaden the rights of those who suffered persecution or violence during the Spanish Civil War and the dictatorship and to establish measures in favour of them.

References

Aurel. 2020a. 'Director's intentions', Press kit in English of the film *Josep*, 2–8. Unifrance. Accessed 12 June 2023. https://en.unifrance.org/movie/48049/josep.

Baetens, Jan, and Domingo Sánchez-Mesa Martínez. 2015. 'Literature in the expanded field: Intermediality at the crossroads of literary theory and comparative literature', *Interfaces: Image Texte Language* 36: 289–304. https://doi.org/10.4000/interfaces.245.

Baker, Mona. 1993. *In Other Words*. London: Routledge.

Bassnett, Susan. 2002. *Translation Studies*. London: Routledge.

Bartoli, Josep, and Narcís Molins i Fábrega. 1944. *Campos de concentración (1939–194…)*. México: ACVF.

Bartoli, Georges, and Laurence Garcia. 2009. *La retirada: exode et exil des républicains d'Espagne*. Arles: Actes Sud.

Batalla, Vicenç. 2020. 'Aurel et Bartolí, les dessins de Josep pour survivre'. Paris-Barcelona, 28 September Accessed 2 May 2023. www.paris-barcelona.com/fr/aurel-et-bartoli-les-dessins-de-josep-pour-survivre.

Bezemer, Jeff, and Carey Jewitt. 2018. 'Multimodality: A guide for linguists'. In *Research Methods in Linguistics, 2nd ed.,* edited by Lia Litosseliti, 281–304. London: Bloomsbury.

Bozal, Valeriano. 2020. *Otra España negra*. Zaragoza: Publicaciones de la Universidad de Zaragoza.

Bruhn, Jørgen, and Beate Schirrmacher, eds. 2022. *Intermedial Studies: An introduction to meaning across media*. London: Routledge.

Carrasco, Jesús. 2013. *Intemperie*. Barcelona: Planeta.

Carrasco, Jesús. 2016. *Out in the Open*. Translated from the Spanish by Margaret Jull Costa. London: Vintage.

Champeau, Geneviève. 2019. 'La novela neorrural actual entre distopía y retro-utopía', *HispanismeS* 11: 16–34.
Clarke, Cath. 2021. '*Josep* Review – Haunting tale of an artist adventurer', *The Guardian*, 25 January. Accessed 2 May 2023. www.theguardian.com/film/2021/jan/25/josep-review-animation-josep-bartoli-biopic.
Clüver, Claus 2007. 'Intermediality and Interarts Studies'. In *Changing Borders: Contemporary positions in intermediality*, edited by Jens Arvidson, Mikael Askander, Jørgen Bruhn, and Heidrun Führer, 19–37. Lund: Intermedia Studia Press.
Cope, Bill, and Mary Kalantzis, eds. 2000. *Multiliteracies: Literacy learning and the design of social futures*. London: Routledge.
Cope, Bill, and Mary Kalantzis. 2009. 'Multiliteracies: New literacies, new learning', *Pedagogies: An International Journal* 4, no. 3: 164–95. https://doi.org/10.1080/15544800903076044.
Cope, Bill, and Mary Kalantzis. 2015. 'The things you do to know: An introduction to the pedagogy of multiliteracies'. In *A Pedagogy of Multiliteracies: Learning by design,* edited by Bill Cope and Mary Kalantzis, 1–36. London: Palgrave.
Dena, Christy. 2019. 'Transmedia adaptation: Revisiting the no-adaptation rule'. In *The Routledge Companion to Transmedia Studies*, edited by Matthew Freeman and Renira Rampazzo Gambarato, 195–206. New York: Routledge.
Elleström, Lars. 2019. 'Transmediation: Some theoretical considerations'. In *Transmediations: Communication across media borders*, edited by Lars Elleström, 1–13. London: Routledge.
Esparza, Ramón. 2020. 'The persistence of myth: The legacy of the España Negra myth in twentieth-century Spanish photography', *Photographies* 13, no. 1: 33–59. https://doi.org/10.1080/17540763.2019.1697962.
Freeman, Matthew, and Renira Rampazzo Gambarato, eds. 2019. *The Routledge Companion to Transmedia Studies*. New York: Routledge.
Giannakopoulou, Vasso 2019. 'Introduction: Intersemiotic translation as adaptation,' *Adaptation* 12, no. 3: 199–205. https://doi.org/10.1093/adaptation/apz023.
Herrero, Carmen. 2019. 'Escritura digital: Estrategias de enseñanza-aprendizaje en entornos digitales'. In *Lectoescritura digital*, edited by Secretaría General Técnica, 123–32. Madrid: Ministerio de Educación, Cultura y Deporte.
Herrero, Carmen. 2021. 'La educación transmedia como estrategia innovadora para integrar lengua y cultura en la enseñanza de ELE', *Doblele: Revista de lengua y literatura* 7: 50–66. https://doi.org/10.5565/rev/doblele.83.
Herrero, Carmen. 2022. 'Applications of transmedia practices in higher education'. In *Visual Literacy and Digital Communication: The role of media in new educational practices*, edited by Elena Domínguez Romero, Jelena Bokina, Carmen Herrero, Svetlana Stefanova Radoulska, and Isabelle Vanderschelden, 43–60. Madrid: Comares.
Herrero, Carmen, Marta Suarez, and Alicia Sánchez-Requena. 2023. 'Screen media in language teaching: Towards a student-centred approach'. In *Teaching Languages with Screen Media: Pedagogical reflections and case studies*, edited by Carmen Herrero and Marta Suárez, 17–45. London: Bloomsbury.
Herrero, Carmen, Karina Valverde, Tomás Costal, and Alicia Sánchez-Requena. 2020. 'The Film and Creative Engagement Project: Audiovisual accessibility and telecollaboration', *Research in Education and Learning Innovation Archives* 24: 89–104. https://doi.org/10.7203/realia.24.16744.
Herrero, Carmen, and Isabelle Vanderschelden, eds. 2019. *Using Film and Media in the Language Classroom: Reflections on research-led teaching*. Bristol: Multilingual Matters.
Herrero, Carmen, and Isabelle Vanderschelden. 2023. 'Training language teachers to use short films in the language classroom: Innovations and challenges'. In *Rethinking Multimodal Literacy in Theory and Practice*, edited by Elena Domínguez, Jelena Bobkina, Svetlana Stefanova Radoulska, and Carmen Herrero, 121–39. Bristol: Peter Lang.
Jakobson, Roman. 1959. 'On linguistic aspects of translation'. In *On Translation*, edited by Reuben Brower, 232–39. Cambridge, MA: Harvard University Press.
Jenkins, Henry. 2003. 'Transmedia storytelling: Moving characters from books to films to video games can make them stronger and more compelling', *MIT Technology Review*. Accessed 2 May 2023. www.technologyreview.com/s/401760/transmedia-storytelling.
Jenkins, Henry. 2006. *Convergence Culture: Where old and new media collide*. New York: New York University Press.

Jenkins, Henry. 2011. 'Transmedia 202: Further reflections'. Confessions of anAca-Fan: The Official Weblog of Henry Jenkins. Accessed 2 May 2023. http://henryjenkins.org/2011/08/dening_transmedia_further_re.html.

Jenkins, Henry, Katie Clinton, Ravi Purushtoma, Alice Robison, and Margaret Weigel. 2009. *Confronting the Challenges of Participatory Culture: Media education for the 21st century*. Cambridge, MA: MIT Press.

Jewitt, Carey, ed. 2009. *The Routledge Handbook of Multimodal Analysis*. London: Routledge.

Jewitt, Carey, Jeff Bezemer, and Kay O'Halloran. 2016. *Introducing Multimodality*. London: Routledge.

Jiménez, Jesús. 2016. 'Jesús Carrasco: La adaptación al cómic de "Intemperie" es un regalo', RTVE. Accessed 2 May 2023. https://www.rtve.es/noticias/20160606/jesus-carrasco-adaptacion-comic-intemperie-casi-regalo/1355300.shtml.

Kalantzis, Mary, Bill Cope, Eveline Chan, and Leanne Dalley-Trim. 2016. *Literacies*. 2nd ed. Cambridge: Cambridge University Press.

Kinder, Marsha. 1991. *Playing with Power in Movies, Television, and Video Games: From Muppet Babies to Teenage Mutant Ninja Turtles*. Berkeley, CA: University of California Press.

Kress, Gunther. 2003. *Literacy in the New Media Age*. London: Routledge.

Kress, Gunther, and Theo van Leeuwen. 1996. *Reading Images: The grammar of visual design*. London: Routledge.

Laget, Laurie-Anne. 2018. 'Ce " vide plein de présence": l'écriture de l'Espagne vide dans le roman *Intemperie* de Jesús Carrasco (2013) et son adaptation à la bande dessinée (Javi Rey, 2016)', *HispanismeS* 11: 169–82. https://doi.org/10.4000/hispanismes.3635.

Lankshear, Colin, and Michelle Knobel. 2003. *New Literacies: Changing knowledge and classroom learning*. Buckingham: Open University Press.

Lim, Fei Victor. 2018. 'Developing a systemic functional approach to teach multimodal literacy', *Functional Linguistics* 5, no. 3: 1–17.

Long, Geoffrey. 2007. 'Transmedia storytelling: Business, aesthetics and production at the Jim Henson Company'. Master's dissertation. Cambridge, MA: Massachusetts Institute of Technology.

Malmkjær, Kirsten. 2011. 'Translation universals'. In *The Oxford Handbook of Translation Studies*, edited by Kirsten Malmkjær and Kevin Windle, 83–94. Oxford: Oxford University Press.

Molino, Sergio del. 2016. *La España vacía: viaje por un país que nunca fue*. Madrid: Turner.

New London Group. 1996. 'A pedagogy of multiliteracies: Designing social futures', *Harvard Educational Review* 66, no. 1: 60–92. https://doi.org/10.17763/haer.66.1.17370n67v22j160u.

Pratten, Robert. 2015. *Getting Started with Transmedia Storytelling: How to captivate and engage audiences across multiple platforms*. London: CreateSpace.

Pérez-Trujillo, Axel. 2017. 'Galgos en el llano: la ecología oscura del campo en *Intemperie* de Jesús Carrasco', *Letras Hispanas* 13, no. 1: 244–54.

Puig, Idoya. 2019. 'Teaching literature and language using a multiliteracies framework: Exploring intercultural skills with Cervantes's *La española inglesa*'. In *Spanish Golden Age Texts in the Twenty-First Century: Teaching the old through the new*, edited by Idoya Puig and Karl McLaughlin, 105–21. Oxford: Peter Lang.

Rajewsky, Irina O. 2005. 'Intermediality, intertextuality, and remediation: A literary perspective on intermediality', *Intermédialités* 6: 43–64. https://doi.org/10.7202/1005505.

Rey, Javi. 2016. *Intemperie* (based on the novel by Jesús Carrasco). Barcelona: Planeta.

Rey, Javi. 2018. *Out in the Open* (based on the novel by Jesús Carrasco). Translated from Spanish by Lawrence Schimel. London: SelfMadeHero.

Rippl, Gabriele. 2015. 'Introduction: Why intermediality'. In *Handbook of Intermediality: Literature-image-sound-music*, edited by Gabriele Rippl, 1–31. Berlin: De Gruyter.

Robin, Edina. 2016. 'The modification of translation universals in revised texts', *New Voices in Translation Studies* 15: 1–4. https://doi.org/10.14456/nvts.2016.28.

Scolari, Carlos. 2013. *Narrativas transmedia: cuando todos los medios cuentan*. Barcelona: Deusto.

Scolari, Carlos. 2018. *Transmedia Literacy on the New Media Ecology: White Paper*. H2020 Transliteracy Research Project. Barcelona: Universitat Pompeu Fabra.

Serafini, Frank. 2014. *Reading the Visual: An introduction to teaching multimodal literacy*. New York: Teachers College Press.

Serafini, Frank. 2023. 'Implications of multimodal theories for literacy research and pedagogy'. In *Rethinking Multimodal Literacy in Theory and Practice*, edited by Elena Domínguez, Jelena Bobkina, Svetlana Stefanova Radoulska, and Carmen Herrero, 17–35. Bristol: Peter Lang.

Siegel, Marjorie. 2006. 'Rereading the signs: Multimodal transformations in the field of literacy education', *Language Arts* 84, no. 1: 65–77.
Sorfa, David. 2022. 'Review of *Josep*'. Film Dispatch Online, 14 February. Accessed 2 May 2023. https://blogs.ed.ac.uk/thefilmdispatch/review-josep-2022.
Toury, Gideon. 1995. *Descriptive Translation Studies and Beyond.* Amsterdam: Benjamins.
Vigneron, Denis. 2020. 'Invention et iconicité du franquisme dans Intempérie de Javi Rey', *L'Entre-deux* 2, no. 8.
Whicker, Jules. 2019. 'Technologically assisted translational activity: An approach to teaching Spanish Golden Age literature'. In *Spanish Golden Age Texts in the Twenty-First Century: Teaching the old through the new,* edited by Idoya Puig and Karl McLaughlin, 123–37. Oxford: Peter Lang.
Wolf, Werner. 2011. '(Inter)mediality and the study of literature', *CLCWeb: Comparative Literature and Culture* 13, no. 3: #2. https://doi.org/10.7771/1481-4374.1789.

Filmography

Aurel. 2020b. *Josep*. Les Films d'Ici Méditerranée. 74 minutes.
Zambrano, Benito, dir. 2019. *Intemperie*. Morena Films, Movistar Plus+, RTVE, Aralan Films, Ukbar Filmes. 103 minutes.

Part III
Cross-disciplinary intersections

7
Translation as queer practice: (de) gendering feminist language in the poetry of Xi Xi and Zhai Yongming

Xiaofan Amy Li

Introduction

This chapter explores translation as queer practice in the pedagogical context of teaching poetry translation and discussing feminism in the classroom. By examining different approaches to translating Chinese-language poetry by women poets into English, I argue that translation can be a queer method of reading poetry and a pedagogical practice that both genders and degenders feminist poetic language. As a verb, 'gender' denotes the gendering process in reading and translation. As the literary translator Andrea Lingenfelter (2012, 58) expounds: '"Gendering," as opposed to simply "gender", suggests the placement or creation of gender in a piece of writing, the process of putting gender [...] into a written work. It implies a certain consciousness on the part of the translator.' In other words, gendering in translation is about highlighting and *engendering* dimensions of poetic language and experience that speak to the social constructs of gender. Conversely, degendering means, firstly, as in conventional linguistic use, 'to avoid assigning [...] a gender to; avoid classifying [...] or differentiating on the basis of gender; and to remove gender distinctions from' (*Oxford English Dictionary*). In this sense, degendering can highlight non-binary modes of experience and thought. Secondly, degendering functions, in the context of the poetry discussed in this chapter, to expose heteronormative biases and the sexualisation of poetry written by women, thus demonstrating that their poetry is not limited to readers or translators with a specific biology or gender identity but deserves to be read *as poetry* in the richest possible aesthetic sense.

When I discuss how translation degenders feminist language, therefore, I do not mean that translation reappropriates the text and its feminist ideas into a gender-blind universalist position that ignores sexual and gender minorities. On the contrary, translation becomes a textual force that excavates the queer potential of poetic language, affirms the latter's capacity to question reified gender categories and ideological frameworks and, finally, renders poetry more gender-fluid and accommodating of different perspectives.

To examine poetry translation as a queer practice in pedagogical contexts, I discuss two poems used in the translation classroom, and I peruse student responses that prompt newer reflections about our understanding of translation. The poems are Hong Kongese writer 西西 Xi Xi's (1937–2022) '許多女子' ('Many a Lady') and mainland Chinese poet 翟永明 Zhai Yongming's (1955–) '她的视点' ('Her Viewpoint'). Both Xi Xi and Zhai are acclaimed contemporary Chinese-language women writers and are recognised for their feminist views and bold literary articulations of neglected, underexplored or taboo dimensions of women's experience. In her prize-winning short story 'A Woman Like Me' (1983), Xi Xi explores cultural discrimination in Sinitic societies against women who work in funeral services, and she has recounted her survival of breast cancer in her semi-autobiographical novel *Mourning a Breast* (1992). The social consciousness in Xi Xi's writings prompted her English-language translator Jennifer Feeley (in Xi Xi 2016, xvii) to comment that Xi Xi's poetry 'is anti-establishment, her rebelliousness manifest in the form of artistic expression'. This is further affirmed by Tammy Lai-ming Ho's (2019, 8) explicit recognition of Xi Xi as a feminist whose poetry conveys 'subtle rebelliousness' but not 'dogmatic' politics. As for Zhai, she established herself as the foremost poetic voice of women's lived experiences and subjectivity in her pioneering poem sequence 'Woman' (1984/2008). Since then, she has continued to explore notions of the feminine and gender in her poetry while becoming increasingly critical of binary gender and disposed towards gender fluidity, as Yanhong Zhu (2022) demonstrates. Zhai (2011, xiv) has also affirmed her feminist stance in an interview with her translator Lingenfelter: 'She rejected the "taboo" against feminism (*nüxingzhuyi*) in contemporary China and had no difficulty calling herself a feminist.' On gender and feminism, Xi Xi's and Zhai's writings already thematically and critically resonate with each other, which leads me to bring their poems into comparative discussion.

The two poems analysed in this chapter provide food for thought about critical intersections between poetic language, feminism and translation. Both poems strongly suggest feminist views via their articulations of women's bodies and perspectives, albeit in fragmented and ambiguously gendered ways. When I taught these poems, I asked students to think critically about the poems' relation to feminism and gender in Chinese societal contexts and how English translations visibilise or reshape important aspects of the poetic language and imagery. This class included about 20 students who either had Chinese as their first language and English as their acquired second language or had been brought up bilingually in Chinese and English. Few of them had any academic background in gender and feminist studies, though most were very interested in this field. Following the critical reflections that emerged from this poetry reading and teaching practice, I argue that translation is a queer method when the translator consciously opts for translations that emphasise the inherently queer, non-binary and non-(hetero)normative implications of the original text, sometimes even creating new queer textual effects that do not exist in the original. This queer translation is made possible because both Chinese and English are grammatically genderless languages that use gender pronouns. The implications of queer translation are twofold: by gendering and degendering feminist language in Xi Xi's and Zhai's poems, it sheds new light on their critical and aesthetic significance; when incorporated into the classroom, it embodies the practice of resisting (hetero)normative epistemic biases and their underpinning power hierarchy.

Xi Xi's new woman imagery and Feeley's feminist translation

Table 7.1 presents a portion of Xi Xi's poem and the English translation by Jennifer Feeley.

How is this poem and its translation relevant to feminism? The key message of 'Many a Lady' is rejecting the stereotypical belief that women dream of finding Prince Charming – that is, the ideal romantic partner. As emphasised by the enjambment from line 4 to 5 that juxtaposes '白馬王子' ('Prince Charming') with '倒不如' ('[is] inferior to'), women desire to seek out the Daoist immortal '太乙' (Taiyi, 'Primordial Unity') to refashion their bodies. Women would then become completely self-sufficient and non-derivative, signalled by the gesture of returning to Adam his rib, from which God creates woman in the biblical Genesis. The quest for the Daoist immortal is particularly telling because it is a familiar trope in premodern Chinese literature about seekers travelling to Daoist sites like Mount Mao ('Maoshan'), wishing to obtain elixirs from immortals to achieve youth

許多女子	**Many a Lady**
Line 1	It's common knowledge that
Line 2	Many a lady
Line 3	Has something weighing on her mind
找尋白馬王子 [4]	Finding Prince Charming
倒不如遠赴茅山 [5]	Can't hold a candle to climbing Maoshan
Line 6	To track down the Taoist True Man of the Primordial Unity.
Line 7	Blossom of lotus, three leaves of the selfsame plant
Line 8	To newly mold each miss and madam
Line 9	Pluck a rib from one and all, and give them back to Adam.

Table 7.1 Xi Xi's '許多女子' and its translation, 'Many a Lady', by Jennifer Feeley (Xi Xi 2016, 68–69). © Xi Xi, for the original poem © Jennifer Feeley, for the translation.[1]

and immortality. This quest thus evokes a soteriological act that advances one's own well-being and self-cultivation, which, in the poem, radically shifts women's concern in life from heterosexual romance and marriage to self-love. Addressing the implied popular question 'What do women want?', I argue that Xi Xi's poetic reply is soundly feminist.

Feeley's translation reinforces the feminist view in Xi Xi's poem by introducing designations such as 'lady', 'miss' and 'madam' to accentuate the feminine gender and viewpoint. While a more neutral translation of '女子' in the original poem title is 'women', Feeley's choice of 'many a lady' gives a slightly archaic and poetic impression, which chimes with the fairy tale figure of Prince Charming, typically depicted as a knight in shining armour rescuing a lady in distress. The dramatic effect of the lady actually *not* needing Prince Charming is thus heightened. Additionally, Feeley's rendering of the last stanza explicitly feminises Xi Xi's language. Line 7, '一枝蓮花, 三片荷葉', which back translates as 'One lotus blossom, three lotus leaves', is rendered by Feeley as '[…] three leaves of the selfsame plant'. Besides astutely avoiding repeating 'lotus' (which is signified by two different Chinese characters, 蓮 and 荷, in the original), the descriptor 'selfsame' introduces the idea of autopoiesis, emphasising women's rebirth as autonomous subjects. The next line – 'To newly mold *each miss and madam*' (my italics) – is an amplifying translation that highlights the creation of new women in the plural, which the original text – '重塑凡身', literally: 'To refashion the mortal body' – does not emphasise because it does not use any possessive pronouns or quantifiers. The imperative 'Pluck a rib' in the last line is a collective act by women, affirmed by 'one and all', which echoes 'miss and madam'. Feeley's translation here again enhances the sense of women's agency and contrasts with the milder tone in Xi Xi's text – line 9: '好將肋骨還給亞當'; 'So that the rib can be returned to Adam' – which uses the subjunctive (好將) rather than the imperative and does not mention women as a collectivity. 'Many a Lady' shows the translator's conscious gendering of poetic language.

Feeley's approach reshapes the linguistically gender-neutral aspects of Xi Xi's poem and raises the question of whether the poem can be read in a way that aligns with a more assertive feminist attitude. Delving into Xi Xi's literary and cultural allusions confirms this, in my opinion. The reference to making a new body from the lotus alludes to the child-deity 哪吒 Nezha, a Chinese Oedipal figure symbolising rebellion and patricide, one of the most unusual gods in Chinese mythology and religion. Narrated in the seventeenth-century hagiographic fiction 封神演義 (*The Canonisation of Gods*; Xu 16th C/2001), Nezha is a child who defies all authority and ends up killing himself to save his family from the revenge of the powerful Dragon Kings. He is, however, resurrected by the Daoist immortal Taiyi, who reconstitutes Nezha's body from a lotus. This explains Xi Xi's use of the lotus imagery. Nezha's suicide is a disturbing story because it savagely parodies Confucian filial piety and attacks patriarchy. Gruesomely depicted,[2] Nezha executes himself by slicing away his own flesh and dismembering his bones to return them to his parents, thus repaying the debt of his birth. This evokes the Confucian adage 'Your body and flesh are bestowed by your parents',[3] which is turned on its head when Nezha considers himself to have cleared his ancestral debt after he self-destructs to ensure his parents are not punished for his individual acts. Once reborn, Nezha no longer acknowledges his father, Li Jing, and reacts fiercely to the latter's abusive behaviour, even trying to kill him. As Meir Shahar (2015, ix) observes, the extraordinary popularity of Nezha in China despite his taboo-breaking patricidal attempts should be understood in the context of 'self-murder as protest', especially 'by an inferior against his superior'. As a child, a deviant and a rebel, Nezha is pitted against the authoritarian and conformist world of adults, symbolising the protest of the oppressed against their oppressors.

In Xi Xi's poem, the new woman is like Nezha reborn, for Nezha repaying his physical body to his parents is analogous to the recreated woman returning to Adam his rib. This suggests a patriarchal worldview shared by Confucianism, where children are indebted to their biological parents, and Christianity, according to which Eve derives from Adam and is therefore secondary to him. But the new woman, Xi Xi asserts, owes men nothing because, like Nezha, she has a wholly new body made from lotus, which severs the biological and moral link between Eve and Adam, child and parent. By returning Adam's rib, the new woman dissolves her subservient relationship to man. If Nezha is a violator of Confucian ethics and driven to patricide, then Xi Xi's poem implies that women's real desire is to attack male authority and overthrow the patriarchy it represents. This critical implication is nothing less than a feminist expression in the strongest terms. While Xi Xi's gentle language does not use exhortations or emotive vocabulary, Feeley's feminising translation and emphatic use of 'selfsame' for the new woman's body draw attention to the radical implications of Xi Xi's underlying message.

When teaching this poem, I presented Xi Xi's 'Many a Lady' to students as an example of the literary articulation of feminist ideas which is not argumentative but imaginative. Xi Xi's reuse of the familiar Chinese legend of Nezha to cast the image of women's self-reinvention shows how literature refocuses our attention on narratives and issues which we have been conditioned to take for granted (for instance, understanding Nezha as a paragon of filial piety) or unsee (for instance, the comparability between the child's revolt against oppressive parents and women's fight against patriarchy). In the classroom, a student asked,

> How can women resist the gender bias and sexism embedded in the Chinese language – such as expressions that associate negativity and evil with female imagery – while using the very same language to speak, write and think? After all, Chinese language and literature have been dominated and employed by men for centuries.

Of course, no language is completely male-dominated, and women have always actively participated in the formation of the Chinese language and its literary expression.[4] Additionally, Xi Xi shows that now, when there are more women writers in the Chinese language than ever, women are reclaiming language – especially poetry, the paradigmatic male writer's realm in premodern China – for anti-patriarchal and non-heteronormative purposes. Masculinist modes of speech and writing are open to radical overhauls. In fact, Xi Xi's (2016, 67) poem '女性主義字典抽樣' ('Excerpts from a Feminist Dictionary') provides a concrete illustration of how the feminisation of language creates new vocabulary and concepts to emphasise the presence and perspective of women:

> A hen is a *shen*
> Heir *sheir*
> Heaven *Sheaven*
> [...]
> Mankind *wekind*
> History *herstory*[5]

Playing on the 'he' embedded in various English words, Xi Xi's use of 'she/her' pronouns to coin new terminology explicitly re-genders normative language. This recalls Hélène Cixous's (1976, 875) assertion that 'woman must put herself into the text – as into the world and history' and resonates with contemporary Herstory narratives and initiatives.[6]

Zhai's feminist language and Lingenfelter's degendering translation

I now turn to Zhai Yongming's 'Her Viewpoint'. Table 7.2 reproduces the poem, and the translation by Andrea Lingenfelter, in full.

The poem presents cryptic phrases that suggest sex and castration, stripped bodies and flesh offered as if in sacrifice, and, finally, an intensely corporeal scene of childbirth. Although the title declares a woman's perspective, the text obliquely portrays the female body and subjectivity while using various gender pronouns to shift between different perspectives. These linguistic and stylistic aspects make the poem very propitious for feminist interpretation and translation. Specifically, the poem posits different subject positions. It starts with '她' ('she'), tracing the woman's gaze moving through space, and then jumps to '你' ('you') in the second line; '它们' ('they') in line 6, which specifically refers to non-human entities; '每个人' ('everyone'), which is gender-neutral, in line 8; '他' ('he') in line 11; and, finally, back to '她' ('she') in lines 17 and 20. In the bracketed last stanza, the phrase '他们的孩子' ('Their child') introduces two additional perspectives: the masculine 'they' and the

她的视点	**Her Point of View**
她的视点从床的一端 射向另一端　看着你的身体 从一大堆衣服　手机　鞋 和钥匙中钻出来	From one side of the bed, her point of view Looking through the opposite side　watching your body Emerging from a heap of clothing　cell phone　shoes And keys
还有你的指头 它们修长　刚直 似乎能再次听见 骨盆和白昼的碰撞声	And let's not forget your fingers They're long, slender　and straight It's as if we could hear once again The collision of hipbones and daylight
每个人都被阉割了 每个人的健康都遗失了 每个人都暴露在他的肉体之外	Everyone's been desexed Everyone's unhealthy Everyone's exposed outside their flesh
要去的地方是个苦难窝 即使穿上盔甲　此时也不能 把你的穴道包裹起来 你的每一寸肌肤终究会 慵懒起来　可供抚摸 她也会为此快活一番	The place you're headed is a slough of despond Even your suit of armour cannot Protect your pressure points this time Every square inch of your skin Will grow slack in the end　Perhaps a little stroking Might give her some pleasure as well
关灯吧　进化论的高潮一再说: 你今晚准备献出来的 不是那么重要　对她而言	Turn out the lights　The climax of evolutionary theory repeats ad nauseam: What you're about to offer up tonight Isn't that important　as far as she's concerned
(他们的孩子会看见 生育的全过程 羊水　血　婴儿 唏里哗啦地冲出来 没留下一滴精子可供选择 没留下一寸空间可供栖息)	(Their child could witness The entire process of procreation Amniotic fluid　blood　baby As it all comes splashing out there's Nothing left behind, not one drop of semen Nothing left behind, no space to call a haven)

Table 7.2 Zhai Yongming's '她的视点' and its translation, 'Her Point of View', by Andrea Lingenfelter (Zhai 2011, 139). © Zhai Yongming for the original poem. © Andrea Lingenfelter for the translation.[7]

child's viewpoint. The wide variety of pronouns reveals fragmented and disparate perspectives that cannot be identified with any single gender, subjectivity or body. Despite the poem's title, 'her viewpoint' does not hold together all the experiences mentioned in the poem. This non-totalising feminine viewpoint goes together with the striking absence of the first-person pronoun 我 'I' in the poem. In a lyric poem – which typically zooms in on the poet's first-person persona and subjectivity (see, for instance, Li

2020) – not instating the poetic 'I' is a deliberate gesture that implies a decentring move from self to Other. A gap between 'her viewpoint' and '*my* viewpoint' is opened, which suggests that a woman never sees herself as 'myself' but always from the third-person perspective, as someone who is Othered. Being woman is thus never self-identical, never quite 'being myself' or master of oneself. This resonates with Cixous's (1976) championing of multiplicity and heterogeneity in feminine writing. Thus, while female subjectivity underpins the poem, it is represented obliquely.

In my view, Lingenfelter produces a degendering translation of Zhai's poem that introduces more gender neutrality into the poetic language while maintaining its feminist critical force. Lingenfelter (2012, 59) herself comments that 'a reading of the [original poem] doesn't unearth any clearly gendered language per se', especially due to its elusiveness about the gender and sexual identities of the depicted bodies. This ambiguity is accentuated by Lingenfelter's translation of personal pronouns. Consider the third stanza: line 11 – '每个人都暴露在他的肉体之外' – translates literally as 'Everyone is exposed outside *his* flesh and body' (my emphasis), which contains the grammatically jarring use of 'his' as the possessive adjective of 'everyone'. Lingenfelter's version is, however, 'Everyone's exposed outside *their* flesh' (my emphasis). In Chinese, the reflexive pronoun for 每个人 ('everyone') is 自己 ('oneself', 'one's own'), which is gender neutral. Moreover, when 每个人 is the grammatical subject in a sentence, the reflexive pronoun is often dropped. An idiomatic rendering of Zhai's line 11 would therefore be '每个人都暴露在(自己的)肉体之外'. Zhai's discordant use of the masculine third-person pronoun 他 ('he') here heightens the sense of emasculation in this stanza, signalled by the blunt '每个人都被阉割了' (literally: 'Everyone is castrated') in line 9. While 阉割 typically refers to male castration in Chinese, Lingenfelter's translation – 'desexed' – again opts for a biologically indeterminate and gender-neutral term. A subtle shift of imagery happens: Zhai evokes a castrated, exposed and vulnerable male body, whereas Lingenfelter presents a universally desexualised and degendered body. Zhai's employment of 'he/his' for 'everyone' re-enacts the stereotypical association of 'everyone' with the male subject, understood as universally representative although he is only a partial perspective. Certainly, the emasculation of 'everyone' hints at the invalidity of the supposedly all-encompassing masculine viewpoint. With Lingenfelter's translation, however, the implication is that everyone (male, female, queer and trans bodies) is sexually undifferentiated and enfeebled.

At this point, one might ask whether Lingenfelter adequately conveys the fierce undertones of Zhai's language that strips the male body of its virility. Lingenfelter's translation is not lacking, but simply differs from the original poem because it degenders Zhai's language and opens up more possibilities for queer interpretation. This is also supported by the coherence of Lingenfelter's translation. For instance, her rendering of '他们的孩子' in line 21 as 'Their child' echoes her use of 'their' in line 11. 他们 is the masculine third-person plural pronoun for 'they', which could – if the translator wants to emphasise the masculine gender – translate as '(the) men', '(those) men and women', or 'a heterosexual couple (man and woman)'. But 'their child' demasculinises the possessive pronoun and maintains gender neutrality. A contrast with Zhai's language emerges again: Zhai emphasises 'men's' claim to the 'child', whereas Lingenfelter does not attribute the child to any gender-specific lineage. This implies that 'you' and 'she', the couple who engage in erotic activity in the previous stanzas, are not necessarily heterosexual but could be two women or a non-binary and queer couple.

How does Lingenfelter's degendering and queer translation of pronouns connect meaningfully to the poem's female imagery and its implied feminist ideas? A translation that queers the original text can simultaneously be a solidly feminist translation. As Susan Bassnett (2014, 70) observes, 'Barbara Godard [...] uses the term "transformance" to emphasize the construction of meaning in feminist translation, which is seen as a productive, not a reproductive, activity.' This concept of feminist translation sees the original/translation hierarchy as analogous to the male/female binary and rejects both, affirming that neither source nor target text is necessarily fixed but, rather, open to creative processes of change. Seen in this light, Lingenfelter's queer transformation of Zhai's language is also feminist, for it is not subservient to the authority of the source text and interrogates existing gender and sexual norms, especially the masculine.

Pronouns and female imagery complement each other in both the original poem and Lingenfelter's translation. Zhai features the female body indirectly, through the absence of descriptions of any clearly identified female body. This is effectively a refusal to sexualise the woman, 'she', as a biologically determined identity in the poem. The only explicitly female imagery is the mother's body in the bracketed last stanza; the body is not described but is a creative agent in the most active sense: '生育的全过程/羊水　血　婴儿/唏里哗啦地冲出来' ('The entire birthing process / Amniotic fluid　blood　infant / Charging out splashing and spattering').[8] Notably, this scene of birth, with violently overflowing bodily fluids, is a blunt, non-romanticising portrayal ('amniotic fluid' are markedly unpoetic words) that implies the pain of childbirth. The exaggerated blank spaces imply a temporal process of birthing that is painfully prolonged, demanding intensified attention at each stage. Birth is not celebrated joyously but stated as the bloody mess that it is and as a forceful ejection from the womb. Most importantly, the birthing body is seen from the third-person viewpoint by the 'child' (line 21), who confronts the gory spectacle of their own coming-to-existence. Zhai's articulation of childbirth is feminist because it brings to light a process that is typically glossed over, sanitised and kept behind the scenes; instead, Zhai's poem makes the mothering body heard ('splashing') and visible.[9] It counters the normative congratulatory response to an infant's birth by suggesting instead reactions such as 'How bearable is this sight to others?' or 'How painful is it?'. Contrasting this birthing imagery with the masculine possessive pronoun in Zhai's '他们的孩子' ('those men's/the man and woman's/their child'), the male claim to the child pales beside the birthing female body and almost connotes irony. With Lingenfelter's gender-neutral 'their child', however, the male/female contrast is pre-empted. The visual shock of witnessing 'procreation', which amplifies the meaning of '生育' ('childbearing'), adds the notion that the child is a witness of their progenitors' copulation through to childbirth itself, which sustains the taboo-breaking approach to the female body in this stanza.

The last stanza is enclosed by brackets and calls for attention. Brackets are commonly used to add clarifying or explanatory information that is non-essential or to make an aside statement, as in stage directions, where some words are intended to be inaudible to others. Formally speaking, Zhai's poem ends with '对她而言' ('to her') in line 20. The last stanza about childbirth is a parenthetical addition – that is, a textual behind-the-scenes. The violence and chaos of birth is thus made secondary and contained formally by brackets. While this hints at Zhai's ironic use of brackets to textually perform what is typically rendered parenthetical in female bodily experiences, when read as an aside explanation of the immediately preceding line 20 the bracketed last stanza suggests that procreation is '不是那么重要' ('not that important') to 'her' (the woman). We may relate this to the feminist view that women's bodies are self-serving and an end in themselves, not to be seen primarily as an instrument for procreation. Lingenfelter's degendering translation 'Their child' further de-emphasises the engendering dimension of language and the act of procreation it represents, aligning with the parenthetical nature of the whole stanza.

'My Viewpoint' can be used in the translation classroom by asking students to read the original poem and Lingenfelter's translation, before back-translating the poem into Chinese from Lingenfelter. This exercise aims to encourage students to think about how the English translation reshapes the source text and whether retranslation into Chinese deepens our understanding of translational techniques and the poem's evocativeness. In this section, I discuss selected comments and retranslations from students.

Firstly, almost all students (from a cohort of 19) viewed Zhai's poem as feminist or predisposed to feminist interpretation. As one student argued, 'The poem tends to promote feminism by unveiling the sexual scene and describing it from a female perspective.'[10] Some students accentuated feminine agency and emotional impact in their retranslations. For instance, Student A explained their translation of verbs in line 2 as follows: to 'connotat[e] the burning intensity of the woman's gaze, I chose to use "刺向" ("thrust at"), "透穿" ("penetrate") to illustrate how direct and piercing the woman's stare was and to further create an atmosphere of insightfulness.' The woman's gaze is made more forceful than is implied by Zhai's verbs '射向' ('shoot/cast towards') and '看着' ('looking at'). Secondly, a few students expressed the view that both Zhai's poem and Lingenfelter's translation were not feminist *enough*, but in fact embedded some gender bias. They took issue with lines 16 and 17 in particular: '可供抚摸/她也会为此快活一番'. One criticism (Student B) read:

> Being a feminist, Zhai's original [line] "可供抚摸 她也会为此快活一番" places the woman in the dominant position during sex, [in which] usually men dominate. [...] In Lingenfelter's translation, the woman is given pleasure rather than creating her own pleasure, which changes the author's original perspective.

If we examine Lingenfelter's rendering – 'Perhaps a little stroking / Might give her some pleasure as well' – it indeed implies that 'you' in the poem 'strokes' the woman ('her'). But Zhai's '可供抚摸' ('offered to the caress') has a grammatical passive, which means 'you' – a man in Student B's understanding – are offered to the woman's touch. Lingenfelter's translation here somewhat misleadingly reverses the agent and recipient.

Student C, interestingly, criticised both Lingenfelter's translation and Zhai's original phrasing because she understood the body 'offered to the caress' as a woman's body. She commented that Zhai's phrase may 'show disrespect for women, as if women are regarded as a plaything to please men. However, according to feminist translation theory, the translator should deconstruct the source text with feminist thinking and reshape the image of the woman.' The point about feminist translators' deconstruction of the source text is excellent. Nevertheless, the sex scene implied here does not necessarily involve a man. Indeed, precisely because the student already understands the body that is 'offered' as a *woman*'s body, she dislikes its sacrificial image. But if 'you' is a woman who sexually engages with 'her', another woman, then the sexist rhetoric about offering women to please men no longer stands. Instead, we have women pleasuring each other.

This debate about the gender of the offered body in the poem made me reflect upon some students' comments that feminism and sexuality are 'marginalised topics in the Chinese context'. Tellingly, despite occasional hints of queer sexuality in some students' translations and commentaries, nobody explicitly stated that the implied sex scene in the poem could be non-heterosexual. Students' retranslations of 'Their child' into Chinese were also invariably '他们的孩子', using the masculine pronoun, even though '她们的孩子' ('the women's child') with the feminine pronoun and 'TA们的孩子' – using the newly coined non-binary 'ta们' ('them') in Chinese[11] – are equally possible translations. This shows some level of unconscious heteronormative bias that, through discussions and feedback with students, the reader can recognise and then deconstruct, as the aforementioned student states. This reminds me that upon my first reading of Zhai's poem and its translations, I also initially pictured a heterosexual couple. Only upon rereading did I start thinking that the poem could articulate radically queer and non-binary relations. Reading and translating Zhai's poem show a process of exposing heteronormative perception and then undoing it by non-normative interpretations. This is putting queer translation into practice, and here students' coursework and reflections play an important role. As a pedagogical process, queer translation promotes equality, diversity and inclusion because it helps students to appreciate difference, gain increased awareness of implicit biases and develop the skills of listening to other voices and assessing information without prior judgement.

My comparison of Xi Xi's and Zhai's poems and their translations shows that both poets' language and imagery have much to do with feminist thought, although their translators' approaches differ. Von Flotow (1991) identifies three practices of feminist translators: 'supplementing', 'prefacing and footnoting' and 'hijacking'. Feeley's translation of Xi Xi here is generally a supplementing one, for it reinforces the feminine gender in the poetic language. Lingenfelter's translation of Zhai is, however, closer to hijacking, but not in Von Flotow's sense of inventing feminist meaning in a source text that lacks it in the first place. Rather, Lingenfelter sustains the poem's feminist significance by subtracting gender from the language and achieving a queerer and more gender-fluid effect. Both engendering and degendering translations demonstrate how feminism and queerness can constructively intersect.

Practising queer translation: the inherent queerness of poetic language

To maximise the critical synergy between feminist language and queer translation, this section explores whether there are inherently queer and non-binary aspects in 'Many a Lady' and 'Her Viewpoint' that have *not* featured in Feeley's and Lingenfelter's translations. In other words, I ask if translation as a queer practice not only creatively rewrites the source text but also fundamentally destabilises and changes the latter so that, regardless of the original author's intentions and biases, it is no longer possible to unsee the potential queerness of the source text itself. This hypothesis stems from the critical view that queerness is not limited to gender expression or the sexually queer, but is also an intellectual attitude, a mode of being and a critical method that challenges rigid identity categories and unequal power relations (see Ahmed 2006). Queer translation, therefore, does not merely provide another interpretive option on top of the normative reading, but should dislodge the normative from its dominant position.

In Xi Xi's 'Many a Lady', besides the feminist language and Feeley's feminising translation, the original poem does not contain explicitly queer content such as queer sexuality or affirmations of non-binary identity. Nevertheless, Xi Xi's analogy of the reborn Nezha and the new woman taps into queer imagery. As an ambiguous being who does not align with a single identity or category, Nezha is a paradigmatically queer figure. He is both child and god – fragile due to youthful naïveté but naturally endowed with demonic strength. Notably, he is also both Chinese and Indian, and therefore originally foreign to Chinese literary and religious contexts, as he is traced to the Indian mythological figure Nalakūbara, a 'semidivine semidemonic *yakṣa* spirit' who appears in 'Sanskrit epics of the first millennium BCE' (Shahar 2015, x). Nezha is thus a transcultural hybrid who is part human, part demon, part divine. Although he is initially born male, his resurrection via a lotus effectively makes him desexed and non-human. In visual and popular representations of Nezha, he is often depicted androgynously, which has prompted the search question on baidu.com (the biggest search engine in mainland China) '哪吒是男是女' ('Is Nezha male or female?'). Recently, after the huge success of the animation film 哪吒之魔童降世 (*Nezha: Birth of the Demon Child*, 2019) in China, online queer fandom exploded and numerous fan-made depictions and fictional narratives about Nezha's homoerotic relationship with his friend/enemy Aobing were generated (see Cheng 2019). These new representations of Nezha re-understand him as a queer figure, which complements the established images of Nezha as a patricidal revolutionary, a rebellious youth (see Sheng 2013), a suicide protestor and even a stand-in for the 'desperate courtesan' (Shahar 2015, 37). These are all positions where 'the self is at odds with everything around it', according to bell hooks's (2014) explanation of being queer.

Returning to read Xi Xi's poem with queer Nezha in mind, the new woman who models after Nezha takes on queer, non-anthropocentric and somewhat unworldly dimensions. In fact, line 8 – '重塑凡身' – does not use any word that would specify the gender and sex of the newly fashioned person. To expand translational options and interpretations of the poem, I therefore propose a degendering translation of the last stanza to emphasise the gender ambiguity of the new body:

> One lotus blossom, three lotus leaves
> To refashion their flesh and body
> So they can return to Adam his rib.

As contrasted with Feeley's translation:

> Blossom of lotus, three leaves of the selfsame plant
> To newly mold each miss and madam
> Pluck a rib from one and all, and give them back to Adam.

By using the pronouns 'their' and 'they', I refrain from feminising Xi Xi's language and suggest that the new woman is non-binary. I also emphasise the 'flesh' to echo the concrete image of 'rib' in the last line and remind readers that the new material from which the body is constituted is the 'lotus', which is non-human and beyond gender categories, not least because the lotus is a bisexual flower in botanical terms. This translation is queer due to the re-understanding of the symbolism of Nezha and the recreation of the grammatically genderless aspects of Xi Xi's Chinese language in non-binary English expressions.

While Lingenfelter's translation of Zhai's 'Her Viewpoint' is already degendering and queer, I would like to build upon it by further excavating the queer potential of Zhai's language. My departure point is the pronoun 'you' in the poem. While 'you' is the implied sexual partner, it is also a direct address to the reader, who could be of any gender and sexuality. In the first stanza, when 'her' gaze watches 'your' body emerge from 'clothes, cell phone, and shoes', the implication is that 'her' gaze strips you, the reader, naked. But this nakedness does not reveal a specific sex, for 'your' body combines masculine and feminine features: 'You' have '刚直' ('hard and straight') fingers that conjure '骨盆和白昼的碰撞声' 'the clashing sound of pelvis and daylight', which correlates with masculine imagery; whereas later, 'you' are vulnerable and even 'armour' cannot wrap up 'your' '穴道', a term that can mean 'acupuncture point', 'tunnel' or 'cavity'.[12] The latter presents feminine imagery, especially because Zhai (1984/2010) associates femininity with 'black night' and darkness. Finally, 'your' flesh and skin '会/慵懒起来' ('will / become languid'), meaning softened and indolent, which contrasts sharply with the hardness and clashing movement in lines 6 and 8. The body here is uncategorisable and in flux, which is properly queer. To reflect this, I hereby offer retranslated lines 12 to 16:

> The place you are headed is a den of misery
> Even if clothed in armour   now you still cannot
> Cocoon your body cavities
> Every inch of your flesh and skin will ultimately
> Become languid   offered to the caress

'Den' echoes 'cavity', while 'clothe' mirrors 'cocoon' and conveys the attempt to protect the vulnerable body. 'Flesh and skin' emphasise the body's materiality, which is malleable. These retranslations offer concrete examples of queer translation and will be incorporated into my future teaching of these poems in the translation classroom.

Re-reading Zhai's poem from a degendering translational perspective, we see that it is already inherently queer. Incidentally, this is also affirmed by the sinologist, poet and poetry translator Wolfgang Kubin. In a poetry reading event with Zhai on 22 December 2022, Kubin was asked by the host: '翟永明的诗歌饱含丰富的女性意识, 他作为男性, 如何把翟永明的诗句转换成德语呢' ('Zhai's poetry abounds with female consciousness. As a man, how do you convert Zhai's verse lines into German'?) (Teehaus Lit 2022). Kubin replied:

> Zunächst, – ich verstehe mich gar nicht als Mann. Nach dem zweiten Weltkrieg gab es keine Männer, es gab nur Frauen, die uns erzogen haben. Deswegen ist mein Bewusstsein grundsätzlich ein weibliches Bewußtsein. Deswegen finde ich in der Lyrik von Zhai Yongming das wieder, was ich bei meiner Mutter, bei meiner Großmutter usw. erfahren hab. Ich habe mich selbst als Mann nie gemocht. Für mich ist das Übersetzen der Poesie von Zhai Yongming eine Befreiung.
>
> (Firstly, I don't see myself as a man at all. After WWII, [in Germany] there were no men, only women who brought us up. So my consciousness is fundamentally a feminine consciousness. And therefore I find in Zhai's poetry what I experienced from my mother and grandmother. I've never liked men, nor liked myself as a man. For me, translating Zhai's poetry is a liberation.) (My translation)

That translating Zhai means for Kubin a breaking away from the strictures of the masculine gender shows a process of queering – both in terms of the gender fluidity in Zhai's language and the practice of translating it with a non-binary consciousness. Returning to the poem's title, 'Her Viewpoint', this non-totalising feminine viewpoint goes hand in hand with queer perspectives. Here, not being master of oneself is a strength rather than a lack, for 'being master' perpetuates the masculinist assumption that agency is about having power over the self and the Other, rather than having power *to act for* oneself and others. The feminine third-person viewpoint rejects the logic of domination and posits instead affective relations.

Conclusion

To conclude, although Xi Xi and Zhai Yongming differ noticeably in terms of poetic style and cultural allusions, they both employ an inherently queer language with rich feminist implications. Thinking about their poems through translation, which is an active interpretive movement that goes beyond the production of the target text, demonstrates that translation itself is a practice of queering. This practice complements feminist translational pedagogy, which, as Emek Ergun and Olga Castro (2017) argue, uses translation to re-examine borders and unlearn artificial oppositions. The ways in which translation between Chinese and English can both engender and degender poetic language 'enabl[e] us to see and hear and imagine a whole range of ways of being; being in between the ones we live now' (Kedem 2019, 180), which is precisely the work of queer translation, according to Nir Kedem. Pedagogically speaking, incorporating poetry into the translation classroom to spark discussions about feminist and (de)gendering approaches to translation constitutes a queer practice in the most concrete sense. Ultimately, practising queer translation in the classroom emphasises the aesthetics of poetry – the intimate space of relation opened up by poetic language – and does not endorse ideological stances or identity categories but offers different possibilities of experience from varying gender perspectives, including the degendered and desexualised. This openness of language that questions and looks beyond hierarchies and this flux of aesthetic experience that accommodates the reader are at the heart of queerness.

Acknowledgements

I thank my colleague Dr Yuan He and students Yixian Li, Mingzhi Li, Xiyang Du, Tristan Sorenson and Yinqi Zhou for co-organising a discussion event on Chinese feminism at UCL, 3 February 2022, which prompted me to think about reading Xi Xi and Zhai Yongming in relation to feminism. I also acknowledge the work of all my students (2022–2023 cohort) on translating Zhai Yongming's 'Her Viewpoint' in the module CMII0176: Advanced Translation into Chinese at UCL. Finally, many thanks to translators Dr Andrea Lingenfelter and Dr Jennifer Feeley, and the Chinese University of Hong Kong Press for granting me permission to cite their translations of Zhai Yongming's 'Her Point of View' and of Xi Xi's 'Many a Lady', as well as Zhai Yongming's original Chinese poem.

Notes

1 As the copyright holder for Xi Xi's Chinese poem in *Not Written Words* was uncontactable, the full poem is not cited here. For the full poem, see its oral presentation here: https://www.youtube.com/watch?v=l1SLreIiX5E (Accessed 11 February 2024).
2 The story appears in popular folklore and various sixteenth-century texts such as *The Canonisation of Gods* (Xu 16th C/2001) and the early modern novel *Journey to the West*.
3 See the Xiao Jing at the Chinese Text Project: https://ctext.org/xiao-jing (Accessed 26 March 2024).
4 As evidenced by extensive literary writings by premodern Chinese women such as Cai Yan, Xue Tao and Li Qingzhao, among others.
5 Feeley's translation. The italicised words are originally in English in Xi Xi's poem.
6 See, for instance, the storytelling platform https://www.herstory.ie/mission (accessed 16 February 2023).
7 This poem originally appeared in the poetry collection 终于使我周转不灵 (Zhai 2002).
8 My own translation.

9 Studies and discussions about pregnancy and childbirth repeatedly highlight that mothers' pain and emotions, as well as post-birth complications, have not received due attention. See, for instance, Kuhn (2004) and Goutaudier et al. (2019).

10 Citations from students' homework have been anonymised and slightly rephrased for conciseness.

11 The romanised 'ta', which is a homophone with all gendered and inanimate third-person pronouns (她, 他, 它, 牠), is currently used in Chinese to refer to queer, non-binary, gender-questioning people and drag queens/kings.

12 My translations.

References

Ahmed, Sara. 2006. 'Orientations: Toward a queer phenomenology', *GLQ* 12, no. 4: 543–74. https://doi.org/10.1215/10642684-2006-002.

Bassnett, Susan. 2014. *Translation Studies*. 4th ed. London: Routledge.

Cheng, Meng. 2019. '"腐女"会是《哪吒之魔童降世》20亿票房的主力军吗?' Accessed 10 April 2024. https://www.sohu.com/a/329215431_500918.

Cixous, Hélène. 1976. 'Laugh of the Medusa', translated by Keith Cohen and Paula Cohen, *Signs* 1, no. 4: 875–93.

Ergun, Emek, and Olga Castro. 2017. 'Pedagogies of feminist translation: Rethinking difference and commonality across borders'. In *Feminist Translation Studies*, edited by Olga Castro and Emek Ergun, 93–108. London: Routledge.

Goutaudier, Nelly, Charlene Bertoli, Natalène Séjourné, and Henri Chabrol. 2019. 'Childbirth as a forthcoming traumatic event: Pretraumatic stress disorder during pregnancy and its psychological correlates', *Journal of Reproductive and Infant Psychology* 37, no. 1: 44–55. https://doi.org/10.1080/02646838.2018.1504284.

Ho, Tammy Lai-ming. 2019. 'Xi Xi, the poet of Hong Kong: Nomination of Xi Xi for the 2019 Newman Prize for Chinese Literature', *Chinese Literature Today* 8, no. 1: 6–9. https://doi.org/10.1080/21514399.2019.1607110.

hooks, bell. 2014. 'Are you still a slave?' Accessed 20 February 2023. www.youtube.com/watch?v=rJk0hNROvzs.

Kedem, Nir. 2019. 'What is queer translation?' *Symploke* 27, no. 1–2: 157–83. https://doi:10.5250/symploke.27.1-2.0157.

Kuhn, Elizabeth. 2004. 'Breaking the silence: Women's poetry tells it like it is', *Women and Language* 27, no. 1: 71.

Li, Xiaofan Amy. 2020. 'A disintegrating lyric? – Henri Michaux and Chinese lyricism', *Comparative Critical Studies* 17, no. 2: 285–302.

Lingenfelter, Andrea. 2012. 'Sensibility and point of view: A practitioner's take on gender and translation', *Chinese Literature Today* 2, no. 2: 58–61. https://doi.org/10.1080/21514399.2012.11833975.

Shahar, Meir. 2015. *Oedipal God: The Chinese Nezha and his Indian origins*. Honolulu: University of Hawai'i Press.

Sheng, Kai. 2013. 'The different faces of Nezha in modern Taiwanese culture', *Archiv orientální* 81, no. 3: 391–410.

Teehaus Lit. 2022. 'Zhai Yongming & Wolfang Kubin: "Zu guter Letzt bringst du mich in Nöte"', 22 December. Accessed 21 February 2023. https://teehaus-lit.podigee.io/2-neue-episode.

Von Flotow, Luise. 1991. 'Feminist translation: Contexts, practices and theories', *Traduction, Terminologie, Redaction* 4, no. 2: 69–85. https://doi.org/10.7202/037094ar.

Xi Xi. 2016. *Not Written Words: Selected poetry of Xi Xi/不是文字: 西西詩選*, translated by Jennifer Feeley. Brookline, MA: Zephyr Press.

Xu, Zhonglin (attributed). 16th C/2001. 封神演義 (*Canonisation of the Gods*), edited by Li Guoqing, 2 vols. Beijing: Beijing tushuguan.

Zhai, Yongming. 1984/2008. 女人 (*Woman*). Beijing: Zuojia Chubanshe.

Zhai, Yongming. 1984/2010. '黑夜意识' ('Black Night Consciousness'), translated by Andrea Lingenfelter. In *Chinese Writers on Writing*, edited by Arthur Sze, 158–61. San Antonio, TX: Trinity University Press.

Zhai, Yongming. 2002. 终于使我周转不灵 (*In the End it Brings Me Up Short*). Shijiazhuang: Hebei jiaoyu chubanshe.

Zhai, Yongming. 2011. *The Changing Room: Selected poetry of Zhai Yongming*, translated by Andrea Lingenfelter. Hong Kong: Chinese University Press.

Zhu, Yanhong. 2022. 'Performing a poetic temporal weave: Gender and femininity in Zhai Yongming's poetry', *Rocky Mountain Review* 76, no. 1: 41–61. https://doi:10.1353/rmr.2022.0002.

8

Translating intersectional feminism: a 'modern' language classroom

Mazal Oaknín

Introduction

This chapter presents a proposal for an English-into-Spanish translation lesson in which students with an advanced level of Spanish are offered opportunities to identify equality, diversity and inclusion (EDI) issues and expand their own understanding of the world through intersectional discourses. Taking two excerpts from acclaimed Black British author Bernardine Evaristo's recent novel *Girl, Woman, Other* (2019) as source text, the chapter presents a series of pre-translation exercises. Besides equipping our students with the means to produce a satisfactory target text, through the students' textual analysis the exercises also have the potential to prompt classroom discussion on the micro-politics and everyday sexism and misogyny described in the novel. The text follows the lives and struggles of 12 characters – 11 women and one non-binary person – all of whom share a common denominator: they are Black and British. This polyphonic novel spans different decades and contexts and presents the protagonists' struggles and acts of resistance as instances of intersectional feminism in modern Britain. Their stories are often interconnected and are defined by the concepts of identity and Otherness. However, said Otherness is not subject to one single interpretation in the novel; the women are matter-of-factly 'Othered' in different ways, and even by each other at times. This chapter proposes that, at a time when most universities are increasingly committed to EDI agendas, the use of novels that have appealed to the public, such as Evaristo's 2019 novel, constitutes an excellent opportunity to expose would-be linguists to more inclusionary feminist politics while raising awareness of difference (e.g. Otherness and Blackness as opposed to normalness and Whiteness) and allowing them to fine-tune their translation skills.

Questions of gender and intersectionality are blended into this chapter's exploration of the pre-translation exercise. Here, feminist translation is used as a pedagogical act in support of social and gender equality, therefore highlighting the power of translation to bring about social, political and cultural transformation. After providing a definition of the concept of the *liberation of the curriculum* and emphasising the importance of intersectionality as a vehicle to grasp invisible power relations and the ways in which inequality can be shaped by them, I present a series of pre-translation exercises that seek to offer an introduction to the novel's themes and unconventional style. The use of mediation as a tool to guide students' approach to translating EDI issues is advocated. Indeed, in order to fully understand the excerpts selected (which include instances of discrimination and oppression) and to achieve a successful translation in spite of the many cultural references and unique literary style, I posit that the use of mediation is necessary not only for students to acquire linguistic and translation competence but also for them to develop interlinguistic and intercultural knowledge and know-how as well as documentation skills.

This chapter ultimately aims to demonstrate how literary translation education can benefit greatly from translating intersectionality. On the one hand, in exploring intersectional feminism, tutors can play a pivotal role as agents of resistance and societal change. On the other, these translation exercises give students the ability to bring about change using the powerful tool of 'other' words.

Liberating the curriculum through translation

In 2023, UCL received an overall score of 95 in the QS World University Rankings, where it was recognised as the eighth top university worldwide (see https://www.qs.com/rankings/). With regards to enrolment numbers, UCL occupies first place in the UK at postgraduate level, and second place in the UK in terms of total enrolment (UCL 2024). The university's commitment to EDI values includes a series of programmes spanning EDI networks; support for students, staff and managers; EDI training; and policies aimed at the prevention of bullying, harassment and sexual misconduct. As part of its commitment to this EDI agenda, the Liberating the Curriculum programme was launched at UCL in 2016 (see UCL n.d.).

In EDI projects across different faculties, degrees and subjects, students and staff work together in order to achieve a more diverse and inclusive curriculum. Liberating the Curriculum has three main objectives:

1. To complement traditional Eurocentric, male- and white-dominated programmes
2. To promote the representation of traditionally marginalised authors
3. To achieve greater inclusion in our programmes in terms of factors such as race, religion, gender, sexuality, ability and neurodiversity, among others.

At the time of writing, this university-wide initiative had given students the opportunity to make their own contributions to the decolonisation of curricula, with some activities such as the diversification of reading lists and teaching materials having a notably direct impact on their sense of belonging, which Tate (2019) claims is a key requirement for the elimination of the awarding gap in respect of BAME-BIPOC (Black, Asian and Minority Ethnic; Black and Indigenous People of Colour). When designing activities aimed at liberating curricula, teachers are encouraged to adopt the following guidelines (Oaknín 2019):

- Activities should promote student–teacher collaboration. Studies by Burke et al. (2016), Zepke and Leach (2010), Halawah (2006) and Strauss and Volkwein (2004) have highlighted the many benefits of positive student–teacher interactions, which include an improved sense of belonging, higher motivation and greater intellectual development, among others.
- Exercises should work towards the elimination of the ethnicity gap, which, according to Tate (2019), results from different factors such as micro-racism, lack of support for BAME students, *invisible* racism and stereotyping. These factors alienate students, thus negatively affecting their sense of belonging and making them more likely to drop out and less likely to achieve higher grades and to pursue postgraduate studies. Activities that emphasise representation and encourage the development of students' sense of belonging are especially relevant.
- Exercises should have long-term potential. Indeed, our efforts to broaden our intellectual vision to include a wider range of perspectives should lead us to challenge power relations and to call for deeper thinking about the content and delivery of future courses (Muldoon 2019).

- Educators should be mindful of possible triggers and endeavour to set up a safe space in the classroom. According to Mendes and Lau (2022), teachers should not only avoid self-silencing and censoring, but also deflect any potential attempts at contention and provocation.
- Activities should offer students the opportunity to foster and develop transferable skills. Highly valued skills such as communication, adaptability, decision-making, negotiation, problem-solving or mediation are linked to higher employability.
- Content should explore intersectionality. This leads to greater opportunities to engage with subjects from different perspectives and showcase a wider range of authors and materials.

Intersectionality in the translation classroom

The benefits of an intersectional approach to pedagogy have recently been remarked upon by numerous studies, such as those by Begum and Saini (2019), Shay (2016), Arday and Safia Mirza (2018), Bhambra et al. (2018), Icaza and de Jong (2019) and Banks (2020).

In translation studies (TS), the use of translation as a pedagogical tool in foreign-language education is a well-established practice (see, among others, Naimushin 2002; Baker 2006; Gaspar 2009; Leonardi 2010; Ayachia 2018). However, and perhaps due to the speed of societal changes, the embedding of research in the translation classroom (i.e. research-led education) appears to be still scarce in the TS body of scholarship, not to mention the lack of literature on the pedagogical implications of including sensitive topics such as gender, feminism, intersectionality, accessibility or LGBTQI+ issues in the language and translation classroom. Naga and McGill (2018) and Schechter (2018) address cultural difference and interpretive diversity in educational environments. In my own teaching and research activities, I have found that modern languages and translation interact effectively with EDI approaches and disciplines such as gender and queer studies. Drawing on the Canadian School of Feminist Translation, more recent events such as the Schools of Feminist Translation (Warwick University, 2023), the e-Expert Seminar Series: Translation and Language Teaching: LGBTQI+ Issues in Modern Languages and Translation Education (UCL and the University of Córdoba, Spain, 2021) and the Gendering Agency and Activism in Translation and Interpreting Conference (University of Ferrara, Italy, 2022) attest to the fact that there is a growing interest in using feminist translation and teaching materials that recognise LGBTQI+ identities as vehicles to pursue social and gender equality and to empower minority groups.

In my own advanced-level English-to-Spanish translation lessons at UCL, I endeavour to explore new connections with feminist translation theory and showcase my commitment to EDI values. Bearing in mind the above guidelines, in the novel *Girl, Woman, Other* (Evaristo 2019) I have found a warmly welcomed opportunity to experiment with interdisciplinarity. There are many ways of liberating the curriculum and further integrating and embracing inclusivity in the classroom and in academic research when educators use materials that put the emphasis on the concept of intersectionality.

The term 'intersectionality' was first coined by Professor Kimberlé Crenshaw in 1989, and it is now central to several disciplines such as gender studies, economics, political science and anthropology (see Crenshaw 1989). The following definition was added to the *Oxford English Dictionary* in 2015: 'Intersectionality is the network of connections between social categories such as race, class and gender, especially when this may result in additional disadvantage or discrimination.' Different versions of the wheel of power and privilege – a sketchnote first designed by Canadian teacher and author Sylvia Duckworth (see https://sylviaduckworth.com) which serves as an accessible visual tool to take into consideration these intersectionalities – have proliferated. Following the third wave of feminism in the 1990s, intersectionality provided answers to the question of how to respond to the perceived failures of the second wave of feminism, and particularly to a rather narrow definition of femininity that emphasised the experiences of upper-middle-class white women. In recent years, renowned authors and activists such as Eddo-Lodge (2018), Saad (2020) and Gay (2014) have unmasked mainstream feminism as a principally white feminism that has traditionally only concerned itself with disparities and oppression of gender, failing to take into account the disparities and oppression of other intersections, such as BAME-BIPOC or LGBTQI+ women, which are just as crucial. Saad (2020) cites the case of the suffragette Alice Paul, who vehemently opposed the idea of White women and Black women marching together in the first suffrage parade held in Washington, DC, and also points out that the Black maternity crisis is only now starting to receive public attention. Through their opposition to mainstream feminism's celebration of a universalised Western model of women's liberation that favours individuality and modernity, these authors reject the universalisation of women and a belief in a universal sisterhood, just as they reject a universal notion of patriarchy that affects all women in the same manner.

Whilst new and innovative language and translation practices mushroom, and as universities are increasingly committed to developing an EDI agenda and to making the content of research and research-led curricula more inclusive, it seems more pressing than ever to consider that the teaching of feminist translation should be intersectional. Women's lives are intersectional, so matters arising from race, ethnicity, class, religion, gender and nationality are all significant factors to consider in translation exercises.

A practical proposal: preparing to translate by understanding intersectionality

The translation exercises showcased in this chapter were carried out as part of a mandatory English-to-Spanish translation component of an undergraduate course in Spanish offered at UCL's Department of Spanish, Portuguese and Latin American Studies (SPLAS), part of the School of European Languages, Cultures and Societies (SELCS). The component forms part of an advanced-level Spanish-language module designed for finalists (C1–C2 according to the *Common European Framework of Reference for Languages*, or CEFR; see Council of Europe 2001). The module's main pedagogical objectives are:

- to improve students' linguistic and translation skills (from English into Spanish)
- to introduce students to a variety of text types and textual conventions
- to foster collaborative learning and teamwork
- to teach students to use reliable sources and to develop their dictionary and documentation skills
- to use translation as a valuable communicative skill in order to develop students' interlinguistic and intercultural abilities (including mediation).

On average, seminar groups are composed of 12 students. As per UCL's Student Registry Services, in the 2022/2023 academic year the university boasted a student body with 55 per cent international students (see UCL 2024). As can be inferred by this percentage, English is not the mother tongue of a considerable number of the students in our classrooms. Indeed, students often speak English as a second or third language. Furthermore, the Year Abroad – a third year spent in a Spanish-speaking country in order to improve students' linguistic and cultural understanding – is an integral, compulsory element of the four-year language degree programmes offered by the School. In the case of those students combining Spanish with another language, the Year Abroad is split between two different countries. It is, hence, logical to expect that these lessons are plurilingual environments where mediation can be maximised as a vehicle to understand students' different perspectives and to bridge potential cultural, epistemological or linguistic gaps.

In 2018, the *CEFR Companion Volume with New Descriptors* (Council of Europe 2018), the official extension of the CEFR (Council of Europe 2001), incorporated the concept of mediation as a mode of communication. Yet, in the UK, the integration of mediation remains to be explored and investigated as a communication skill in the curricula of modern foreign languages (North and Piccardo 2016). From a pedagogical perspective, complex communicative skills are understood to be the traditional language skills – reading, writing, listening and speaking – combined with more complex skills such as reformulating ideas, condensing information, providing definitions, explaining extralinguistic and cultural references and shifting registers. Mediation therefore becomes applicable to teamwork in translation education, as each group of students must overcome communication obstacles in order to successfully complete a task. Trovato (2016) understands mediation as a type of interaction that occurs between people who are unable to communicate with each other due to various reasons.

Drawing from Gould and Tahmasebian's (2020) understanding of translators and interpreters as activists, and bearing in mind our goal to make the translation classroom a more equal, diverse and inclusive space, students were asked to analyse and translate two excerpts from *Girl, Woman, Other* (Evaristo 2019). In the brief, students were advised that their translation choices had to reflect their role as champions of political and cultural change, promoters of gender diversity, voice-givers of minorities and oppressed groups and advocators of gender equality. This idea also follows in the footsteps of Castro and Ergun's *Feminist Translation Studies: Local and transnational perspectives* (2017), which campaigns for a feminist approach towards translation as a means of challenging different forms of discrimination. By pinpointing different systems of gender discrimination and finding alternative ways of furthering gender equality, these practices contribute to the discussion on the interplay between feminist translation, agency and activism as academic fields of enquiry.

Girl, Woman, Other was a joint winner of the Man Booker Prize in 2019. The immense popularity enjoyed by the novel is evidenced by its high sales: it was 12th on the bestsellers list for hardback fiction in the UK in 2019 and for five weeks in the summer of 2020 it was the number 1 bestselling paperback in the UK. It has also been praised not only by literary critics, but by important public figures such as Barack Obama, Roxane Gay and Nicola Sturgeon (see Flood 2019). Evaristo (2021, 144) has defined the novel as a polyphonic paean to Black British womanhood and to non-binary people, in all our flawed complexity, and she has interpreted her joint win – and iconic hug – with Canadian novelist Margaret Atwood as a life-changing moment for both literature and feminism:

> I'll never forget how elated I felt when my name was called out by the Chair of the jury. Margaret and I met at the steps of the stage and hugged – two women, two races, two nations, two generations – and then we ascended the stage hand-in-hand to rapturous applause. It was a landmark historical moment for literature and the sisterhood. (Evaristo 2021, 145)

In order to begin the preparatory exercise, students were asked to read the following excerpts from the novel:

> **Excerpt 1**
> DOMINIQUE
> Dominique came across Nzinga at Victoria station in the rush hour as she was being knocked down by the steamrollering effect of London's ruthless commuters determined to catch their trains at all costs
> her bag fell open and everything fell out: passport, A–Z, Rough Guide to London, hemp purse, tampons, Zenith E camera, Palmer's hand cream, evil eye charm, ivory-handled hunting knife
> Nzinga was profusely grateful when a passing Dominique approached to help, the pair of them scrambling about on the station floor gathering up her belongings
> when that was done, and Nzinga was once more upright and composed, Dominique found herself in front of an extraordinary vision
> the woman was statuesque, her skin glowed, her robes flowed, her features were sculptural, lips fulsome, thin ropes of dreadlocks fell freely down to her hips, silver amulets and bright beads sewn
> into them

Dominique had never seen anyone like her before, offered to buy her coffee, confident she'd say yes because lesbians, and she suspected this one was, usually did
they sat opposite each other in the station café as Nzinga sipped on a glass of hot water with a slice of lemon in it, the only hot drink she allowed to pass her lips, she said, I don't abuse my body
meanwhile
Dominique, drinking a cup of granulated coffee into which she'd dissolved two sugars and was dunking a succession of digestive biscuits (a packet of Maltesers at the side for dessert), felt guilty about the rubbish she was unthinkingly putting into her body – abusing it, yes, abusing it

Excerpt 2

Bummi
did not foresee the long-term negative impact of her daughter
going to the famous university for rich people
especially when she returned home after her first term wailing that
she could not go back because she did not belong there
whereupon Bummi applied a tissue or two to her daughter's eyes and
cheeks and asked her outright and forthrightly, Carole, have I raised a
fighter or a quitter? You must return to the university and get your degree
by hook or by crook or I cannot vouch for the consequences of my actions
Bummi did not subsequently expect Carole to return home after
her second term speaking out of her nose like there was a sneeze
trapped up inside of it instead of using the powerful vibrations of her Nigerian
vocal power, all the while looking haughtily around their cosy little
flat as if it was now a fleapit
did she think her mama did not notice the external manifestations of
her internal mind? eh! eh!, you do not raise a child without becoming
an expert in the non-verbal signals they think you are too stupid to see
that first summer holiday Carole worked in Marks & Spencer in
Lewisham, not to start paying off her student debt like a responsible

adult, but to buy clothes from those expensive fashion shops called Oasis
and Zara, instead of getting bargains at New Look and Peacock
in her second year she barely came home at all and by her final year she was spending weekends and holidays at her friend Rosie's family manor in the countryside, which had more rooms than a housing estate, she said, it's simply divine, *Mother*, simply divine
(*Mother* – was she being ironical?)

Students are prompted to work on their understanding of the texts above and on the identification of the main translation challenges that will be posed by these excerpts. Once the potential difficulties are pinpointed, a discussion of the possible techniques and strategies ensues. Based on PACTE's (2001) classification of four types of translation problems and on Carreres et al.'s (2018, 27) preparatory activities methodology, the activity follows a discussion-based approach that aims to foster students' translation skills, to improve their command of Spanish and to raise their awareness of difference and diversity. The emphasis is put on translation both as communication and as learning and collaboration. The subsections that follow contain condensed versions of the exhaustive list of questions put forward by Carreres et al. (2018, 27). The questions posed to students followed the structure outlined in Table 8.1.

In class, after reading the selected excerpts, students were divided into small groups. Each group was comprised of students of different nationalities and mother tongues. Mediation techniques were used to bridge any linguistic, cultural or epistemological gaps among group members while fostering discussions on intersectionality. Students were asked to discuss the list of questions below by fine-tuning their complex language skills such as paraphrasing, summarising, defining, explaining, changing registers and so forth. As each group shared their answers with the rest of the class, the class was briefed on the novel's main themes and on Evaristo's intention to 'put as many Black British women into a single novel as possible because [she] was fed up with the fact [they] weren't really present in British literature and [she] knew for [them] to be present [they] had to write those stories [themselves]' (in Hall 2022). Indeed, all the main characters are Black and British, and White characters remain on the periphery and are not part of the main narrative. The 12th character, Morgan, identifies as non-binary. In spite of its 452 pages, this is a readable novel that is driven by a simple structure, composed of 12 character portraits divided equally among 4 chapters. Each chapter describes three characters (usually Black, British, female) who are interconnected.

Challenge	Resulting from
Linguistic	• Lexical choices • Morphosyntactic structures • Comprehension and/or reformulation
Textual	• Coherence • Cohesion • Thematic progression • Genre conventions • Author's style
Extralinguistic	• Subject knowledge • Cultural references and general knowledge of the source and target cultures
Pragmatic	• Lack of consideration of the context in which the translation is carried out • The target text not taking into account the translation's ultimate aims

Table 8.1 Types of translation challenges in source texts (Carreres et al. 2018)

Linguistic challenges

The linguistic questions below seek to develop students' contrastive awareness of the differences between English and Spanish, as well as their awareness of conventions linked to genre and text type and appreciation of the texts' stylistic features:

- What do Dominique and Bummi have in common? What makes them different?
- In which ways are their voices different?
- What does the first excerpt tell us about Dominique as a character? How do you envision her future relationship with Nzinga?
- How is London depicted in the first excerpt? And in the second excerpt?
- What is Bummi's relationship with her daughter Carole like?
- Why does Bummi feel alienated from her daughter?
- In your translation, in which instances should the different past tenses (*pretérito imperfecto* or *pretérito perfecto simple*) be used?

In the class discussion, it was explained to students that this is a choral novel that follows the lives and struggles of 12 characters. Besides Dominique and Bummi, there are a further nine characters who identify as women and a non-binary character.

As can be noted in an initial reading of the excerpts, the differences between Dominique and Bummi highlight the novel's polyphonic qualities. Although the action spans different decades, geographical spaces and contexts, what characters have in common above all are their experiences of struggle and resilience. All the characters are interconnected for different reasons, be it friendship, love, family, mentorship, solidarity or their opinions. The combination of the universality of the novel's main themes and the specific focus on Great Britain makes mediation a particularly useful vehicle to enhance understanding among those students who do not yet have complete proficiency in English or Spanish, or a full understanding of British culture, history and societal norms. Likewise, Dominique and Bummi, just like the other protagonists in the novel, are complex, rich characters, and as Bucknell (2019) explains, 'none of these characters supports all Black womanhood, or Black personhood; there are always some identities they will not stand for, or – because they are figures in a novel – stand in for'. The insertion of such characters supports Kramsch and Kramsch's (2000) view of literature in the language classroom as a means of providing students with the chance to reflect on their personal viewpoints and learn about others and different worldviews, whilst considering their own use of language.

Textual challenges

The questions below prompt students to work on their close-reading skills and textual analysis:

- Are the excerpts written in a conventional style? Which features support your opinion? Is it important to maintain this style in your translation?
- How is the use of capital letters incorporated? How is punctuation used?
- How are dialogues inserted in the texts?
- How are direct and indirect speech combined?

Students tended to remark upon the novel's unconventional style. Full stops are not used; instead, line breaks dictate rhythm and beat in a more poetic fashion. This fusion fiction utilises line breaks to convey difficult, painful experiences, direct and indirect speech, run-on sentences, and streams of consciousness, and has been one of the novel's most praised artefacts (Alam 2019; Rhodes 2019). This style not only succeeds in tackling societal concerns in Evaristo's fiction, but also possesses accessible, inclusive qualities, as Evaristo (2021, 143) has remarked:

> I have also discovered that the decision to remove aspects of traditional punctuation can have the effect of changing the reader's experience, as people have informed me, making it more quickly immersive. A dyslexic reader told me that she found herself whizzing through the novel because the absence of orthodox punctuation meant she wasn't tripped up by it as she went along.

In fact, both Dominique and Bummi are characters that have just arrived in the literary canon. Dominique is a Black lesbian woman who, after meeting Nzinga, ceases to be a carefree, social, professionally successful woman and ends up becoming a victim of domestic violence and a vulnerable shell of her old self. Bummi is a Nigerian immigrant who, in spite of her high level of education, accepts low-paid, precarious cleaning jobs in London in order to support her family and put her daughter Carole through school and university. Proud Bummi is flabbergasted when Carole's academic and social success comes at the price of her leaving her Black heritage behind. The inclusion of these characters not only allows Evaristo to tackle key societal concerns in her fiction, but also provides language students – especially those belonging to ethnic minorities and the LGBTQI+ community – with the opportunity to be mirrored in the public sphere of literature. As explained by Kondo (2019):

> Identities are formed by watching sports, going to the theatre, watching TV and YouTube; by playing videogames, dancing and listening to music. Those are more than just forms of entertainment, they stage 'visions of possibility' for what and who we can become. Because marginalized populations have fewer role models in the workplace and society in general, we need more expansive and generous visions of possibility that tell stories of people from different races, genders, sexualities, classes, abilities, cultures. Everyone should have the opportunity to be recognized as fully human.

In the case of Dominique, a Black lesbian female scriptwriter, we are offering our students a peek into a worldview that is different from accounts in mainstream, contemporary, patriarchal, racialised and heteronormative societies. Students emerge from these excerpts with a richer understanding of the range of experiences that Black and Brown women have in the UK. Whilst the excerpts tackle current social issues as grave as psychological abuse, gender, sexuality, cultural origin, immigration, belonging and elitism, the complex approach with which they are handled allows for a variety of interpretive experiences and makes in-class discussion particularly rich. In this sense, Gray (2021) argues the case for the use of well-chosen literary texts as a vehicle for fighting the erasure of LGBTQI+ identities and themes in the language classroom. Through this inclusion, LGBTQI+ students can be given important opportunities for recognition and identification, whereas those students who are not part of the LGBTQI+ community are offered the chance to come to comprehend those who are. As Gray (2021, 143) posits:

> From the point of LGBTQI+ students, whose erasure is a reminder of their marginalized status, opportunities for identification are particularly important, as it is through identification that we (partly) construct identities and become culturally intelligible to ourselves and others [...] in addition to providing LGBTQI+ students with opportunities for identification through self-recognition, literary texts have the potential to play a key role in enabling non-LGBTQI+ students to see the world through different eyes, enlisting their empathy and capacity for Other-recognition.

Extralinguistic and pragmatic challenges

On the one hand, the questions below prompt students to work on extralinguistic problems:

- Which elements from the original text highlight intersectionality and should be maintained in your translation?
- Which cultural references can be challenging to translate, and why?

On the other hand, the questions below prompt students to work on pragmatic problems:

- How is humour used to introduce important social issues in the two chapters?
- What do Nzinga's outfit, accessories, hairstyle and belongings tell us about her?

- What is the significance of the way in which Dominique's last words echo Nzinga's comment?
- Bummi is shocked to hear Carole call her *Mother*. What are the implications of using this appellative? How can it be accurately translated into Spanish?

The two categories above are aimed at fostering students' pragmatic and intercultural competences. The selected excerpts raise issues of culture, race, sex, culture, social class, physical ability, sexuality and education that go beyond gender. Students are encouraged to work collaboratively, with both their tutor and their peers, to fully understand the texts in order to achieve a translation that enhances intersectionality. Humour is utilised as comic relief to introduce difficult, controversial social issues; in-class discussion of these issues also broadens our students' understanding of difference, especially of Otherness and Blackness as opposed to normalness and Whiteness. There is notable diversity in today's students at UCL, in terms of native language, background, nationality and culture. Therefore, taking into account that 'humour in its various forms – joke, wordplay, is significantly defined by culture and language' (Kovács 2020), the translation of humour is a complex task, requiring mediation between different groups of students if they are to provide well-rounded answers to these sets of questions.

In spite of having graduated from secondary school with excellent grades, Carole, just like so many other BAME-BIPOC students in Great Britain, experiences an intense lack of belonging during her first term at university (see Gabriel and Tate 2017; Arday et al. 2022). She is at serious risk of dropping out, so she refuses to engage with her cultural and racial heritage in order to escape the BAME awarding gap that threatens to destroy her chance to escape a life of poverty and precarity. Her mother, Bummi, takes her daughter's immersion into the white, elitist, privileged society of the university as a personal affront. As for Dominique, her romance with Nzinga will soon turn sour when – as already hinted at in the first excerpt – the latter reveals herself to be a controlling, emotionally abusive narcissist. Whilst the eradication of domestic violence occupies a predominant place in mainstream feminist agendas, and it impacts the lives of all women regardless of background, race, culture, religion, sexuality or class, not all survivors receive the same level of help or recognition. This is because stereotypes can create obstacles to assistance, which makes some groups more prone to suffering domestic violence (Simpson and Helfrich 2014). For instance, 44 per cent of lesbian women experience intimate partner violence, compared to 35 per cent of heterosexual women (HRC Foundation 2010). Furthermore, it is Black LGBTQI+ victims who are more likely to suffer physical intimate partner violence (NCADV 2018). Given that the domestic violence awareness movement has focused primarily on heterosexual relationships, it is hardly surprising that the literary inclusion of LGBTQI+ characters who are survivors of intimate partner violence is still scarce. Through the translation of these excerpts, our students develop essential linguistic skills, such as reading comprehension, textual and syntactic analysis, team collaboration and intercultural and pragmatic competence. Furthermore, the overarching idea is that language and translation educators can work on key social-emotional skills such as empathy, integrity and openness while educating students on healthy relationships and acting as allies and EDI advocators.

Sample source text analysis

This chapter has argued that literary texts can be carefully selected in the translation classroom to capitalise on a plurality of life experiences and worldviews. In particular, intersectionality can help our students to not only enhance their translation skills and improve their command of a foreign language (in this case, Spanish) but also embrace EDI values, appreciate difference and develop emotional skills. Taking two excerpts from Black British novelist and scholar Bernardine Evaristo's *Girl, Woman, Other* (2019) as a case study, a pre-translation exercise, to be carried out by small, heterogeneously assigned groups of students, has been proposed. The exercise aims to make students reflect on four main categories of translation challenges that they are likely to encounter. For practical purposes, and as practised in my lessons, the excerpts are reproduced again below, with the textual elements that are more likely to pose challenges for students highlighted in different colours according to the category of problem they represent. The colours have been assigned as follows:

- Linguistic problems
- Textual problems
- Extralinguistic problems
- Pragmatic problems

Excerpt 1

DOMINIQUE

Dominique came across Nzinga at Victoria station in the rush hour as she was being knocked down by the steamrollering effect of London's ruthless commuters determined to catch their trains at all costs

her bag fell open and everything fell out: passport, A–Z, Rough Guide to London, hemp purse, tampons, Zenith E camera, Palmer's hand cream, evil eye charm, ivory-handled hunting knife

Nzinga was profusely grateful when a passing Dominique approached to help, the pair of them scrambling about on the station

floor gathering up her belongings

when that was done, and Nzinga was once more upright and composed, Dominique found herself in front of an extraordinary vision

the woman was statuesque, her skin glowed, her robes flowed, her features were sculptural, lips fulsome, thin ropes of dreadlocks fell freely down to her hips, silver amulets and bright beads sewn into them

Dominique had never seen anyone like her before, offered to buy her coffee, confident she'd say yes because lesbians, and she suspected this one was, usually did

they sat opposite each other in the station café as Nzinga sipped on a glass of hot water with a slice of lemon in it, the only hot drink she allowed to pass her lips, she said, I don't abuse my body

meanwhile

Dominique, drinking a cup of granulated coffee into which she'd dissolved two sugars and was dunking a succession of digestive biscuits (a packet of Maltesers at the side for dessert), felt guilty about the rubbish she was unthinkingly putting into her body – abusing it, yes, abusing it

Excerpt 2

Bummi

did not foresee the long-term negative impact of her daughter going to the famous university for rich people

especially when she returned home after her first term wailing that she could not go back because she did not belong there

whereupon Bummi applied a tissue or two to her daughter's eyes and

cheeks and asked her outright and forthrightly, Carole, have I
raised a
fighter or a quitter? You must return to the university and get your
degree
by hook or by crook or I cannot vouch for the consequences of my
actions
Bummi did not subsequently expect Carole to return home after
her second term speaking out of her nose like there was a sneeze
trapped up inside of it instead of using the powerful vibrations of
her Nigerian
vocal power, all the while looking haughtily around their cosy little
flat as if it was now a fleapit
did she think her mama did not notice the external manifestations of
her internal mind? eh! eh!, you do not raise a child without
becoming
an expert in the non-verbal signals they think you are too stupid
to see
that first summer holiday Carole worked in Marks & Spencer in
Lewisham, not to start paying off her student debt like a responsible
adult, but to buy clothes from those expensive fashion shops
called Oasis
and Zara, instead of getting bargains at New Look and Peacock
in her second year she barely came home at all and by her final
year she was spending weekends and holidays at her friend Rosie's
family manor in the countryside, which had more rooms than a housing state, she said, it's simply divine, Mother, simply divine
(*Mother* – was she being ironical?)

Conclusion

To conclude, the value of this type of preparatory exercise is twofold. First, it promotes classroom discussion, as part of a pre-translation analysis, on the micro-politics and everyday sexism and misogyny described in the novel. That is to say that students and tutors are provided with the means to foster gender equality, acknowledge gender diversity and empower minorities through peer discussions. Secondly, the novel's unconventional, experimental style is a form of protest against our contemporary patriarchal, racialised society. The instances of different language conventions – or lack thereof – used to challenge normative writing include erratic line breaks, direct and indirect speech mix-ups with little punctuation, and run-on sentences, among other features. The author's peculiar representation of her stream of consciousness is ever-present throughout the novel, and so is her mastery of a myriad of cultural and ideological terms, which she also uses to tackle societal concerns in her fiction. Through mediation, students develop a contrastive awareness of the differences between English and Spanish, while improving their awareness of textual conventions, fine-tuning their stylistic awareness, fostering their pragmatic and intercultural competence, practising their reading skills, developing their creativity and collaborating with their peers. Finally, and most importantly, I would like to highlight that it is the educator's social responsibility to create opportunities for students to identify EDI issues and expand their own understanding of the world through intersectional discourses. The material included in this chapter is an example of activities that educators can create to achieve this goal.

References

Alam, Rumaan. 2019. 'Bernardine Evaristo's *Girl, Woman, Other* deserves all the prizes', *New Republic,* 5 November. Accessed 3 October 2023. https://newrepublic.com/article/155596/bernardine-evaristos-girl-woman-deserves-prizes.

Arday, Jason, Charlotte Branchu, and Vikki Boliver. 2022. 'What do we know about Black and Minority Ethnic (BAME) participation in UK higher education?', *Social Policy and Society* 21, no. 1: 12–25. https://doi.org/10.1017/S1474746421000579.

Arday, Jason, and Heidi Safia Mirza. 2018. *Dismantling Race in Higher Education: Racism, whiteness and decolonising the academy*. London: Palgrave Macmillan.

Ayachia, Houda. 2018. 'The revival of translation as a fifth skill in the foreign language classroom: A review of literature', *AWEJ for Translation and Literary Studies* 2, no. 2: 187–98.

Baker, Philippa. 2006. 'Jumping the language barrier: The "fifth skill"', *English Teaching Matters* 7, no. 1: 22–24.

Banks, James A. 2020. *Diversity, Transformative Knowledge, and Civic Education: Selected essays*. London: Routledge.

Begum, Neema, and Rima Saini. 2019. 'Decolonising the curriculum', *Political Studies Review* 17, no. 2: 196–201. https://doi.org/10.1177/1478929918808459.

Bhambra, Gurminder, Dalia Gebrial, and Kerem Nişancıoğlu. 2018. *Decolonising the University*. London: Pluto Press.

Bucknell, Claire. 2019. 'Fusion fiction', *London Review of Books* 41, no. 20, 24 October. Accessed 25 March 2024. https://www.lrb.co.uk/the-paper/v41/n20/clare-bucknell/fusion-fiction.

Burke, Penny Jane, Anna Bennett, Cathy Burgess, Kim Gray, and Erica Southgate. 2016. *Capability, Belonging and Equity in Higher Education: Developing inclusive approaches*. [Report]. Newcastle: University of Newcastle, Australia.

Carreres, Ángeles, María Noriega-Sánchez, and Carme Calduch. 2018. *Mundos en palabras: Learning advanced Spanish through translation*. London: Routledge.

Castro, Olga, and Emek Ergun, eds. 2017. *Feminist Translation Studies: Local and transnational perspectives*. London: Routledge.

Council of Europe. 2001. *Common European Framework of Reference for Languages: Learning, teaching, assessment*. Strasbourg: Council of Europe.

Council of Europe. 2018. *Common European Framework of Reference for Languages: Learning, teaching, assessment. Companion volume with new descriptors*. Strasbourg: Council of Europe.

Crenshaw, Kimberlé. 1989. 'Demarginalizing the intersection of race and sex: A black feminist critique of antidiscrimination doctrine, feminist theory and antiracist politics', *University of Chicago Legal Forum*, 1989, 1: #8. Accessed 25 March 2024. http://chicagounbound.uchicago.edu/uclf/vol1989/iss1/8.

Eddo-Lodge, Reni. 2018. *Why I'm No Longer Talking to White People About Race*. London: Bloomsbury.

Evaristo, Bernardine. 2019. *Girl, Woman, Other*. London: Penguin.

Evaristo, Bernardine. 2021. *Manifesto: On never giving up*. London: Penguin.

Flood, Alison. 2019. 'Bernardine Evaristo doubles lifetime sales in five days after joint Booker win', *The Guardian*, 22 October. Accessed 3 October 2023. https://www.theguardian.com/books/2019/oct/22/bernardine-evaristo-doubles-lifetime-sales-in-five-days-after-joint-booker-win.

Gabriel, Deborah, and Shirley Anne Tate. 2017. *Inside the Ivory Tower: Narratives of women of colour surviving and thriving in British academia*. London: Trentham Books.

Gaspar, Neida Ferreira. 2009, 'Translation as a fifth skill in EFL classes at secondary school level'. In *Translation in Second Language Learning and Teaching*, edited by Arnd Witte, Theo Harden, and Alessandra Ramos de Oliveira Harden, 173–80. Bern: Peter Lang.

Gay, Roxane. 2014. *Bad Feminist: Essays*. New York: Harper Perennial.

Gould, Rebecca, and Kayvan Tahmasebian, eds. 2020. *The Routledge Handbook of Translation and Activism*. London: Routledge. https://doi.org/10.4324/9781315149660.

Gray, John. 2021. 'Addressing LGBTQ erasure through literature in the ELT classroom', *ELT Journal* 75, no. 2: 142–51. https://doi.org/10.1093/elt/ccaa079.

Halawah, Ibtesam. 2006. 'The impact of student–faculty informal interpersonal relationships on intellectual and personal development', *College Student Journal* 40, no. 3: 670–8.

Hall, Rachel. 2022. 'Bernardine Evaristo fears publishers may lose interest in Black authors', *The Guardian*, 4 June. Accessed 3 October 2023. https://www.theguardian.com/books/2022/jun/04/bernardine-evaristo-fears-publishers-may-lose-interest-in-black-authors.

HRC Foundation. 2010. 'Understanding intimate partner violence in the LGBTQ+ community'. Human Rights Campaign. Accessed 10 April 2024. https://www.hrc.org/resources/understanding-intimate-partner-violence-in-the-lgbtq-community.

Icaza, Rosalba, and Sara de Jong. 2019. 'Introduction: Decolonization and feminisms in global teaching and learning: A radical space of possibility'. In *Decolonization and Feminisms in Global Teaching and Learning*, edited by Sara de Jong, Rosalba Icaza, and Olivia Rutazibwa, xv–xxxiv. New York: Routledge.

Kondo, Dorinne. 2018. *World-Making: Race, performance and the work of creativity*. Durham, NC: Duke University Press.

Kondo, Dorinne. 2019. 'Oscars 2019: Beyond the stats, why diversity matters', The Conversation, 21 February. Accessed 20 April 2024. https://theconversation.com/oscars-2019-beyond-the-stats-why-diversity-matters-111943.

Kovács, Gabriella. 2020. 'Translating humour: A didactic perspective', *Acta Universitatis Sapientiae, Philologica* 12, no. 2: 68–83. https://doi.org/10.2478/ausp-2020-0013.

Kramsch, Claire, and Olivier Kramsch. 2000. 'The avatars of literature in language study', *Modern Language Journal* 84, no. 4: 553–73. https://doi.org/10.1111/0026-7902.00087.

Leonardi, Vanessa. 2010. *The Role of Pedagogical Translation in Second Language Acquisition: From theory to practice*. Bern: Peter Lang.

Mendes, Ana, and Lisa Lau. 2022. 'Wither the plurality of decolonising the curriculum? Safe spaces and identitarian politics in the arts and humanities classroom', *Arts and Humanities in Higher Education* 21, no. 3: 223–39. https://doi.org/10.1177/14740222221100711.

Muldoon, James. 2019. 'Academics: It's time to get behind decolonising the curriculum', *The Guardian*, 20 March. Accessed 3 October 2023. https://www.theguardian.com/education/2019/mar/20/academics-its-time-to-get-behind-decolonising-the-curriculum.

Naga, Noor, and Robert McGill. 2018. 'Negotiating cultural difference in creative writing workshops, close reading translations and interpretive diversity', *Pedagogy: Critical Approaches to Teaching Literature, Language, Composition, and Culture* 18, no. 1: 69–86. https://doi.org/10.1215/15314200-4216946.

Naimushin, Boris. 2002. 'Translation in foreign language teaching: The fifth skill', *Modern English Teacher* 11, no. 4: 46–9.

NCADV (National Coalition Against Domestic Violence). 2018. Domestic violence and the LGBTQ community'. Blog, 6 June. Accessed 10 April 2024. https://ncadv.org/blog/posts/domestic-violence-and-the-lgbtq-community.

North, Brian, and Enrica Piccardo. 2016. 'Developing illustrative descriptors of aspects of mediation for the Common European Framework of Reference (CEFR): A Council of Europe Project', *Language Teaching* 49, no. 3: 1–5.
Oaknín, Mazal. 2019. 'Nuevos recursos en la enseñanza de lenguas y de traducción'. In *Translation and Language Teaching: Pedagogical translation and foreign language education*, edited by Mazal Oaknín and Azahara Veroz González. [Video]. Córdoba: UCOPress.
PACTE [Allison Beeby, Laura Berenguer, Doris Ensinger, Olivia Fox, Amparo Hurtado Albir, Nicole Martínez Melis, Wilhem Neunzig, Mariana Orozco, and Marisa Presas]. 2001. 'La competencia traductora y su adquisición', *Quadernos* 6: 39–45.
Rhodes, Emily. 2019. '*Girl, Woman, Other* by Bernardine Evaristo: A celebration of soul sisters', *Financial Times*, 17 May. Accessed 3 October 2023. https://www.ft.com/content/8b808cac-7587-11e9-b0ec-7dff87b9a4a2.
Saad, Layla. 2020. *Me and White Supremacy*. London: Hachette.
Schechter, Laura. 2018. '"On the outside facing the wooded ridge": Close reading translations and interpretive diversity', *Pedagogy: Critical Approaches to Teaching Literature, Language, Composition, and Culture* 18, no. 1: 51–68. https://doi.org/10.1215/15314200-4216930.
Shay, Suellen. 2016. 'Decolonising the curriculum: It's time for a strategy', The Conversation, 13 June. Accessed 3 October 2023. https://theconversation.com/decolonising-the-curriculum-its-time-for-a-strategy-60598.
Simpson, Emily Katherynn, and Christine A. Helfrich. 2014. 'Oppression and barriers to service for black, lesbian survivors of intimate partner violence', *Journal of Gay and Lesbian Social Services* 26, no 4: 441–65. https://doi.org/10.1080/10538720.2014.951816.
Strauss, Linda C., and Fredericks Volkwein. 2004. 'Predictors of student commitment at two-year and four- year institutions', *The Journal of Higher Education* 75, no. 2: 203–27.
Tate, Shirley Anne. 2019. 'Tackling the "BPOC" attainment gap in UK universities', TEDTalk [Video], 18 March. Accessed 3 October 2023. www.youtube.com/watch?v=UPMuuJrfawQ.
Trovato, Giuseppe. 2016. *Mediación lingüística y enseñanza de Español/LE: cuadernos de didáctica del Español/LE*. Madrid: Arco/Libros.
UCL. n.d. 'Liberating the curriculum'. Accessed 26 March 2024. https://www.ucl.ac.uk/teaching-learning/research-based-education/liberating-curriculum.
UCL. 2024. 'Key statistics'. Accessed 26 March 2024. https://www.ucl.ac.uk/about/what/key-statistics#student-numbers.
Zepke, Nick, and Linda Leach. 2010. 'Improving student engagement: Ten proposals for action', *Active Learning in Higher Education* 11, no. 3: 167–77.

9

Queer challenges and affordances of literary translation in the foreign language classroom

John Gray

Introduction

The title of this chapter raises three issues that have been considered taboo in many foreign language classrooms over several decades. These are the representation of non-normative sexualities and gender identities in pedagogical materials, the use of literary texts as linguistic content (particularly in commercial language teaching settings) and the incorporation of translation as a legitimate language learning activity. That said, things are beginning to change, particularly with regard to the latter (see Carreres et al. 2021), as translation comes to be seen as the 'fifth language skill' (Ayachia 2018). In exploring these issues together, the chapter makes the case for translation activities linked to the reading of literary texts as a way of addressing ongoing LGBTQI+ invisibility in language teaching materials. I do so specifically with regard to Anglo-American English language teaching (ELT), which has been traditionally averse to bilingual approaches, although much of what I have to say applies to the teaching of modern foreign languages in general.

Before continuing, it is important to state that many categories of person, social groups, identities, events, injustices and histories are also rendered invisible in the curriculum, and that the approach that I am advocating here, specifically with regard to the taboo on LGBTQI+ representation, could also be applied to them. After dealing with the three specific taboos I have chosen to address, I move on to look specifically at queer aspects of translation (Baer and Kaindl 2017) and the challenges and affordances of translating literary texts in the foreign language classroom. By way of example, I do this with reference to translating elements of two English-language texts into Spanish and French, given that many Spanish-speaking and French-speaking language learners are students of English. The texts are Jarlath Gregory's (2021) novel *What Love Looks Like*, which contains what might be described as explicitly queer content, and Edward Lear's (1867) poem 'The Owl and the Pussy-Cat', whose content is more implicitly queer. With regard to the first of these, explicitly queer refers to content that features openly LGBTQI+ characters and addresses aspects of LGBTQI+ experience, such as coming out, prejudice and insult. Implicitly queer content, on the other hand, makes no reference to gender and sexual minorities, but conveys ideas about the legitimacy of non-normative ways of being (Gray 2021). The reason behind the choice of two such different texts is that although working with overtly queer content is possible for teachers in many settings, it is not an option for all. However, I argue that this need not preclude teachers who wish to address issues of gender and sexual diversity from doing potentially useful work with their students.

Overall, the chapter makes the case for an *educational* view of foreign language teaching in which students are sensitised to the linguistic choices available for encoding the complexities of the social world with regard to gender and sexual diversity. Such a view is contrary to the currently dominant *instrumental* view, in which foreign languages are narrowly conceptualised as skills to be acquired for deployment in the neoliberal marketplace (Park 2016).

The sexual and gender diversity taboo

It is worth commenting on terminology at the outset. In many cases, the word 'queer' is used in the literature as a blanket term for the diverse forms of sexual orientation and gender identity contained in the acronym LGBTQI+. But 'queer' is also much more than that and comes with its own evolving history. Originally an insult, queer was reappropriated by gay people in the 1990s against the backdrop of the AIDS crisis. At the time, Halperin (1995, 62) explained that queer is 'by definition *whatever* is at odds with the normal, the legitimate, the dominant' and demarcates 'not a positivity but a positionality vis-à-vis the normative – a positionality that is not restricted to lesbians and gay men but is in fact available to anyone who is or feels marginalized by her or his sexual practices'. Queer theory (Warner 1993), as it came to be known, initially focused on critiquing heteronormativity but quickly evolved to include a focus on homonormativity (the promotion of sexual diversity from an apolitical assimilationist stance in which individualism, domesticity and consumerism are foregrounded) and cisnormativity (understood as adherence to an essentialist sex/gender binary as a biologically determined human norm). Today queer theory may be said to incorporate all of these critiques as well as the ways in which they intersect with critiques of other types of oppression (for instance racism, colonialism and discrimination against migrants) (see Puar 2007; Rao 2020). So although 'queer' can be used as a blanket term, it also seeks to convey a political stance that aims to trouble the (sexual and gender) status quo as a well as a sense of the provisionality of all labelling. I use the term 'queer' in both these senses in this chapter.

Regardless of what concerned educational institutions and individual teachers are able to do in some settings (Moore 2016), the erasure of non-normative sexualities and gender diversity in ELT is to a large extent established and maintained by the Anglo-American ELT publishing industry (Gray 2010, 2013). While products such as textbooks are assiduous in representing women and men as equal (particularly in the workplace), great care is taken to ensure that sexual and gender minorities are not included when materials are being designed for global consumption. Profit margins – rather than any educational remit – militate against the production of differentiated materials with regard to sexual and gender norms, which results in the perceived requirements of socially conservative markets determining the form all textbooks take. Paradoxically, this erasure takes place against the backdrop of protective legislation introduced in many countries from the late twentieth century onwards, including the granting of specific rights to LGBTQI+ people (for instance forms of civil partnership and same-sex marriage, the right to adopt children or the rights of transgender people to obtain new documentation in line with their gender identification). However, as a UNESCO (2016) global report speculates, instances of violence in educational settings based on sexual orientation and gender identity/expression might be reduced if teacher education programmes prepared teachers to address these issues explicitly, and if the pedagogical materials they were required to use reflected LGBTQI+ diversity more comprehensively.

At the same time, it needs to be stated that the aforementioned wave of legislative reform is currently being met in some countries by a conservative backlash against so-called 'gender ideology' (Borba 2022). This has been described as 'a trope to anathematize feminist and LGBTQIA+ agendas and to uphold an essentialist (rather than social and political) view of sexual orders' (Borba 2022, 59). In such a scenario it is highly unlikely that the publishing practices of Anglo-American ELT will change in the short term. Teachers who wish to address such taboos in their classes are forced to consider alternatives to the crop of textbooks currently on offer. One option is to introduce literary texts that address diversity (Gray 2021), but here too another taboo rears its head – that of literature in the language classroom.

The literature taboo

From the days of the Reform Movement in the late nineteenth century, language has been understood largely as speech, rather than as writing. This view, which has underpinned the waves of methods for teaching foreign languages since then (for instance the direct method and audiolingualism), has largely eschewed the use of literature, increasingly understood as a specialised form of writing, far removed from the needs of everyday speakers. The arrival of communicative language teaching (CLT) in the 1970s–1980s is particularly significant in this regard. As an approach to teaching language, it was profoundly influenced by Hymes's (1972) view that using a language was not solely a matter of linguistic competence, but also one of communicative competence. This was understood as knowing 'when to speak, when not, and as to what to talk about with whom, when, where, in what manner' (Hymes 1972, 277) – thus underlining again the primacy of language as speech. Such a perspective also resonated with the Council of Europe's advocacy of a functional-notional syllabus (Wilkins 1976) in which the focus was on using language in concrete situations to fulfil various functions such as inquiring or inviting, and to talk about notions such as duration, distance and time. In terms of an approach to teaching and in terms of syllabus and curriculum these two would become powerful global exports – on the one hand, the functional-notional syllabus evolved into the widely disseminated *Common European Framework of Reference for Languages* (CEFR) published by the Council of Europe (2001, 2018), while CLT, and contemporary offshoots such as task-based learning, are promoted globally by Anglo-American ELT as the most effective and up-to-date ways to teach foreign languages.

That said, literature did not entirely disappear from the foreign language classroom. A small group of scholars continued to make the case for literature as a rich source of so-called authentic material, capable of engaging language learners imaginatively in ways that standard textbooks could not (Lazar 1993; Koutsompou 2015; Paran and Robinson 2016). These writers also took the view that the use of literature in foreign language teaching was not incompatible with a broadly communicative methodology. Despite the strength of their case, there is no denying that literature has been significantly sidelined by the CLT movement, as well as by the way in which foreign languages came to be understood from the perspective of contemporary neoliberal capitalism. In this view, languages – and in particular global languages such as English – are key skills that can be added to the jobseeker's toolkit. Not only are individual languages seen as skills in themselves, they can also be used in the acquisition of additional skills (Shin 2016). At the same time, CLT can also be said to have impacted on foreign language teaching in another significant way. As an inheritor of the Reform Movement's privileging of language as speech, CLT also inherited its repudiation of (grammar) translation as a language learning activity. It is to this aspect that I turn in the following section.

The translation taboo

Pennycook (2019, 175) has argued, plausibly, that 'one of the great crimes of the global hegemony of communicative language teaching' is the way in which it served to 'promote a monolingual, native-speaker norm-based, and educationally shallow version of English'. The prejudice against the mother tongue(s) in the second-language classroom is long established and stems from the 'direct method' (Howatt 1984), which emerged from the Reform Movement. This prejudice is, as Cook (2007) astutely points out, not unrelated to the growth of late-nineteenth-century nationalist political ideology. The direct method aimed to bypass the L1 where possible, keeping the focus firmly on the L2. Translation was frowned on, as it brought the L1 openly into the foreground and was, additionally, associated with writing. From the middle of the twentieth century onward the burgeoning field of second-language acquisition (SLA) – which, it could be argued, purports to provide a key element in the knowledge base of foreign language teaching – has tended to view the L1 as a source of interference. Its research agenda has also, as Cook (2007) notes, ignored the role that translation might play in instructed second-language learning. This is something of a paradox, because although monolingual CLT has been marketed very effectively globally, it never succeeded in completely eradicating pedagogical practices that entailed translation, and many successful language learners have been educated in settings where it remains a feature.

Today, monolingual approaches to foreign language teaching are increasingly being challenged (North and Piccardo 2017). The current case for decolonising the curriculum (Macedo 2019) is opposed to monolingualism in the foreign language classroom and generally subscribes to the arguments put forward by those who advocate a pedagogy informed by translanguaging as a means of redress (García et al. 2021). From the translanguaging perspective, named languages are viewed as sociopolitical constructs and the language use of bi- and multilingual speakers is understood as a contextually qualified activity in which the deployment of named languages is characterised by a high degree of mutual porosity. García et al. (2021, 217) do not deny the existence of named languages – rather, their focus is on asserting the value of a pedagogy in which students are permitted to draw on the full range of their linguistic repertoires in their learning. This is seen by those working in this paradigm as making sense from cognitive, educational and social justice perspectives. Such a view of language (again very much focused on speaking) might seem to be initially incompatible with translation, which is concerned predominantly with named languages and with written text. However, Baynham and Lee (2019, 14) argue that this need not be the case, because

> [t]ranslation, regardless of its manifest form, is an activity driven by an aspiration to reach a terminus point (A→B) and to culminate in some material outcome; yet it is also the accruement of a series of intercultural moments in time. Within each moment dwells a translanguaging space where languages (as well as language varieties, registers, discourses, and modalities) converge in temporal suspension and negotiate within a whirlpool of semiotic tension – a repertoire. […] Translation can therefore be seen as embedded within a translanguaging space, at the same time as it is composed of successive translanguaging moments.

From this perspective, classroom activities in which students make decisions about the necessarily complex issue (if not the impossibility) of deciding on L1–L2 equivalences (Krein-Kühle 2014) could easily be undertaken within a translanguaging orientation to talk about translation. However, regardless of one's position on translanguaging as a specific pedagogical approach, the fact that translation (viewed as falling within a translanguaging space or not) is openly undertaken in the foreign language classroom as a legitimate learning activity in itself can be seen as providing (at least the basis for) a decolonising challenge to the monolingual orthodoxy associated with CLT (Macedo 2019). So what then of queer perspectives on translation and the translation of literary texts in the foreign language classroom? It is to this that I now turn.

Queer perspectives on literary translation

Baer and Kaindl (2017) argue that the application of queer perspectives to translation studies entails two requirements. Firstly, there is the need to address specifically queer phenomena, by which they mean 'phenomena that are typically ignored, marginalized, or domesticated by the dominant regime(s) of knowledge/power' (Baer and Kaindl 2017, 3). Secondly, there is the need to do this 'queerly' – that is, by considering how 'the rendering of queer phenomena across languages and cultures [might] challenge our understanding of translation as theory and practice' (Baer and Kaindl 2017, 3). The second of these involves considerations of how translation itself might be queered and a recognition of its ideological nature and the active role of the translator as a (re)shaper or troubler of meanings. As Santaemilia (2015, 142) puts it:

> [t]ranslating sex(uality) tends to be an activity in which gender-related prejudices and configurations are routinely reproduced and projected. Through translation, social norms defining what is (im) moral or in(decent) are usually reinforced but may also – at least potentially – be challenged or defied. No translator is ever a neutral agent, but this is even more the case when dealing with sex-related language – when s/he needs to make decisions as to social attitudes or interdictions, to the existence (or absence) of (self-)censorship, political or ideological constraints, to economic or institutional pressures, and other factors.

From the perspective of the queer challenges and affordances of literary translation in the classroom, there are two points to bear in mind. On the one hand, addressing queer phenomena openly is already a troubling of classroom practice, given the kind of taboo mentioned above. It provides access to language and content that is normally withheld from students by textbook publishers, who tend to present a sanitised version of the language to be learnt. Addressing queer phenomena entails not only the specific language of sex and sexuality, but also (in many cases) the language of prejudice and insult. With regard to the centrality of the latter in queer experience, Eribon (2004, 15–16) argues:

> [I]t all begins with an insult. The insult that any gay man or lesbian can hear at any moment of his or her life, the sign of his or her social and psychological vulnerability. [...] One of the consequences of insult is to shape the relation one has to others and to the world and thereby to shape the personality, the subjectivity, the very being of the individual in question. [...] The insult lets me know that I am not like others, not normal. I am *queer*: strange, bizarre, sick, abnormal.

In addition, by providing an opportunity to discuss and critique translations of literary texts in which the focus is on queer content, language learners can be sensitised to the ideological nature of translation and the ways in which their own translations can engage with texts and (re)shape the meanings created by others. In this way, it could be argued that many of the problems identified by Pennycook (2019) can be dealt with, while at the same time addressing the ongoing issue of LGBTQI+ erasure and the ills that flow from that. As I have suggested elsewhere (Gray 2021), these ills include the denial of (much-needed) recognition of LGBTQI+ students as well as the perpetuation of ignorance among non-LGBTQI+ students about sexual and gender diversity more generally. My point is that queer inclusion is important for *all* students, providing recognition for those who are LGBTQI+ as well as educating those who are not about the complexity of human sexual orientation and gender identity.

In the following section, I turn to the first of the two literary texts, with some reflections on the issues raised and how they might be approached in the foreign language classroom.

Teaching scenario 1: *What Love Looks Like*

Jarlath Gregory is a young queer Irish novelist who writes mainly for older teenagers and young adults. In the author's note at the end of the novel, Gregory explains that with this book he wanted to write a narrative with a happy ending, but one in which some stories about modern Ireland were still not being told. 'Where' he asks, 'were the LGBTQ friendships groups and supportive parents? Where were the amateur drag queens and working-class kids? Where were the people of colour?' (Gregory 2021, 238) (cf. discussion of intersectionality in Chapter 8, this volume). This is the gap the novel seeks to fill. *What Love Looks Like* is set in modern Ireland, post the 2015 referendum in which the majority of people voted for equal marriage. With regard to second-language learners, it would be suitable for those at CEFR level B2 in terms of linguistic challenge.

The opening sets the tone for much of what follows: 'When Ireland voted to let gay people get married, my stepdad hugged me and said, "Your turn next, Ben! Get yourself a boyfriend. Make us proud"' (Gregory 2021, 7). Ben is the seventeen-year-old working-class boy at the centre of the story. He lives with his mother, who is divorced, his Jamaican stepfather and his younger mixed-race stepsister. Taking a year out between school and university, Ben spends most of his time with Soda, a twenty-something, mixed-race part-time drag artist, and Chelsea, his butch female best friend who comes out as a trans man towards the end of the novel. Post-referendum Ireland is not free from prejudice though. Racist graffiti appear on Dublin's streets, and profiles on gay dating sites contain items such as 'No fats, no femmes, no Asians' (Gregory 2021, 144) – and here too we find the recurring theme of queer insult, although (as will be seen below) the treatment of this is determinedly optimistic. The novel deals with Ben's quest for love and when we first meet him, he has just had a date with the handsome nineteen-year-old Peter. For all his manly attractiveness, it emerges over the course of the narrative that Peter is closeted. Moreover, it is his adherence to hegemonic masculinity (Connell 2005) that underpins his negative attitudes towards many of Ben's friends and aspects of the Dublin gay scene, where drag queens mix with leather men in bars and clubs. Much of the action deals with the difficulties Ben has with Peter and the events that lead to their eventual separation. In terms of using the novel in the language classroom, much of the advice that teachers are given with regard to extensive reading applies (Paran and Robinson 2016). Vocabulary needs are best addressed prior to reading, which can be done as part of homework, and then opportunities can be made available in class to discuss comprehension and student responses.

In terms of translation and its specific challenges and affordances, I suggest that certain sections relating to queer phenomena are best undertaken as part of classroom activities in which students can discuss linguistic choices. At the time of writing, the novel has not been translated. However, the translations provided by Google Translate (GT) can be used as the basis for discussion. GT uses neural machine translation engines (González-Pastor 2021) that endeavour to provide natural-sounding language. However, such engines, while producing translations in language that is grammatically well formed, can fail to capture textual implicature, idiomaticity and lexical innovations. As will be seen, GT provides translations that are uneven – at times they are highly appropriate, and at others they are too literal to capture the sense of the original. However, this unevenness is useful from a pedagogical perspective, as the GT versions can be problematised and students can then be asked to provide their own post-edited versions, based on their discussion and their own research. As Hu and Cadwell (2016) explain, post-editing within the translation industry has become widely adopted as a means of improving the quality of machine translation (see also Krings 2001; Koponen 2015; González-Pastor 2021). As well as being an important skill for second-language students to develop, it is particularly useful in terms of queer translation, as discussion about linguistic choices can draw attention to the ideological nature of language and of translation itself. In the following examples I consider the ways in which extracts from the novel have been rendered in Spanish and French in GT and the issues the translations raise.

After his first date with Peter, Ben is called 'faggot' by a passer-by in the street as he returns home. He reflects on this insult as follows, using the word 'faggot' four times and the word 'gay' once. I have highlighted in bold the key elements in the original and in the translations.

> See, here's the thing about the word **faggot**. First time someone calls you a **faggot**, you get upset because you feel like you did something wrong. After that, you learn to start hiding all **the things that make you a faggot**. And it's only later, when you find out that your real friends don't care how **gay** you are and that your family still loves you, that someone shouting '**faggot**' at you in the street doesn't hurt as much, and you can walk away with your head held high. It still stings though, no matter how many times you hear it. (Gregory 2021, 14)

GT provides the following versions:

> Mira, esto es lo que pasa con la palabra **maricón**. La primera vez que alguien te llama **maricón**, te enojas porque sientes que hiciste algo mal. Después de eso, aprendes a empezar a esconder todas **las cosas que te hacen marica**. Y es solo más tarde, cuando descubres que a tus verdaderos amigos no les importa lo **gay** que eres y que tu familia todavía te quiere, que alguien te grite '**maricón**' en la calle no duele tanto, y puedes marcharse con la frente en alto. Sin embargo, todavía duele, no importa cuántas veces lo escuches.
>
> Voyez, voici la chose à propos du mot **pédé**. La première fois que quelqu'un vous traite de **pédé**, vous vous énervez parce que vous avez l'impression d'avoir fait quelque chose de mal. Après cela, vous

> apprenez à commencer à cacher toutes **les choses qui font de vous un pédé**. Et ce n'est que plus tard, quand tu découvres que tes vrais amis s'en fichent de ton **homosexualité** et que ta famille t'aime toujours, que quelqu'un qui te crie « **tapette** » dans la rue ne te fait pas autant mal, et tu peux repartez la tête haute. Il pique toujours cependant, peu importe combien de fois vous l'entendez.

The Spanish translation proceeds on the basis that *maricón* is the most appropriate equivalent for 'faggot' in all cases with the exception of one. Although the fit between terms of abuse in different languages is never perfect, and dictionary definitions suggest that *maricón*, depending on the context of use, has broader coverage than 'faggot' (which is always a sexual insult), it is an appropriately strong choice with a primary meaning that is sexually pejorative. However, rendering the 'the things that make you a faggot' as '*las cosas que te hacen marica*' involves the use of a quasi-synonym (*marica*), which it could be argued changes the meaning somewhat. Although a pejorative sexual term (and one which is semantically linked to *maricón*), it could be argued that *marica* specifically connotes effeminacy in a way that *maricón* does not, and that it is more aligned with terms such as 'pansy' or 'nancy boy' in English. In similar vein with regard to the French translation, *pédé* is a strong insult, although it has been reappropriated in French in a way similar to the reappropriation of 'queer' in English. It carries no necessary connotation of effeminacy, whereas *tapette* (as with *marica* in the Spanish translation) implies precisely an effeminate man. Although a strongly pejorative term, this substitution can also be seen as extending the sense of 'faggot' in the original text in the direction of explicit effeminacy.

Also of interest is the French translation's rendition of 'your real friends don't care how gay you are' as '*tes vrais amis s'en fichent de ton homosexualité*'. The syntactical rearrangement apart, the use of the term *homosexualité* again raises the issue of how terms resonate in different languages. 'Homosexual/homosexuality' as alternatives for 'gay/gayness' in English are particularly meaningful, with the former terms having been ascribed originally to those who were same-sex attracted in a pathological sense, whereas the latter terms were claimed by the community itself at a particular historical moment when such pathologising was being rejected. This is not the case in French, where *homosexuel/homosexualité* are terms that are currently used by many members of the LGBTQI+ community. Although there *is* lexical borrowing from English in the French *gai* or *gay* and the Spanish *gay*, the GT French translation eschews *gai* or *gay*. This could usefully generate discussion about the implications of such choices, as well as the meanings that accrue to borrowings specifically from English (often viewed as problematic from the perspective of linguistic gatekeepers in France). A teacher could ask students why they think terms are borrowed from other languages and what meanings can be attached to such descriptive labels, especially when they are ascribed by non-group members or claimed by in-group members themselves.

With regard to prejudice, in this case within the LGBTQI+ community itself, the above-mentioned 'No fats, no femmes, no Asians' (Gregory 2021, 139) is rendered literally (and therefore problematically) in both GT translations as follows:

> Sin grasas, sin mujeres, sin asiáticos.
> Pas de graisses, pas de femmes, pas d'Asiatiques.

Here we see what happens when, as Pym (2011) suggests, technology imposes the paradigmatic on translation in a decontextualised way. Technology, according to Pym (2011, 2), 'disrupts linearity by imposing what Saussure called the paradigmatic axis of language – the metaphorically vertical dimension from which items are selected. The paradigmatic is where language is systemic and things start to slow down.' GT was unable to recognise 'fats' as a noun referring to fat people in this particular context, and in both translations (Spanish *grasas* and French *graisses*) selects terms that refer to food fats, when terms such as *gordos* (Spanish) and *gros* or *obèses* (French) would have been more accurate. Similarly, the French word *femmes* (meaning 'women'), which is used in English by LGBTQI+ people to refer to effeminate or camp gay men (and feminine lesbians as distinct from butch lesbians) is rendered as *mujeres* ('women') in Spanish and is not translated in the French version. Appropriate translations in Spanish and French might be *afeminados* and *efféminées* (effeminate types) respectively. The use of *sin* (meaning 'without' in Spanish) also fails to capture the nature of the message being conveyed and it could be argued that the substitution of *nada de* (literally 'nothing of') would have been more grammatically and stylistically appropriate. Thus, possible translations could be:

> Nada de gordos, nada de afeminados, nada de asiáticos.
> Pas de gros, pas d'efféminées, pas d'Asiatiques.

It is also worth pointing out that 'Asians' means different things in different geographical areas depending on migration patterns. Given that the prejudice on the online dating site is referred to by Soda, who has

East Asian heritage, it is likely that East Asians are being referred to here. Decisions about the most appropriate translations could also give rise to discussions about prejudice within the LGBTQI+ community (and in society more generally) with regard to the ways in which body types and gendered mannerisms and ways of speaking can articulate with racism in the social construction of attractiveness and sexual desirability.

Moving on then to terms and expressions associated with the body and LGBTQI+ experience, and the ways in which these are translated, the following extract is taken from a scene in the novel in which Chelsea challenges Peter about his dismissive attitude to Soda's drag act in a gay bar. Peter describes Soda's routine as 'total shit', and Chelsea accuses him of being a 'Neanderthal', his hyper-masculinity based on a fear of ever appearing feminine. Again, I have highlighted key terms in bold.

> Being a man isn't about **having the world's biggest dick**. And **acting like the world's biggest dick** doesn't make you a man. **It takes balls** for Soda to dress up and get on stage. Meanwhile, **you're not even out to your parents**. (Gregory 2021, 85)

GT renders this as follows:

> Ser hombre no se trata de **tener el pene más grande del mundo**. Y **actuar como el mayor idiota del mundo** no te convierte en un hombre. Soda **necesita pelotas** para vestirse y subir al escenario. Mientras tanto, **ni siquiera hablas con tus padres**.
>
> Être un homme, ce n'est pas **avoir la plus grosse bite du monde**. Et **agir comme le plus gros con du monde** ne fait pas de vous un homme. **Il faut des couilles** à Soda pour se déguiser et monter sur scène. Pendant ce temps, **vous n'êtes même pas sorti avec vos parents**.

Again, we see the problem posed by machine translation. Maintaining the semantic link between 'dick' as an informal term for 'penis' and 'acting like a dick' in the sense of behaving stupidly cannot be straightforwardly translated into either Spanish or French, thus necessitating a degree of ingenuity on the part of human translators and post-editors. In addition, a number of other issues also present themselves here. By avoiding an informal term in favour of *pene* ('penis'), the Spanish translation clearly departs from the tone of the original. It could be argued that *polla* ('dick' or 'cock') would be a more appropriate translation. Similarly, the choice of *idiota* ('idiot') for 'dick' fails to retain the specifically derogatory and vulgar sense of the original insult. It could be argued that *gilipollas* ('dickhead'), which has the virtue of maintaining a semantic link with *polla*, would be more effective. In this respect, the French translation is truer to the sense of the original, although with a significant difference. *Bite* ('dick' or 'cock') is appropriate in terms of register, but *con* ('twat' or 'cunt') has an altogether different sexual association. That said, it is a coarse and insulting way of describing someone and might be said to work more effectively in terms of tone than the Spanish version. *Pelotas* ('balls') and *couilles* ('balls') are appropriately informal terms; however, GT fails to capture the meaning of 'you're not even out to your parents' in both translations. 'To be out to someone' or 'to come out to someone' requires the addition of *el armario* ('closet' or 'wardrobe') in Spanish and *le placard* ('closet' or 'cupboard') in French. It would also be more appropriate for Chelsea to use the *tu* form rather than the *vous* form with Peter in the French translation. Thus, possible translations might be:

> ... ni siquiera **has salido del armario** frente a tus padres.
>
> ... **tu n'es même pas sorti du placard** devant tes parents.

Sticking with terms associated with the body, sexual arousal can also be difficult to translate. Furthermore, it is an issue that is generally not addressed in the foreign language classroom, and certainly not one found in published pedagogical materials. To include such language, which many students might reasonably wish to have access to, is clearly a queering of classroom practice and one in line with the educational view of foreign language learning espoused in this chapter. In an early scene in the novel, Ben returns home in a state of excitement after a date with Peter, while at the same time mulling over the fact that he appears to be closeted.

> Anyway, I told myself, fishing my door key out of my pocket, **my hard-on for Peter** still threatening to poke a hole in my jeans, why shouldn't a fella stay in the closet if he wanted to? (Gregory 2021, 20)

This is translated as follows by GT:

> De todos modos, me dije, sacando la llave de la puerta de mi bolsillo, **mi erección por Peter** todavía amenazando con hacerme un agujero en los jeans, ¿por qué un tipo no debería quedarse en el armario si quisiera?

> Quoi qu'il en soit, me suis-je dit en sortant la clé de ma porte de ma poche, **mon sexe pour Peter** menaçant toujours de faire un trou dans mon jean, pourquoi un mec ne resterait-il pas dans le placard s'il le voulait?

Ponérsela dura ('to get it hard') or *empalmarse* ('to get a hard-on') are the most common ways in informal Spanish to indicate male sexual arousal. However, a significant degree of lexical and syntactic reformulation is needed if the technical sense of *erección* is to be avoided and the informal sense of the original is to be retained. Thus 'my hard-on for Peter', and the remainder of the sentence, could be translated as '*el calentón que tenía pensando en Peter hacía que la polla amenazara con hacerme un agujero en los vaqueros*' (literally 'the horniness I had thinking about Peter made it that my cock was threatening to make a hole in my jeans'), thereby avoiding the issue of an exact equivalent to 'hard-on'. Another option entailing this specific sense could be '*con la polla empalmada solo de pensar en Peter y todavía amenazando con hacerme un agujero en los vaqueros*' (literally 'with my cock stiff from thinking about Peter and still threatening to make a hole in my jeans'). Regardless of what is selected, the use of informal alternatives to *erección* ('erection') would be more in keeping with the register of the original. As regards the French translation, *mon sexe* (literally 'my genitals') does not succeed in capturing the sense of the original, as *sexe* does not entail sexual arousal, which is key here. Informal terms for 'hard-on' are *trique* (derived from 'stick') or *gaule* (derived from 'sapling'). Options in this case might be '*la trique* [or *la gaule*] *que j'avais en pensant à Peter*'.

So far, I have looked at the translation of elements of what I have referred to as an explicitly queer text. But as I have suggested, such activities will not be possible in some educational settings. Some teachers may work in contexts where there is no legal protection for LGBTQI+ people or in settings where there is state-sponsored homophobia and transphobia. In such settings, teachers will have to be careful and work under the radar, as it were, if they seek to address the needs of LGBTQI+ students while sensitising all their students to the legitimacy of diverse ways of being and feeling. In the following section I look at existing translations of an implicitly queer text in which there is no mention of LGBTQI+ people or issues relating to them.

Teaching scenario 2: 'The Owl and the Pussy-Cat'

This is an example of what is referred to in English as nonsense verse. Such poetry is generally humorous and frequently contains invented words, fantastical elements and clear rhyming schemes and repetitions. Popular from the nineteenth century onwards, it is generally written to entertain children. One of the poets most associated with the genre is Edward Lear, whose collection *The Book of Nonsense* first appeared in 1846. Although characterised by a pervasive whimsicality and accompanied by Lear's drawings, many of the short poems in the collection have a darker meaning, which scholars have often associated with Lear's own personal unhappiness (Noakes 1968; Swaab 2016). As well as being frequently ill, he also suffered from unrequited love for two other men throughout long periods of his life. This darkness can be seen in a poem such as 'There Was an Old Man of Whitehaven' (Lear 1846, 71):

> There was an Old Man of Whitehaven,
> Who danced a quadrille with a Raven;
> But they said – 'It's absurd, to encourage this bird!'
> So they smashed that Old Man of Whitehaven.

This poem is also typical of the inter-species contact, which is frequently romantic, found throughout Lear's work, and the accompanying drawing shows the pair dancing exuberantly together. However, the unnamed 'they' find this somehow unacceptable and violently put a stop to it. In fact, the unlikely and frankly queer pairings – such as 'The Duck and The Kangaroo' – that typify so many of Lear's poems are shown to have happier endings when the couples embark on journeys abroad together. Swaab (2016, 114) notes that 'Lear's nonsense is full of loneliness, maladjustment, unrequited affection, and madness, but he also has a rhapsodic vein, with escapes, elopements, and excitements, and visions of marvellous unlikely love. "The Owl and the Pussy-cat" is the best-known example.'

This poem is one of Lear's most popular and features a seemingly impossible love story that has a happy ending. Having decided to go to sea, the aforementioned owl and the cat eventually arrive in a remote land; there they are married by a turkey, with a pig providing the wedding ring. Here I focus on the first of the three stanzas, as this is the one that raises the key issues with regard to translation running throughout the poem. There are many translations in both Spanish and French and for this chapter I have selected two by professional translators.

The **Owl** and the **Pussy-cat** went to sea
In a beautiful pea-green boat,
They took some honey, and plenty of money,
Wrapped up in a five-pound note.
The **Owl** looked up to the stars above,
And sang to a small guitar,
'O **lovely Pussy**! O **Pussy, my love**,
What a **beautiful Pussy** you are,
You are,
You are!
What a **beautiful Pussy** you are!'

One of the most salient features of this couple is that they are not gendered – and this is reinforced by Lear's drawing, which does not in any way attempt to represent either animal as male or female. Although the owl serenades the cat in the first stanza, a role that might be traditionally associated with the male, in the second stanza it is the cat who proposes marriage – again, a stereotypically masculine role (certainly as far as nineteenth-century norms were concerned). However, in the two translations reproduced here, the pair are gendered so that the owl is male and the cat female. This is typical of many translations and of the numerous animated cartoons of the poem on YouTube (see, for instance, Ives 1963).

El Búho y **la Gatita** se hicieron a la mar,
En un lindo barquito de verde guisante.
Llevaron dulce miel y dinero constante,
Envueltos en un billetito al instante.
El Búho las estrellas miró,
Y al son de una guitarrita cantó:
'¡Oh **mi Gatita preciosa**! ¡Oh **mi minina hermosa**!
¡Qué **linda Gatita** eres tú!
Eres tú,
Eres tú,
¡Qué **linda Gatita** eres tú!'
(Guerrero Quijano 2012)

Hibou et **Minou** allèrent à la mer
Dans une barque peinte en jaune-canari;
Ils prirent du miel roux et beaucoup de sous
Enroulés dans une lettre de crédit.

Le hibou contemplait les astres du ciel,
En chantait, en grattant sa guitare,
'Ô **Minou chérie**, ô **minou ma belle**,
Ô **Poussiquette**, comme tu es rare,
Es rare,
Es rare!
Ô **Poussiquette**, comme tu es rare!'
(Steergmuller 1961)

The prefix 'pussy', when added to 'cat', indicates that the cat in question is a domestic one – and throughout the English-speaking world, any domestic cat (regardless of sex) whose name is unknown can be addressed by a human as 'pussy' or 'puss' (cf. the fairy tale 'Puss in Boots'). In the Spanish translation (Guerrero Quijano 2012) the owl (*el búho*) is male, in keeping with its grammatical gender, but the cat (*el gato*) has been made female (*gatita*, literally 'little female cat'). This means that when the owl addresses the cat using the adjectives *preciosa* ('lovely'), *hermosa* ('beautiful') and *linda* ('pretty'), these very appropriate translations are in their feminine form. In gendering the couple along such heteronormative lines, the possibilities for a queer reading are significantly undermined. We see precisely the same manipulation in the French version (Steergmuller 1961). Here the cat is given the name *Minou* ('kitty' or 'pussy-cat') and referred to by the owl using the inventive neologism *Poussiquette*, a term consonant with Lear's own frequent poetic word coinage. The diminutive suffix *-ette* is a clear indication that the cat in question is female. This is also reinforced through the choices of *chérie* (grammatically feminine 'darling') and *ma belle* ('my beautiful one', also grammatically feminine).

These translations are particularly useful in the foreign language classroom for a number of reasons. With regard to the practice of translation itself, they glaringly draw attention to the ideological position of the translator and their role in favouring particular readings. As Santaemilia (2003, 1) explains:

> the idea of 'manipulation' is inherent to the phenomenon of 'translation'. Both *manipulare* and *translatare* share a common lexical ground: an (artful) adaptation, change, transformation, transmission – to suit one's purpose or advantage. In some sense, the two terms are quasi synonyms, which are also associated with transgression, perversion or subversion. In spite of its widespread critical presence, 'fidelity' is a rather useless term, since all texts are both faithful and unfaithful – faithful to some interests

> and unfaithful to others. [...] a translator *creates* but *copies* (or *rewrites*), reproduces *faithfully* but has scope for *intervention*, aims at *equivalence* but ends up producing *difference*.

Foreign language students can be asked to compare the original and the translated version and to identify the differences in terms of grammar, syntax and lexis, but with a special focus on grammatical gender and its impact on meaning-making. They can also be invited to offer possible explanations for the changes that have been made. 'The Owl and the Pussy-Cat' is also particularly appropriate for sensitising students to the concept of non-normative romantic relationships, without mentioning LGBTQI+ issues in any way. As I have suggested elsewhere (Gray 2021), carefully worded questions set by the teacher can enable students to speculate on the reasons the owl and the cat leave their country of origin, the possibilities of their future return, their potential for happiness together and the challenges they might face as an inter-species couple. Handled sensitively by a teacher concerned about queer erasure, some students may be enabled to read queerly between the lines and think differently about themselves or those whose desires and identities fall outside the socially sanctioned norm.

Conclusion

This chapter arises from a primary concern with the ongoing erasure of non-normative sexualities and gender identities in foreign language teaching and in the curriculum generally. Taking my cue from Eisenmann and Ludwig (2018), I concur with their assessment that it is only by LGBTQI+ identities becoming explicitly present in the curriculum that much of the legislative reform of recent years can become socially embedded – and that LGBTQI+ students can be recognised, while those who are not can be sensitised to the diversity of sexual orientations and gender identifications and the issues these raise.

In this chapter, I have argued that literary texts are particularly useful in this respect, particularly if they are well chosen, as they have the potential to engage students with real-world issues in ways that conventional pedagogical materials do not. At the same time, the addition of translation activities can help draw attention to specifically queer phenomena and how these are addressed both linguistically and ideologically in the L1 and the L2. Such an approach overall – that is, one that combines queer content with the use of literature and translation activities – has, I would suggest, the potential to contest the instrumental way in which much foreign language teaching is framed, certainly as far as Anglo-American ELT is concerned. This approach is based on an educational view of language teaching in which the many taboos and erasures (such as gender, sexuality, class, race, disability, age) currently characterising foreign language teaching can be tackled. Amid much discussion of the need to liberate the curriculum, such an approach has the potential to begin to address the ways in which the curriculum is colonised not only through the deployment of discourses of European superiority, monolingualism, individualism, consumerism and neoliberalism (Gray and Block 2014; Macedo 2019; Pennycook 2021; Ortaçtepe Hart 2023), but also through the relentless reproduction of damaging and limiting discourses of heteronormativity and cisnormativity. The two very different texts I have chosen allow teachers in different contexts to address these issues in ways that are direct, in the case of the Gregory novel, and indirect, in the case of the Lear poem. In both instances they represent a queering of the second-language classroom and have the potential to open up spaces for the exploration of non-normative ways of being and the manner in which these are encoded in language and represented in translation.

Acknowledgements

I would like to thank José Santaemilia for making it possible for me to write much of this chapter at the University of Valencia in spring 2023 and for his advice. I would also like to thank Miguel Fuster, Sergio Maruenda and Carmina Gregori for their many kindnesses during my stay. Thanks too to Mike Baynham, David Block, Elena Mira Climent and David Rodríquez-Velasco for their helpful comments along the way.

References

Ayachia, Houda. 2018. 'The revival of translation as a fifth skill in the foreign language classroom: A review of literature', *AWEJ for Translation & Literary Studies* 2, no. 2: 187–98. https://doi.org/10.24093/awejtls/vol2no2.

Baer, Brian James, and Klaus Kaindl, eds. 2017. *Queering Translation, Translating the Queer: Theory, practice, activism*. London: Routledge.

Baynham, Mike, and Tong King Lee. 2019. *Translation and Translanguaging*. London: Routledge.

Borba, Rodrigo. 2022. 'Enregistering "gender ideology": The emergence and circulation of a transnational anti-gender language', *Journal of Language and Sexuality* 11, no. 1: 57–79. https://doi.org/10.1075/jls.21003.bor.

Carreres, Ángeles, María Noriega-Sánchez, and Lucía Pintado Gutiérrez. 2021. 'Introduction: Translation and plurilingual approaches to language teaching and learning', *Translation and Translanguaging in Multilingual Contexts* 7, no. 1: 1–16. https://doi.org/10.1075/ttmc.7.1

Connell, Raewyn W. 2005. *Masculinities*. Los Angeles, CA: University of California Press.

Cook, Guy. 2007. 'Viewpoint. A thing of the future: Translation in language learning', *International Journal of Applied Linguistics* 17, no. 3: 396–401. https://doi.org/10.1111/j.1473-4192.2007.00160.x.

Council of Europe. 2001. *Common European Framework of Reference for Languages: Learning, teaching, assessment.* Strasbourg: Council of Europe.

Council of Europe. 2018. *Common European Framework of Reference for Languages: Learning, teaching, assessment. Companion volume with new descriptors.* Strasbourg: Council of Europe.

Eisenmann, Maria, and Christian Ludwig, eds. 2018. *Queer Beats: Gender and literature in the EFL classroom*. Bern: Peter Lang.

Eribon, Didier. 2004. *Insult and the Making of the Gay Self.* Durham, NC: Duke University Press.

García, Ofelia, Nelson Flores, Kate Seltzer, Li Wei, Ricardo Otheguy, and Jonathan Rosa. 2021. 'Rejecting abyssal thinking in the language and education of racialized bilinguals: A manifesto', *Critical Inquiry in Language Studies* 18, no. 3: 203–28. https://doi.org/10.1080/15427587.2021.1935957.

González-Pastor, Diana. 2021. 'Introducing machine translation in the translation classroom: A survey on students' attitudes and perceptions', *Tradumàtica* 19: 47–65. https://doi.org/10.5565/rev/tradumatica.273.

Gray, John. 2010. *The Construction of English: Culture, consumerism and promotion in the ELT global coursebook*. Basingstoke: Palgrave Macmillan.

Gray, John. 2013. 'LGBT invisibility and heteronormativity in ELT materials'. In *Critical Perspectives on Language Teaching Materials*, edited by John Gray, 40–63. Basingstoke: Palgrave Macmillan.

Gray, John. 2021. 'Addressing LGBTQ erasure through literature in the ELT classroom', *ELT Journal* 75, no. 2: 142–51. https://doi.org/10.1093/elt/ccaa079.

Gray, John, and David Block. 2014. 'All middle class now? Evolving representations of the working class in the neoliberal era: The case of ELT textbooks'. In *English Language Teaching Textbooks: Content, consumption, production*, edited by Nigel Harwood, 45–71. Basingstoke: Palgrave Macmillan.

Gregory, Jarlath. 2021. *What Love Looks Like.* Dublin: O'Brien Press.

Guerrero Quijano, Eleonora. 2012. 'El Búho y La Gatita de Edward Lear'. Accessed 11 September 2023. http://armadillosvoladores.blogspot.com/2012/06/el-buho-y-la-gatita-de-edward-lear.html.

Halperin, David M. 1995. *Saint Foucault: Towards a gay hagiography*. Oxford: Oxford University Press.

Howatt, Anthony P. R. 1984. *A History of English Language Teaching*. Oxford: Oxford University Press.

Hu, Ke, and Patrick Cadwell. 2016. 'A comparative study of post-editing guidelines', *Baltic Journal of Modern Computing* 42, no. 2: 346–53.

Hymes, Dell H. 1972. 'On communicative competence'. In *Sociolinguistics: Selected readings*, edited by John B. Pride and Janet Holmes, 269–93. Harmondsworth: Penguin.

Ives, Burl. 1963. 'The Owl and the Pussy-Cat', [Video]. Accessed 11 September 2023. https://www.youtube.com/watch?v=9diwlVXCrBQ.

Koponen, Maarit. 2015. 'How to teach machine translation post-editing? Experiences from a post-editing course'. In *Proceedings of the 4th Workshop on Post-editing Technology and Practice*, 2–15. Miami, FL: MTSummit.

Koutsompou, Violetta-Irene. 2015. 'The use of literature in the language classroom: Methods and aims', *International Journal of Information and Education Technology* 5, no. 1: 74–9. https://doi.org/10.7763/IJIET.2015.V5.479.

Krein-Kühle, Monika. 2014 'Translation and equivalence'. In *Translation: A multidisciplinary approach*, edited by Juliane House, 15–25. Basingstoke: Palgrave Macmillan.

Krings, Hans P. 2001. *Repairing Texts: Empirical investigations of machine translation post-editing processes*. Kent, OH: Kent State University Press.

Lazar, Gillian. 1993. *Literature and Language Teaching: A guide for teachers and trainers*. Cambridge: Cambridge University Press.

Lear, Edward. 1846. *The Book of Nonsense*. London: F. Warne and Co.

Lear, Edward. 1867. 'The Owl and the Pussycat'. Poetry Foundation. Accessed 11 September 2023. https://www.poetryfoundation.org/poems/43188/the-owl-and-the-pussy-cat.

Macedo, Donaldo, ed. 2019. *Decolonizing Foreign Language Education: The misteaching of English and other colonial languages.* London: Routledge.

Moore, Ashley R. 2016. 'Inclusion and exclusion: A case study of an English class for LGBT learners', *TESOL Quarterly* 50, no. 1: 86–108. https://doi.org/10.1002/tesq.208.

Noakes, Vivien. 1968. *Edward Lear: The life of a wanderer.* London: Collins.

North, Brian, and Enrica Piccardo. 2017. 'Mediation and exploiting one's plurilingual repertoire: Exploring classroom potential and proposed new CEFR descriptors'. In *ALTE 6th International Conference: Conference Proceedings*, edited by Esther Gutiérrez Eugenio, 87–95. Cambridge: Association of Language Testers in Europe.

Ortaçtepe Hart, Deniz. 2023. *Social Justice and the Language Classroom.* Edinburgh: Edinburgh University Press.

Paran, Amos, and Pauline Robinson. 2016. *Literature*. Oxford: Oxford University Press.

Park, Joseph Sung-Yul. 2016. 'Language as pure potential', *Journal of Multilingual and Multicultural Development* 37, no. 5: 453–66. https://doi.org/10.1080/01434632.2015.1071824.

Pennycook, Alastair. 2019. 'From translanguaging to translingual activism'. In *Decolonizing Foreign Language Education: The misteaching of English and other colonial languages*, edited by Donaldo Macedo, 169–85. London: Routledge.

Pennycook, Alastair. 2021. *Critical Applied Linguistics: A critical re-introduction*. London: Routledge.

Puar, Jasbir K. 2007. *Terrorist Assemblages: Homonationalism in queer times.* Durham, NC: Duke University Press.

Pym, Anthony. 2011. 'What technology does to translation', *Translation and Interpreting* 3, no. 1: 1–9.

Rao, Rahul. 2020. *Out of Time: The queer politics of postcoloniality*. Oxford: Oxford University Press.

Santaemilia, José. 2003. *Gender, Sex and Translation: The manipulation of identities*. Manchester: St Jerome.

Santaemilia, José. 2015. 'Translating sexuality from English into Spanish and vice-versa: A cultural and ideological challenge', *Atlantis: Journal of the Spanish Association of Anglo-Saxon Studies* 37, no. 1: 139–56.

Shin, H. 2016. 'Language "skills" and the neoliberal English education industry', *Journal of Multilingual and Multicultural Development* 37, no. 5: 509–22. https://doi.org/10.1080/01434632.2015.1071828.

Steergmuller, Francis. 1961. *Le Hibou et La Pousiquette*. London: Rupert Hart-Davis.

Swaab, Peter. 2016. '"Some think him … queer": Loners and love in Edward Lear'. In *Edward Lear and the Play of Poetry*, edited by James Williams and Matthew Bevis, 89–114. Oxford: Oxford University Press. https://doi.org/10.1093/acprof:oso/9780198708568.003.0005.

UNESCO. 2016. *Out in the Open: Education sector responses to violence based on sexual orientation and gender identity/expression*. [Report]. Accessed 11 September 2023. https://unesdoc.unesco.org/ark:/48223/pf0000244756.

Warner, Michael, ed. 1993. *Fear of a Queer Planet: Queer politics and social theory*. Minneapolis, MN: University of Minnesota Press.

Wilkins, David Arthur. 1976. *Notional Syllabuses*. Oxford: Oxford University Press.

10
Final reflections: why I am still talking to white people about race

Haydn Kirnon

In the summer of 2022, I was asked by my colleagues, Dr Mazal Oaknín and Dr Alejandro Bolaños García-Escribano of the Spanish, Portuguese and Latin American Studies (SPLAS) programme, on which we teach in the School of European Languages, Culture and Society (SELCS) at UCL, for my reflections on the teaching of translation. I teach Spanish–English translation at undergraduate level.

Along with a fourth colleague on the SPLAS programme, Dr Marga Navarrete, we have, in the last academic year, begun to implement a programme of initiatives in line with the project titled Tackling the BAME-BIPOC[1] Awarding Gap at the university, the principal aim of which is to address the so-called 'cold climate' in our classrooms that, according to Tate (2019), is the leading contributing factor when it comes to the awarding gap at universities in Britain. This 'cold climate' has been brought about by, among other factors, micro-agressions, insufficient support for BAME-BIPOC students, 'invisible' racism and stereotyping, all of which can alienate students and so have a negative impact on their sense of belonging in the student community. It can also lead to the increased likelihood of students dropping out or failing to achieve the 2:1/first-class degree needed to pursue postgraduate studies.

In addition, during my time at UCL I have been involved in the e-Expert Seminar Series: Translation and Language Teaching, a collaboration between UCL and the University of Córdoba (UCO), Spain, the aim of which has been the creation of a space in which to reflect on topics related to translation and language teaching. Specifically, in May 2022, I participated in a round-table discussion in the sixth iteration of the series, which took as its theme 'Feminism and Gender Awareness in

Modern Foreign Languages and Translation'. This gave me an opportunity to address what I see as a glaring omission in the curriculum when I was, myself, an undergraduate on a Modern Languages programme at a British university in the mid- to late 1980s: the lack of women's voices in the curriculum, both in content modules and in the teaching of translation.

I began to teach on the SPLAS programme in October 2017, and my tenure as a language teacher is, as I see it, the latest stage in a career as a language practitioner that spans over 30 years. It started with my time as a lexicographer at Collier Macmillan, immediately after graduating from the University of Leeds with a degree in Spanish Language and Literature with Subsidiary French, followed by several years as a subtitler of films and television programmes and as a freelance translator.

Here, I wish to discuss how, as a language graduate, my career has evolved over the years, with each stage being, in a sense, a *starting again* of sorts involving the acquisition of new skills and fresh knowledge each time. With each successive change, I have been able to use those skills to build on knowledge and skills already acquired; however, this also required that that previous knowledge not be 'set in aspic' as it were. That it not be used, in my teaching practice, as an incontrovertible set of truths to be held forever more but, instead, be constantly revisited and reviewed and reconfigured in the practice of my teaching and, specifically, in relation to the themes of equality, diversity and inclusion. My practice as a teacher is and should always be evolving in accordance with the world and environment in which we live *now*.

My journey, then, I feel, for the purposes of my reflections, must begin with where I found myself towards the end of a rather staid and conservative undergraduate programme of study, when I encountered what would prove to be a significant determiner in my eventual choice of career: María Moliner's *Diccionario del uso del español* (1966/2016).

In an age – long before the advent of the internet and its endless playground of resources – in which reliable dictionaries were vital when it came to the decoding and re-encoding of unfamiliar (and sometimes even familiar!) words encountered in the source language of study, but not readily available or accessible, Moliner's dictionary was, to me, a compelling and engaging work. Comprised of two weighty tomes, it seemed to me to be a *Wunderkammer* of wordsmithery, constructed in such a way that a search for a particular lexical unit, once successfully despatched, would almost invariably take you, pleasurably, on yet another journey in search of the meaning of another lexical unit you had encountered in the process. To this day, in my teaching, I urge my students to emulate this journey. I stress the importance, when learning another language at an advanced level, of acquainting yourself with a good monolingual dictionary. The purpose should be twofold: almost invariably, you will be able to decode the lexical unit that took you to the dictionary in the first place, from the definition therein, but – and I always stress the importance of this – in the *source* language itself, thus not interrupting your engagement with that language by deferring to your language of habitual use. Secondly, in that process, there is a good chance that you will encounter at least one word with which you may not have been familiar previously, but which you can now add to your lexicon.

Born in Zaragoza, Spain, María Moliner (1900–1981) trained as a librarian and in 1950 she began to work on the *Diccionario de uso del español* (1966/2016). Its two volumes would eventually see the light of day under the auspices of the Gredos publishing house, in 1966 and 1967 respectively. In her article 'Maria Moliner and her contribution to the history of Spain's public libraries', María R. Osuna Alarcón (2009, 227–8) writes:

> The first edition underwent twenty reprints; it was issued on CD-ROM in 1995 and revised and expanded editions were published in 1998 and 2007. Now, after four decades, the dictionary's originality is still upheld; it uses 'a very broad criterion when including words,' among them foreign ones, colloquial usage, slang and acronyms not contemplated in the dictionary of the Spanish Royal Academy. As Joaquín da Costa, lexicographer and coordinator of the latest edition, explains in the foreword: 'It is a very unusual dictionary, because not only does it include the meaning of the words, but also allows one to find which word to use to express an idea, through a system of indexes and synonyms.' The dictionary was revolutionary because Moliner set out to improve upon the latest edition of the Royal Academy dictionary, which dated from ten years earlier and was 'complicated, very conservative and antiquated.' Her purpose was to 'make a profound revision' and prepare one with 'much clearer and more up-to-date language,' according to Da Costa.

Writing on the occasion of Moliner's death, Colombian Nobel laureate Gabriel García Márquez (1981; my translation) wrote: 'She performed an almost unprecedented feat: alone, at home and by hand, she wrote the most comprehensive, useful, enthusiastic, and entertaining dictionary of the Spanish language.'

It is only many years later that I came to know just to what extent the dictionary was, effectively, the enterprise and brainchild of one woman working largely alone, and how her work came to prevail and endure against incredible odds, at a time when this would have been uncommon. However, as Osuna Alarcón encapsulates, it is clear to me now, all these years later, how much I as an undergraduate responded to Moliner's originality in creating a dictionary that educated, enthralled and entertained.

As a burgeoning Hispanist in the 1980s – and I feel it is important to recognise this shortcoming here in myself, as a cisgender male and the product of a very conservative upbringing and society – it simply never occurred to me to question the significant lack of women in the syllabus. Spanish women writers such as Emilia Pardo Bazán, Carmen Martín Gaite and Carmen Laforet – all of whom had been published to acclaim in the first part of the twentieth century – failed to find their way onto a module on the twentieth-century Spanish novel alongside, to name a few, Pío Baroja, Camilo José Cela and Juan Goytisolo. In this regard, then, it is important to highlight how my discovery of María Moliner – whose work I now place front and centre in my own practice as a language teacher – was pretty much by happenstance, in the university library, in no way connected to the practice of translation. That discovery, though, sparked my curiosity about dictionaries, about their composition, purpose and possibilities.

Furthermore, I would argue that the way in which Moliner's work was ignored for years by the Establishment (in particular the Royal Spanish Academy) parallels the way in which the work of the aforementioned Spanish women writers of the first half of the twentieth century failed to find its way onto the syllabus when I was an undergraduate. Later, I aim to show how I attempt to specifically redress this imbalance in the language classroom, and I discuss responses to it from students.

At the beginning of my final year at university, everyone, almost overnight, seemed to be galvanised into the high-powered-career mode that was in keeping with the zeitgeist, it being the 1980s. It was a time when blue-chip companies – Mars, Coats Viyella and the like – would visit university campuses with a sort of travelling fair, trawling for prospective candidates for their graduate programmes in a process known as the 'milk round' (to my mind, as soulless, dispiriting and pedestrian a venture as the task from which it takes its name – the milkman of old's daily delivery). I had no idea what I wanted to do once I left university, but the milk round was, I knew, decidedly not for me. So, as many of my peers suddenly acquired a suit and naked professional ambition, I continued to acquaint myself with Moliner's seminal dictionary. In doing so, it gradually dawned on me that what I *did* want to do was stalk, seize upon and eventually get to the heart of words and their essence, *à la* Moliner. I wanted to compile dictionaries.

And so it is that I found myself, in the summer of 1989 following my graduation, answering an ad in the job section of the *Guardian* newspaper. This led to me joining a small yet mighty little Spanish-English dictionary project at a company called Collier Macmillan. The project had been going for about five years when I joined as a translation editor, and so I found my dream job.

So, what purpose does this meander down memory lane serve? Well, I do not, sadly, have time to explain in detail just how much of an impact the seven years that I spent working at that company had on me; however, it feels important to mention this job because I learnt so much about translation and about how to work and how to *live* from that job – things that have become the bedrock not only of how I translate, but of how I approach life in general. And about how I approach being a language student to this day. Because, yes: as a translator, as a teacher and, specifically, as a language teacher, I place a lot of emphasis in my teaching on the importance of being a lifelong student of my second language and of always seeing myself as such. If you are to be a successful teacher of translation, a successful learner of a second language, you must strive to refresh your knowledge of and acquaintance with the second language as it evolves and changes. I feel that this is a practice that has served and continues to serve me well. I do not present myself as having infinite knowledge of the language and, certainly, I see the language teacher as, always, learning as their students learn – and often learning *from* them. I see myself, and I tell the students this, as the moderator in the seminar room based on my many years of experience. This does, I hope, make the language teacher useful to them in many respects; however, I am also always learning and they often bring contemporary, pertinent, fresh observations and knowledge to the table that I am discovering for the first time. I see this exchange as necessary and empowering for all of us: for the students and for the educator.

In talking to students about my time as a lexicographer at the beginning of my career, I realise that I am revealing to them a work culture that really does seem like something from a bygone age. At that time, as a young graduate, you would go into an environment with, I like to think, some potential that your employer had already glimpsed, but understanding that you were there to learn and to be mentored by people who knew more than you did, who had lived more than you had and who would affect you in deep and meaningful ways, and that this would involve long periods of discussion and reflection before you, finally, produced work with which you were satisfied. However, this is not what many of my students are likely to find when they enter the workplace. In the classroom, though, I seek to recreate this environment as much as I can given the time and goal-focused constraints. I want to model the way in which I was mentored by older, more experienced lexicographers who didn't simply relate to me *de haut en bas*, as it were, but instead gave me the benefit of their experience, whilst encouraging my own creativity and originality as a translator, in the expectation that I would one day be doing their job. And doing it as successfully and passionately as they did. This should be the teacher's guiding principle in the language classroom.

The dictionary went through various ups and downs whilst I worked on it, and changed ownership a couple of times. At one point, we came under the aegis of the Mirror Group for a year, just before the demise of its then owner, tycoon Robert Maxwell, and were known as Maxwell Dictionaries. At the end of that year Maxwell met a rather unfortunate end, falling to his death from his yacht in the Canary Islands in the autumn of 1991. Our dictionary, however, had a happier ending, as it was acquired by Oxford University Press. The dictionary on which I and my colleagues had worked painstakingly and meticulously for many years thus eventually became the *Oxford Spanish Dictionary* (Galimberti Jarman and Russell 1994). The senior editors Beatriz Galimberti Jarman and Roy Russell, who headed up the English–Spanish and Spanish–English teams respectively, were not merely managers. They were teachers, mentors and, eventually, friends, and they corralled us all, skilfully, diplomatically – firmly – but also sensitively and with affection, in our pursuit of the best possible translation of a headword. We would spend hours sitting around having conversations about definitions and etymology, and sometimes debate would be passionate and heated. I loved the enthusiasm and vigour with which corners would sometimes be defended, as we would then attempt to pour that passion into the final product. Again, these are qualities and a practice that I seek to bring into the translation classroom; when this is successful I derive heartfelt pleasure and satisfaction from the connectivity between my work at Oxford University Press and my work with SPLAS.

We would work like scribes, on pieces of paper, with these pieces of paper eventually making their way to a team of in-house keyboarders who would type our work up before it was then sent out of house. It was the kind of leisurely pace that simply would not be tenable now, but it was an invaluable education for me as an aspiring young translator.

Having worked in several capacities within the translation industry (chiefly as a film subtitler and freelance translator) since my time at Oxford University Press and before arriving at UCL, I have come to see the language classroom as a platform for promoting enquiry and interest among students, offering insight into what language tutors have done outside the classroom. Hopefully, some of them may feel inspired to become translators themselves. For those – and this will be, doubtless, the majority – who do not, irrespective of whether they *think* translation is for them or not, the goal is that they should see the discipline as a useful and vital tool in the context of learning a language, a notion championed by other authors in previous chapters such as those by Bolaños García-Escribano and Cerezo Merchán, Ogea and Talaván, and Oaknín. The translation module should be seen as, at the very least, a useful and necessary companion to other modules students might take, irrespective of whether the undergraduate is interested in becoming a professional translator or not. The successful decoding and re-encoding of a source text, which is at the heart of the tasks in which we engage in class, encourage and enhance linguistic skills in the language of study; these are invaluable for communication and research. But, in tandem with the necessary harnessing of two languages involved in the process of translating, I think it is also my role to highlight the beauty, charm and uniqueness of each language as much as possible.

Often, the time in the translation classroom is, for me, an opportunity to encourage students to occasionally depart from the translator's practice and stop to consider the aesthetics, utility and even humour of each language. In a recent fourth-year seminar, for example, the discussion of a single cartoon by feminist Spanish cartoonist Flavita Banana which had appeared in a Spanish-language daily that week, with two characters depicted – one silent, one uttering a mere six words – initiated a conversation between myself and the students, and among the students, about gender, sexual orientation and patriarchy that was informal yet thought-provoking. And often quite simply hilarious. All, I might add, before we even began to consider just what the optimal translation into the target language might be – which, in turn, led to a discussion of what the various virtues or shortcomings of the target language might be, in this regard.

As someone from an African-Caribbean background, I feel that my ethnic and cultural identities inform my practice in the language classroom. Certainly, my experiences as an undergraduate and, subsequently, throughout my career, have proved a useful point of departure from which to engage in the Tackling the BAME-BIPOC

Awarding Gap project at UCL and how it relates, specifically, to the initiatives that we have begun to implement on the SPLAS programme. When I was a student – and, indeed, throughout most of my career as a translator and as an educator – I have found myself to be the sole BAME-BIPOC person in many environments.

In an ideal world, these experiences should inform the language teacher's practice and then, by extension, be brought to bear on the decolonisation of the curriculum; the BAME-BIPOC language teacher would be seen as a role model and so on. However, this can be a burden of expectation, not only for the educator but for the BAME-BIPOC student as well, caught in the glare of the 'headline blare' of the phrase 'awarding gap'. For BAME-BIPOC students, having their often undeniable visibility magnified can, sometimes, be almost unbearable.

Furthermore, the very term BAME-BIPOC is such a broad church, effectively bringing together under one umbrella an almost endless array of ethnic and cultural identities, with what can seem a one-size-fits-all approach. If you then apply this to the notion of decolonising a curriculum, it is not always – at least to me – clear quite what this means or how it should be done. Drawing on my very personal experiences as an African-Caribbean cisgender man does, certainly, have a value in this context, and I can and do draw upon these experiences in the language classroom. Inevitably, though, it can never be a catch-all for addressing all the aspects of this issue successfully, which is why there will always be a need for a more diverse teaching body. I, too, am therefore at the beginning of a long journey in which I have much to learn about other people's BAME-BIPOC identities and how to address and handle them with sensitivity in the language classroom.

This was brought home to me, when, in a final-year Spanish language class, I chose an extract for discussion and translation into English from *Viajes: De la Amazonia a las Malvinas* (Sarlo 2014). In the extract, there is a reference to an indigenous Bolivian man as having *ojos achinados*, which back-translates into English as 'Chinese-like eyes'. According to the Royal Spanish Academy's *Diccionario de la lengua española*, the verb *achinar*, of which *achinado* is the past participle and adjectival form, is defined thus: 'dar rasgos o características semejantes a las de los chinos (naturales de China)'; also 'dicho de los ojos: ponerse oblicuos'. Very crudely, this is 'to ascribe features or characteristics similar to those of the Chinese to'; and, in the second instance, 'when used of eyes: to slant'.

Almost invariably – and sometimes with anxiety, via email, in advance of a seminar – students will indicate that they have difficulty finding a 'politically correct' way of translating this word, to which the hard truth of my response is that the task in which they are engaged is neither about political correctness nor about their own personal sensitivities, in the first instance. It is about accuracy. It is also, obviously, about context and the brief that they have been given. Here, I feel that what they are being introduced to is the need to translate accurately and honestly and that, sometimes, doing so may be painful. We talk about the gaze of the user of the word, and about Othering. We talk about the importance of not flinching from the uncomfortableness that words such as this provoke and whether their continued use is problematic. It is also important for us all, though, in the language classroom, to understand that these conversations are nonetheless respectful – that we do not proselytise when discussing the usage of these words with speakers whose language of habitual use is Spanish (which does not preclude respectful discussion, of course). We seek to balance our critique of the work with as comprehensive an appraisal as can be made of Sarlo's activity as a left-wing activist in Argentina in the 1970s, her feminist beliefs and her status as a revered public intellectual. The intention is neither to condemn nor to condone, but simply to analyse usage and its context; however, in so doing, what can and should ensue is a discussion about how this dilemma might be taken out of the classroom and into 'the real world'.

This usually segues neatly into an examination of the possibilities for translating this word into English and the realisation that the English language does not come up smelling of roses in this respect either. Often, I will talk about the use of the word 'nigger', in the expression 'a nigger in the woodpile', of how I recall coming across the use of this expression in a 1960s edition of crime novelist Agatha Christie's novel *Dumb Witness* (1937) and, as someone of African-Caribbean descent, my perception of this expression.

I usually preface my discussion of this word by making it, I hope, very clear that my intention is not to be inflammatory or provocative, or to make anyone in the classroom feel uncomfortable. At this point in the programme of study – the final year – I have, I hope, gained the trust and confidence of my students in my ability to handle this topic sensitively, so that these conversations take place in a space that is safe for *everyone*, BAME-BIPOC and otherwise. I say this because, at this point, it is also important that these conversations draw upon the allyship (or potential allyship) of non-BAME-BIPOC people in the classroom. It is a discussion that does (or should) involve all of us if real progress is to be made. These conversations have almost always been keenly engaged in, often to an extent that I could not have foreseen, and heart-warmingly so.

Also, though, to give the conversation some academic underpinning, I reference Randall Kennedy's *Nigger: The strange career of a troublesome word* (2002), in which Kennedy, an African American and the Michael R. Klein Professor of Law at Harvard University, takes an unflinching look at 'the nuclear bomb of racial epithets' (Chideya 1999, 9).

Comparing and contrasting, then, the use of *achinado* and 'nigger' has, in my experience, served as a useful and insightful gateway into discussing how usage of these problematic words has (or has not) evolved in varying contexts, allowing students – in particular, but by no means exclusively – from BAME-BIPOC backgrounds to bring their own experiences and perceptions of these and similar words into an academic setting.

Using texts taken from Desirée Bela-Lobedde's *Ser mujer negra en España* (2018) has also driven similarly interesting debate in the classroom. Born to Equatorial Guinean parents in Barcelona in 1978, Bela-Lobedde writes movingly about what it meant to be a young Black girl growing up in Spain in the 1980s and 1990s. She addresses, often unflinchingly, racial abuse, sexuality and the politics surrounding Afro hair, amongst other topics, and her writing has often elicited insightful and, at times, moving observations not only from BAME-BIPOC students, many of whom find her immediately relatable, but from the wider classroom population too, many of whom will confess that these topics are ones that they have either never considered or of which they have little understanding. Again, I begin the classes in which we look at these texts by stating that, while I feel it is both interesting and important to introduce these themes into the translation classroom, it is paramount that everyone understands that we must proceed with respect and sensitivity as well as tolerance and emotional intelligence. On my part, as the educator, I see my role here as twofold: making sure that BAME-BIPOC students feel neither inhibited nor provoked when discussing these topics with non-BAME-BIPOC people and that the latter group, in turn, do not feel afraid to participate because they do not have prior knowledge or because they feel that they 'might say the wrong thing'. Let common sense, honesty and sensitivity be your guide, I say, and this will lead to an enriching experience for everyone – one that may at times be frank, but which need never leave anyone feeling vulnerable or defensive.

It is exciting to see how students approach the texts by both Sarlo and Bela-Lobedde, moving organically between discussing the language used, how our target text might best be achieved and the social contexts in which the works have been conceived.

Equally rewarding and invigorating for me and, I believe, my students has been the use of extracts from screenwriter and journalist Diana López Varela's *No es país para coños* (2016). In this work López Varela, born in 1986, looks at the state of feminism in Spain in the early twenty-first century. Her perspective as a cisgender, heterosexual woman and her sometimes very salty prose again make for very interesting classroom discussion and analysis. Her position as a fourth-wave feminist writer serves as a useful point of departure in two directions: I reference earlier waves of feminism, inviting discussion on how López Varela fits into (or disrupts?) a continuum, and my students bring their own fresh perspectives as people who are familiar with a burgeoning fifth wave of feminism that, often, they feel puts them at odds with assertions made in the text. Coupled with López Varela's very familiar way of addressing her reader and love of sometimes decidedly earthy prose, this has led to rich and eye-opening analysis when we then consider our target text and how it is best achieved. López Varela's use of colloquialisms and, specifically, swearwords generates very useful discussion about how these should be addressed when translating, and about relevant cultural differences between Anglophone and Hispanophone speakers, all of which enriches the students' language learning beyond the requisites of the translation exercise.

This, then, is a snapshot of how in my classroom practice I have begun to address the gender imbalance in the syllabus of yore, which was very much a part of my entrée into academia, as well as the inclusion of BAME-BIPOC voices; however, this is all but an initial pin prick. There is a limit to what can be achieved in 10 seminars of 50 minutes a year.

It is heartening then, at least, to be involved in the Tackling the BAME-BIPOC Awarding Gap initiative, for which we have funding that enables us to empower students outside of the classroom as well as inside. Presently, this includes the appointment of BAME-BIPOC student representatives to conduct interviews among their peers regarding their experiences at the university.

We have also been able to institute a series of talks by highly regarded BAME-BIPOC academics, among which was a compelling and well-attended address by Jason Arday, Professor of Sociology of Education at Cambridge, given at UCL earlier this year. A British sociologist known for his research on race and racism, Arday is the youngest Black person to be appointed to a professorship at Cambridge.

In his talk, Arday (2023) addressed 'misogynoir', amongst other things, as being a serious stumbling block in the path of Black women aspiring to scale the academic ranks. The *Oxford English Dictionary* defines misogynoir as a 'dislike of, contempt for, or ingrained prejudice against black women'. This was set against the backdrop of an Advance HE report citing that in 2020 there were a mere 27 Black female professors in the UK, out of a total of 22,810 (HESA 2022). On this topic, McLetchie-Holder (2023) argued:

> As a Black Caribbean woman lecturer in the UK, the experiences of other Black women colleagues have always been of interest to me. Much of the literature to date, which is largely US-based, is compelling but sadly affirms the hurdles and barriers faced by Black women in academia. It documents their feelings of isolation and marginalisation, brought about by constant challenges to their status, authority, and scholarship. It is acknowledged that as race and gender intersect, Black women are 'double outsiders' who are subjected to both racism and sexism.

Similarly, McLetchie-Holder (2023) stated:

> Keen to learn about the experiences of Black women academics in my faculty, I spoke at length with three high-achieving colleagues as part of my ongoing research. Reassuringly, I found authentic, confident academics who were juggling a multitude of important roles, leading faculty innovations and discussing their jobs with pride and fulfilment. These largely positive experiences of my colleagues must of course be set against the vast evidence of oppression and marginalisation of Black women in academia over the last decade. However, I asked these women how they seemed to be thriving in a predominantly white space … They talked about the importance of their valued 'mentors', 'allies', 'confidants' and 'rocks'. These mentors were used for counsel, guidance, and support with career progression. Not all had Black or women mentors and, although this brought a different dynamic, what really mattered was the quality of the relationship.

Arday (2023) referenced the ways in which Black men themselves may, at times, collude in the hindrance of their Black female counterparts' careers. At this juncture, I believe it is important to state that my intention is not, as a Black cisgender male, to co-opt or mute McLetchie-Holder's assessment of the fate of Black women academics. It is, though, my role to be their ally. I would also like to stress the importance of McLetchie-Holder recognising the value that some of the women she interviewed saw in their relationships with mentors who were not Black or women.

Several years ago, when I was working as a freelance translator, I was asked to translate a piece of writing in which there was a detailed description of the American tennis players Serena and Venus Williams. It was a voice-over script for a sports programme aimed, mainly, at 18–30-year-old men. The language used to describe the sisters' prowess and physicality was, to say the least, problematic. In fact, I found it to be racist, offensive and inflammatory, relying as it did on a dated and very unnecessarily sexualised description of the players' attributes, invoking very particular racist tropes. I have, on occasion, told this anecdote in my final-year classroom by way of illustrating a very particular ethical dilemma that might confront any professional translator. I have then focused explicitly on how it affected me, as a Black man, a Black son and a Black father. I tell them that it was especially challenging because I was asked to work on this translation at a time when I was, to say the least, underemployed; I therefore needed the work. It led to a protracted discussion with my contact at the translation agency. I explained that I would be unable to translate the text as it was written and, therefore, unable to do the work for them. Following a lengthy discussion, they agreed that they could see my point and the offending material was removed and the script rewritten.

Relating this matter back to the use of the word *achinado* in translating Sarlo, and the importance of – in the classroom – accepting that its translation in the context might make us uncomfortable, I point out that in the classroom we can do this because it can lead to the kinds of conversation that, hopefully, will in turn result in professional translators not being presented with a dilemma such as mine. However, I do stress that it wasn't my role to simply translate or edit the text as I saw fit, but to initiate that potentially uncomfortable conversation and, if necessary, to refuse to accept the work.

Echoing Arday's exhortation in his UCL talk to be an ally, this episode does, I feel, illustrate just how and when that allyship might be called upon in a professional context. Furthermore, as well as the specificity of being an ally of Black women in academia and a supporter of BAME-BIPOC women students in the translation classroom, it is also a salutary reminder for me of the importance, as stated earlier, of ensuring that my practice as an educator in the translation classroom also focuses on the historical deficit of women's voices in our syllabuses.

So, my journey, from my beginnings as a lexicographer to where I find myself now as an educator, has not always been a straightforward or happy one. Nonetheless, I feel that it has mostly been an exciting one. Certainly, latterly, I feel very encouraged by where we find ourselves, beginning to look at how we decolonise the curriculum, making it more inclusive. My goal, though, is that this inclusion of women's voices and of BAME-BIPOC voices should be seen as being inclusive not only for women and BAME-BIPOC members of the academic community, but by everyone.

Notes

1 The terms 'Black and Minority Ethnic' (BAME) and 'Black, Indigenous, and People of Colour' (BIPOC) are used interchangeably in the present chapter.

References

Arday, Jason. 2023. 'Advancing the dialogue on the BAME awarding gap'. Lecture, University College London, London, 13 June.

Bela-Lobedde, Desirée. 2018. *Ser mujer negra en España*. Madrid: Ediciones B.

Chideya, Farai. 1999. *The Color of Our Future*. New York: William Morrow.

Christie, Agatha. 1937. *Dumb Witness*. London: Collins.

Galimberti Jarman, Beatriz, and Roy Russell, eds. 1994. *Oxford Spanish Dictionary*. Oxford: Oxford University Press.

García Márquez, Gabriel. 1981. 'La mujer que escribió un diccionario'. *El País*, 10 February. Accessed 3 October 2023. https://elpais.com/diario/1981/02/10/opinion/350607617_850215.html.

HESA (Higher Education Statistics Agency). 2022. 'Higher education staff statistics: UK, 2020/21'. Accessed 13 September 2023. www.hesa.ac.uk/news/01-02-2022/sb261-higher-education-staff-statistics.

Kennedy, Randall. 2002. *Nigger: The strange career of a troublesome word*. New York: Pantheon.

López Varela, Diana. 2016. *No es país para coños*. Barcelona: Ediciones Península.

McLetchie-Holder, Shelley. 2023. 'What we can learn from black women academics in the UK'. *Times Higher Education*, 12 June. Accessed 13 September 2023. www.timeshighereducation.com/campus/what-we-can-learn-black-women-academics-uk.

Moliner, María. 1966/2016. *Diccionario de uso del español*. Gredos: Barcelona.

Osuna Alarcón, María R. 2009. 'María Moliner and her contribution to the History of Spain's public libraries', *Libraries & the Cultural Record* 44, no. 2: 220–33. https://doi.org/10.1353/lac.0.0072.

Sarlo, Beatriz. 2014. *Viajes: de la Amazonia a las Malvinas*. Buenos Aires: Seix Barral.

Tate, Shirley Anne. 2019. 'Tackling the 'BPOC' attainment gap in UK universities', TEDTalk [Video], 18 March. Accessed 3 October 2023. www.youtube.com/watch?v=UPMuuJrfawQ.

Index

Page numbers in italics are figures; with 't' are tables.

www.ingramcontent.com/pod-product-compliance
Lightning Source LLC
LaVergne TN
LVHW052017300826
846742LV00020B/81